Maximum Power

Maximum Power

Emergence and the Victory of the Cross

JOHN W. DANIELS

WIPF & STOCK · Eugene, Oregon

MAXIMUM POWER
Emergence and the Victory of the Cross

Wipf & Stock
An Imprint of Wipf and Stock Publishers
199 W. 8th Ave., Suite 3
Eugene, OR 97401

www.wipfandstock.com

PAPERBACK ISBN: 979-8-3852-6766-8
HARDCOVER ISBN: 979-8-3852-6767-5
EBOOK ISBN: 979-8-3852-6768-2

To Barbara
with love and thanks for supporting me to write this
and for the previous thirty-seven years.

Contents

List of Figures

List of Tables

Preface

Why should you read this book?

If you sometimes—or often—feel that something's gone wrong with the way the human world works, but aren't quite sure why that is, then this book offers an explanation. It also points to a way of putting that right, so that human beings and our nonhuman neighbors can look to a future in which we can survive and thrive together.

Who should read this book?

If you're interested in ideas and in making connections between different silos of knowledge then this book is for you. You should find it a stimulating read. It's intended for a general readership, even though some of the material in here may seem at first blush rather demanding. It covers a range of topics: sociology, biology, ecology, thermodynamics, complexity science, anthropology, economics, philosophy, and theology. It's not intended as a narrowly academic book for specialists, but I hope that any specialists who do read it will find that it gives a fair and accurate account of the subjects covered. It's not intended for a specifically Christian readership either, and Christian faith is not presupposed by much of the content. Equally, Christian readers will hopefully benefit from having connections made between their faith and aspects of modern, secular life which may not otherwise have been obvious. My hope is that non-Christian readers too will read it and come to see the relevance of the Christian faith to living well at this time of polycrisis.

How should you read this book?

You *could* start with the introduction and plow through chapter by chapter to the end; there is a logical progression between chapters, and to appreciate the book's overall argument you'll need to read it all in some sequence or other. That said, depending on what most interests you, you might do better to hop around.

Start with the introduction anyway, as it sets out the rationale for the book and provides a foretaste of the ground covered. It's also relatively short. Chapter 1, although it's the longest, makes sense next, as it introduces some basic ideas about power which go on to reappear frequently afterwards.

Chapters 2 and 3 are the science chapters, and they go together. They introduce some key ideas, such as the Maximum Power Principle and dissipative structures. You'll need to look at these eventually, but if science isn't your thing you may want to limit yourself to the "Summing Up" sections at the end of each chapter initially, and then return to read them in full later.

Chapter 4 is literally and figuratively the centerpiece of the book. It can be read pretty well as a standalone chapter, and I suspect that many people will find it the most accessible and interesting one. After the introduction and chapter 1 you might want to continue your reading here, therefore, and dip into other chapters afterwards.

Chapters 5 and 6, although quite different in content, also go together. Chapter 6 is all about power and the story of Jesus, as read through the lens provided by chapter 5. You'll therefore need to read that first if you're going to make much sense of chapter 6. Chapter 5 may initially seem rather jargon-heavy, but do persevere; it includes lots of examples which will hopefully help make sense of the jargon, and the ideas contained here will definitely enrich your reading of the entire book.

Chapter 7 continues in a theological vein and moves on to summarizing the overall message of the book, specifically what it has to say about power and wisdom.

However you read it, I hope you'll feel afterwards that it was time well spent. Thank you in advance for doing so.

John W. Daniels

Introduction: A Nineteen-Terawatt Society

> It's late at night, and you're driving fast along a country road in a dense fog. Your headlights are strong, but you still can't see much . . . Yet you feel calm and confident—secure, even. After all, this is sleepy farming country, and while you know you're driving a little too fast for the conditions and have never been down this road before, your map tells you it's straight and flat and that there are no side roads from which other cars can emerge. And because it's nighttime, there's little chance of oncoming traffic. Anyway, in spite of the hazards, you want to get where you're going as quickly as you can. Sensible behaviour? Most would say not. Countless things could go wrong. Perhaps the map is wrong, and there's a sharp curve ahead; perhaps a deer will jump into the road suddenly or a stranded motorist step out to flag you down. Driving fast in the fog is, of course, not sensible. But it's exactly what we're doing today.[1]

Those words were written some twenty years prior to my writing what you're now reading. The title of the book from which the extract is taken gives a good idea of its thesis: *The Upside of Down: Catastrophe, Creativity and the Renewal of Civilisation*. It's one of a host of similar titles which, in recent times, have sought to draw our attention to the cul-de-sac which global civilization has entered. More optimistic versions of this story have imagined the possibility of doing an adroit about-turn; others have imagined finding a sneaky way through the seeming cul-de-sac; others again have resigned themselves to the likelihood that this is going to end in tears, but sought to uncover some upsides to the coming crash.

That was twenty years ago. Not much has changed, it could be argued, except that we're traveling faster than ever towards whatever lies ahead. Why is that? It's not as if the book's author, Thomas Homer-Dixon, and others of his ilk were all marginal voices crying in the wilderness. The

1.. Homer-Dixon, *Upside of Down*, 7.

blurb on the back of the book describes the then director of the Trudeau Center for Peace and Conflict Studies as a contributor to the likes of the *New York Times* and *Financial Times*, a frequent lecturer to the World Bank and the World Economic Forum, and even as an advisor to the CIA. He for one did not lack an influential audience. And, to some extent, the message seems to have gotten through: the results of a 2021 survey suggest that 56 percent of young people around the world considered humanity to be doomed.[2]

So why is it that, instead of hitting the brakes, we've instead been pressing ever harder on the throttle? This book aims to answer that question. In a word, the answer is *power*. More accurately it's because of something called the Maximum Power Principle. More accurately still it's down to the default manner in which we, collectively, have put this principle into practice. In order to unpack that claim we'll need to join the dots provided by a number of different disciplines: biology, ecology, thermodynamics, complexity science, anthropology, economics, philosophy, and last, but not least, Christian theology. In doing so I'll argue that the only viable alternative to business as usual involves rethinking how we enact the Maximum Power Principle, and that this rethinking requires us to look again at the story of a certain first-century West Asian tradesman.

But, twenty years on from Homer-Dixon's *The Upside of Down*, it's worth starting off by taking stock afresh of where our joyride in the fog has gotten us. It's not pretty reading, but it's important to be clear about where we stand at the outset, and about the inevitable consequences of our civilization's default approach to power.

THAT WILE E. COYOTE FEELING

Some call it a polycrisis, or metacrisis.[3] Others opt for great simplification, or great unraveling.[4] Others again, perhaps euphemistically, speak of a descent of one form or other.[5] But for Jem Bendell what awaits modern industrialized societies is simply collapse. Bendell, one-time high-flying academic and World Economic Forum Young Global Leader turned organic farmer, prefers the term "collapse" as it conveys the irreversibility of

2. Smith Galer, "56 Percent."

3. Tooze, "What Is the Polycrisis?"; Norrsken, "Introduction to the Metacrisis."

4. Hagens, "Great Simplification"; Heinberg and Miller, *Welcome to the Great Unraveling*.

5. Holmgren, "Future Scenarios."

the process. For process, rather than discrete event, is the form collapse generally takes, "an uneven ending of industrial consumer modes of sustenance, shelter, health, security, pleasure, identity and meaning."[6] What's more, he reckons that the process of collapse was already underway by 2016 and will be largely complete within a generation, that is by 2050.[7]

Collapse has many dimensions. The consequences of climate change, or global heating, are well known and widely acknowledged, as is the rapid decline in biodiversity. But these are only two pieces of a much bigger puzzle. Bendell allots a chapter each to these, alongside others dealing with the collapse of energy supplies, food supplies, the economy and the global financial system and, finally, society itself. Taking these factors together, he mounts a strong argument for the imminent demise of what we've come to regard as civilization.

Although Bendell stands out by drawing this conclusion so emphatically, others too have been documenting humanity's journey towards the precipice. For some years the Stockholm Resilience Center has been charting the encroachment of the human race on the nine planetary boundaries which together constitute what it terms humanity's safe operating space. As of its 2025 update, seven of these nine boundaries have been crossed—those relating to climate change, biodiversity loss, chemical pollution, nitrogen and phosphorus pollution, water use, land use changes, and ocean acidification. "We don't know how long we can keep transgressing these key boundaries before combined pressures lead to irreversible change and harm," concludes the Center's Johan Rockström.[8]

Canadian ecologist Bill Rees is perhaps even more strident in his prognostications than Bendell. For him, humanity is in drastic ecological overshoot, consuming resources and producing wastes at rates far in excess of the rates at which nature can absorb those wastes and renew those resources. Climate change is only one symptom of overshoot, and programs to achieve net zero greenhouse gas emissions through the deployment of renewable energy and other technologies, when abstracted from the larger context of overshoot, amount to little more than displacement activities. Our only hope lies in "a managed contraction of the human

6. Bendell, *Breaking Together*, 24.

7. Bendell, *Breaking Together*, 251–52. Bendell provides a foreword to Servigne and Stevens, *How Everything Can Collapse*, which also pursues the car trouble/car-out-of-control metaphor.

8. Stockholm Resilience Center, "Planetary Boundaries." See also Kitzmann et al., *Planetary Health Check 2025*.

enterprise" entailing "many fewer people consuming far less energy and material resources than at present."[9]

Fans of the *Road Runner* cartoon series will be familiar with scenes in which the protagonist, Wile E. Coyote, overshoots the edge of a cliff in a failed attempt to catch his ever-resourceful prey. This being a cartoon, the laws of physics don't kick in until the point when Wile, having been running horizontally through thin air for some time, realizes that there's nothing beneath his feet. Ecological overshoot works in a somewhat similar manner. Although the global human population has been in collective overshoot since around 1970, the consequences have yet to be felt in a definitive way. Adverse developments are often local in nature, happen in dribs and drabs, or take place so slowly initially that people gradually adjust to them—until, just like when a slow trickle of pebbles abruptly gives way to a full-scale avalanche, a sudden major and widespread societal buckling occurs.

Nonlinear responses like these are typical of complex systems in general, and human societies are no exception.[10] In fact (as we shall see later in this book) their complexity may be augmented in unprecedented ways by the phenomenon of trust. Contemporary human society is based in large part on the exchange of claims on wealth—money, as it's better known. However, as we shall see in chapter 2, much of the actual wealth represented by these claims does not, and never will, exist. Even so we persist in trusting these claims; like Wile E. Coyote we carry on running, miraculously, on thin air. Until, that is, something happens and trust evaporates. That something very nearly happened around 2008, when central banks across the world had to take unprecedented steps to stop the global financial system from plummeting, taking us all with it. Trust, while it lasts, is empowering; but once it fails the only way is down.

NINETEEN TERAWATTS . . . AND COUNTING

Given that the coyote never catches his prey, and so never gets anything to eat, the pedantic viewer might wonder how he manages to survive, let alone keep running. This is where the analogy with global human society breaks down. Humans may not live on bread alone, but they sure do need

9. Seibert and Rees, "Through the Eye of a Needle," 3. See also Wackernagel and Rees, *Our Ecological Footprint*; Global Footprint Network, "Ecological Footprint."

10. On complexity see, e.g., Fieguth, *Introduction to Complex Systems*, 245–69; Holland, *Complexity*, 1–12.

that bread or, in more general terms, sufficient flows of energy coursing through their physical bodies, individually and collectively, in order to live. In fact, human societies only got to be zooming into the fog at this speed by being able to access increasing amounts of energy at faster and faster rates over the course of time. Most of this acceleration has happened only very recently, over the last two hundred years or so. This is pretty remarkable when you bear in mind that settled agriculture became established several thousand years ago, and that the species *Homo sapiens* was around before that for perhaps three hundred thousand years. The rate at which energy is harnessed for whatever counts as useful work is known as *power*, and the following chart speaks volumes about the relevance of power to our current situation.[11]

FIGURE 1

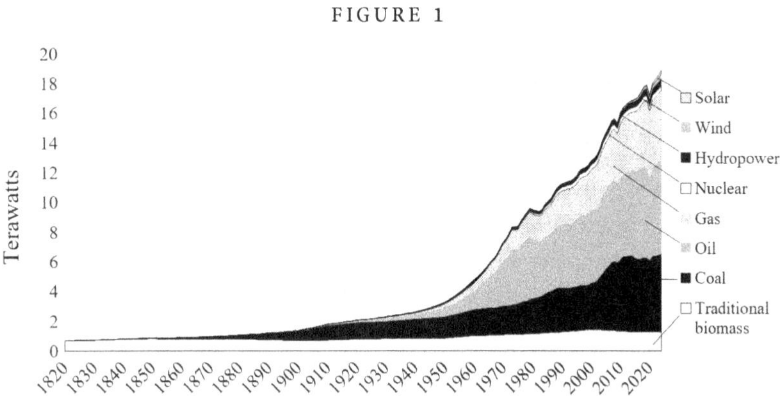

Figure 1: Global primary energy consumption by source, 1820–2024. Sources: see footnote.

One of the things this chart tells us is that by 2024 we were consuming primary energy at a rate of nineteen terawatts—that's nineteen million million watts. An incandescent domestic light bulb typically consumes one hundred watts; an equivalent LED bulb maybe ten watts. Your electric kettle probably runs on two thousand to three thousand watts (two to three kilowatts). So our world in 2024 was consuming primary energy at a rate equivalent to 9.5 billion two-kilowatt kettles running twenty-four hours a day, seven days a week, fifty-two weeks a year, all

11. Energy Institute, "Statistical Review of World Energy"; Smil, *Energy Transitions* (with major processing by Our World in Data); Our World in Data, "Global Direct Primary Energy Consumption."

serving a global population of just over eight billion people.[12] Of course, consumption rates vary hugely across the world, the average American consuming at nineteen times the rate of the average African.[13]

Another thing this chart tells us is that the world's total primary energy consumption rate in 2024 was fully twenty-seven times what it was in 1820. Global population, by comparison, has increased by a factor of less than eight over this period. One last thing to notice is how, at different points over these two centuries, new energy sources have come on stream—coal, oil, natural gas, and so on—yet so far the arrival of each new energy source hasn't resulted in the displacement of older ones.[14] This is crucially important to realize. It's not that human power demand is fixed, and that we've sought to source that via different energy mixes at different times. Rather, new power sources have always gotten harnessed *in addition to* those already in use. It would seem that the world cannot get *enough* power, in other words. By way of illustration, consider that since the year 2000 wind and solar supply has increased from virtually zero to 0.5 terawatts. Far from declining by a comparable amount, coal, oil, and natural gas consumption has increased by almost 5.5 terawatts over the same period—eleven times as much. So much for the renewables transition, thus far at least.

Looked at against a longer time horizon, the human lust for power is even more apparent. Adding the energy contained in human food to primary energy, our hunter-gatherer ancestors got by on some ten to twenty gigajoules per person each year. The advent of agriculture over the millennia since the end of the last Ice Age some 12,000 years ago led to increased power flows through societies, reaching forty to seventy gigajoules per person per annum in eighteenth-century Europe (these figures include the fodder of domesticated animals). Today the share of the average person living in a fully industrialized country is in the region of one hundred and fifty to four hundred gigajoules per annum.[15] Look at it this way: the energy footprint of a contemporary American is twenty to forty times the size of that of one of the original settlers on the continent in the latter part of the last Ice Age.

12. With the caveat that a kettle consumes final energy rather than primary energy. Both are defined in chapter 1.

13. Energy Institute, "Statistical Review of World Energy." Figures for 2024: US—266; Africa—14 gigajoules per capita.

14. York and Bell, "Energy Transitions or Additions?"

15. Haberl et al., "Sociometabolic Transition," 4.

In 1937 George Orwell wrote that "our civilisation . . . is founded on coal, more completely than one realises until one stops to think about it. The machines that keep us alive, and the machines that make machines, are all directly or indirectly dependent upon coal. In the metabolism of the Western world the coal-miner is second in importance only to the man who ploughs the soil."[16] Had he lived today he would surely have referred to oil rather than coal, but his point would have been the same. The industrial harnessing of fossil fuels has been essential for providing us with the power which enables the way of life which we've come to take for granted. Crudely, you could say that power equals prosperity. As the following chart shows, human development in a given country is closely correlated with that country's primary energy consumption footprint (although the correlation weakens for countries with high or very high development indices, i.e., >0.7).[17]

FIGURE 2

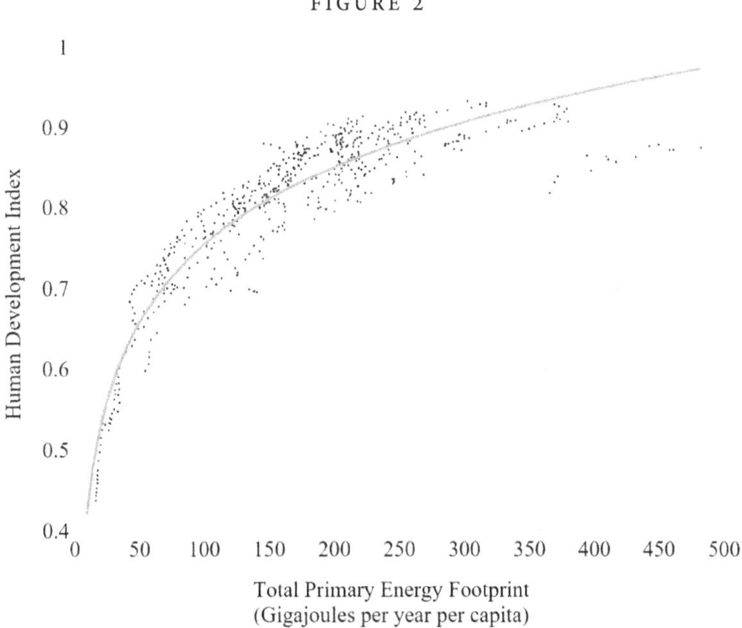

Figure 2: Human Development Index as a function of Total Primary Energy Footprint for forty selected countries, 1995–2008. Each dot represents figures for a given country in a given year. Source: See footnote.

16. Orwell, *Road to Wigan Pier*, 18.

17. Arto et al., "Energy Requirements of a Developed World." "Total Primary Energy Footprint" is defined as the energy consumed worldwide to produce the goods and services demanded by a given country.

This is no mere statistical artifact. In 2020 global primary energy consumption dipped slightly because of pandemic-associated restrictions, as can be seen in figure 1. Since more that 80 percent of primary energy comes from burning fossil fuels global greenhouse gas emissions also declined, by some 5 percent, during that year. Cause for rejoicing? It might be, were it not that those declines were associated with an additional 120 million people being pushed back into extreme poverty. Just imagine, then, the impact of 5 percent reductions in emissions, year on year, as required by the Paris Protocols of 2015: "The global economy would be devastated. Billions would be pushed into poverty, with all the suffering and political instability that would create. It would mean the end of life as we know it in modern societies—aka collapse."[18]

But surely, you might retort, the solution isn't to reduce energy consumption but rather to clean it up. And hasn't renewable energy production taken off in recent years? Sadly the situation isn't that simple. Renewable sources such as wind turbines and solar photovoltaic panels produce electricity, and in 2023 electricity represented only 21 percent of global final energy demand.[19] So that just means that we need to get on with electrifying the energy system, doesn't it? Well yes, but as the table below indicates, the pace of electrification since 1990 has been frustratingly slow; and, to make matters worse, in 2023 as much as 60 percent of electricity was produced by burning fossil fuels—a reduction of only 3 percent over thirty-three years.[20]

	Fossil fuels as percentage of global final energy (excluding electricity generation)	Electricity as percentage of global final energy	Fossil fuels as percentage of global electricity generation	Fossil fuels as percentage of global final energy (including electricity generation)
1990	70	13	63	78
2023	66	21	60	78

Table 1: Global final energy demand, 1990 and 2023. Source: See footnote.

Thus the net result of more than thirty years of effort in greening global energy consumption has been precisely zero: in 2023, 78 percent of final demand still depended on the burning of fossil fuels, exactly the same

18. Bendell, *Breaking Together*, 119.

19. International Energy Agency, "Data and Statistics." "Final energy" is defined in chapter 1.

20. Author's calculations based on International Energy Agency, "Data and Statistics."

proportion as in 1990. Meanwhile, in absolute terms, total final energy demand had grown by no less than 65 percent over this period.

It gets worse yet. Road freight transport cannot realistically be electrified. Neither can aviation or seaborne freight. Heavy industry—the manufacture of iron, steel, and cement in particular—requires high temperatures historically achieved by burning coal or natural gas. Although nonfossil fuel alternatives exist in principle, in practice these are many times more expensive and are burdened by numerous technical challenges.[21]

Worst of all though, the path to a renewably powered future runs in the opposite direction to the path which has led to the modern industrial society which most of us would like to preserve. Consider the *Zero-Carbon Britain* project of the Centre for Alternative Technology near Machynlleth, UK.[22] In the various iterations of this project over the years the authors of this admirably rigorous piece of work have sought to detail how the UK could feasibly achieve a fossil-fuel-free future. For our purposes here, the most salient outcome of their calculations is that, in order to balance power supply and demand, demand has to reduce by a thumping 60 percent relative to recent levels. That's right: a *60 percent* reduction in power consumption. Other factors being equal, just imagine what that would mean for standards of living. Radical changes in ways of life would be necessary, but this fails to figure in much discussion of a green transition.

Hard though such changes would be to swallow, what really makes a program like this stick in the throat is the fact that our inherited economic regime requires, in effect, that power consumption go on *increasing* over time. How so?

In the early modern period Europeans came to adopt a financial system based on interest-bearing debt.[23] From the very start this was linked to accessing new energy subsidies—initially that of wind power, made possible by technical innovations, which enabled long-distance international trade.[24] An underlying economic growth compulsion can be

21. See, e.g., Friedemann, *When Trucks Stop Running*; Centre for Alternative Technology, *Zero-Carbon Britain*, 47–53, 70–72; Hund et al., *Minerals for Climate Action*; Friedmann et al., *Low-Carbon Heat Solutions*; Sandalow et al., *Industrial Heat Decarbonization Roadmap*. See Seibert and Rees, "Through the Eye of a Needle," for a summary of the challenges presented by wholesale decarbonization.

22. Centre for Alternative Technology, *Zero-Carbon Britain*.

23. See chapter 2 below.

24. Robertson, *Three Waves of Globalization*, 78–102; Heinberg, *Party's Over*, 28–29.

traced back to at least this point, with growth becoming an explicit policy goal after World War Two. Following widespread democratizing social changes around the world, economic growth had become essential for social stability. As Edward Heath, prime minister of the UK from 1970 to 1974, put it, "The alternative to expansion is not an England of quiet market towns linked only by trains puffing slowly and peacefully through green meadows. The alternative is slums, dangerous roads, old factories, cramped schools, and stunted lives."[25]

Here's the dilemma: a system based on interest-bearing debt presupposes that there will be more money in circulation next year than there is now. Since money is a claim on wealth, this means a further assumption that we will be wealthier next year than we are now. And since acquiring wealth—however you define it—involves the expending of energy, this implies ever-increasing energy consumption rates. In other words *our financial system requires us to be always accessing more power, and to go on doing that in perpetuity.*[26]

That's why, under the existing financial regime, the goal of net zero emissions is such a pipe dream. As Bendell along with many other hard-headed analysts have shown, it will be impossible to both switch to 100 percent renewable energy sources *and* maintain our current social systems, be they financial, economic, or political.[27] That's why the growth in renewables hasn't staunched the increase in fossil fuel consumption and, of itself, never will. Not under the present social regime, that is. The biophysical power represented by flows of fossil fuels and the social power associated with flows of money are intimately intertwined.

IN THE BEGINNING WAS . . . POWER

The parable of the boy-racer with which this chapter began poses many questions. Questions like: Where is the driver headed? Why the hurry? What's the backstory to this imminently fatal scenario? Burning questions like these make it less a parable than a whodunit, a mystery which demands a solution.

25. Attributed. Douthwaite, *Growth Illusion*, 29.

26. Haberl et al., "Systematic Review," demonstrate the impossibility of decoupling economic growth from resource consumption. See also Hickel and Kallis, "Is Green Growth Possible?"

27. See, e.g., Bendell, *Breaking Together*; Martenson, *Crash Course*; Smil, *Energy and Civilization*; Hagens and White, *Energy Blind*; Jensen et al., *Bright Green Lies*.

This book is an attempt to provide a solution to this mystery. Remarkably though, much of it is already available in summary form in the first three chapters of the book of Genesis. To see why this is so we need to go beyond some of the pious platitudes about the fall of Adam and Eve with which we may be familiar. We need to look instead at how power features in these chapters, and what that might imply for our situation today.

Biblical source critics have long argued that we have not one, but two distinct creation accounts here. The first runs up to the fourth verse of the second chapter, having the form of a liturgical poem which, rather like Ravel's *Bolero*, comprises a series of variations on a repeated pattern, gradually increasing in volume as the piece progresses. The seventh and final iteration of the pattern gives us the paradoxical climax of the poem when, after the epic yet peaceful calling-forth of creation in all its complexity, God the creator rests. For those more interested in action, however, the story peaks on day six with the creation of the human.

Much has been written about these verses, especially the mandate to "have dominion" over every other living thing, to "fill the earth and subdue it." Understandably some have seen this mandate as lying at the root of the polycrisis, as if the human had thereby been ordered to bully the rest of creation into submission.[28] This isn't the place to enter into an extended exegesis of these verses, but we do have to admit that the language used by the author is strong: both "have dominion" (*radah*) and "subdue" (*kabash*) have at their roots the idea of trampling down, of forceful subjugation.[29] Likewise, in the context of the polycrisis, even the relatively innocuous command to "fill" (*male'*) the earth might suggest the supplanting by the human of everything else.

What gets in the way of this kind of interpretation is the realization that the creature charged with this mandate stands out from the rest of creation precisely by bearing God's image and likeness. Carrying out the mandate, therefore, can only be done in ways which authentically express this divinely rooted identity. And what we know about God, on the basis of the earlier parts of this creation account, is his notably *un*forceful manner. Unlike the gods of other ancient Near Eastern creation myths this

28. White, "Historical Roots of Our Ecologic Crisis." On the "Lynn White thesis" see, e.g., LeVasseur and Peterson, *Religion and the Ecological Crisis*; Milbank, "Out of the Greenhouse."

29. "In most contexts in which it [*radah*] occurs it seems to suggest an absolute or even fierce exercise of mastery." Alter, *Genesis*, 5.

one doesn't create through a primordial act of violence.[30] Rather, in the manner of a benign potentate, he commands and it simply is so: what was obscure, formless, and void, *tōhū wābōhū*, becomes distinct and real. This is how the basic gift of identity is conferred. God's style of creation is well summed up in theologian John Macquarrie's phrase—God *lets be*, and in so doing exhibits who and how God is.[31]

By implication human rule over creation should therefore mirror this letting-be, not in the sense of disinterest or neglect but of allowing, through human engagement, the fullness of creation to emerge. This reading also allows us to read the human filling of the earth as its *ful*filling.[32] Most importantly, though, what the first creation account makes clear is that the human is both part of God's creation yet, equally, different to all the rest by virtue of bearing the divine image and likeness. Human rule is therefore most true to its deepest nature when it reflects the divine rule exhibited at creation, and experienced still, as uncoercive providence. This is how God's power works. So long as the divine image and likeness remain intact, the human exercise of power always operates subject to this basic constraint.

So long as they remain intact . . . The second creation account tells the sorry tale of how the call to steward God's creative power issues in tragic failure. In Genesis chapter 2 the human is molded from the dust of the earth and infused with the divine breath. The human is also given a twofold job: to both watch over, or care for (*shamar*), and to cultivate, or work (*ābad*), the garden of Eden. Notice the tension here between simultaneously conserving and somehow altering a given status quo. What kind of work is consistent with caring for the garden? Whatever answer we give, it's a matter of how the human stewards entrusted power. In discharging the divine mandate, the human is permitted to eat from any tree in the garden apart from the tree of the knowledge of good and evil. Without entering headlong into debates regarding the meanings of the fateful tree, the serpent, the story's gender politics, and so on, we can at least notice how this single exception to God's carte blanche highlights two very basic things about being human.

First, the story brings into relief a lacuna in human existence: the space between *can* and *should*. "Can" implies power, the freedom

30. See, e.g., Tamtik, "Enuma Elish."

31. Macquarrie, *Principles of Christian Theology*, 190–210.

32. Which is linguistically quite legitimate. Compare, e.g., the use of *male'* in Gen 25:24, "When her time to give birth was fulfilled, there were twins in her womb."

or technical ability to do something, to act as an agent, to bring about change. "Should" on the other hand implies a constraint on one's freedom, excluding certain actions and/or mandating others. This isn't a physical constraint; rather it's ethical, that is to say, to do with right interpersonal or social relationships, in this case God's relationship to Adam and Eve. The human in Eden *can* eat from the tree but *should not*. That the human *does* so nonetheless is the consequence of desire, specifically a propensity to reach to the very limits of what is technically possible—to exercise maximum power, if you will. The *ascesis* of *not* doing something that can be done doesn't come easily to us. Of course some individuals will find it easier to say no than others; but if I don't do it, someone else almost certainly will. Collectively, therefore, humanity goes on tasting of the forbidden fruit time and time again.

Secondly, Adam and Eve's downfall can be read as a meditation on how particular *kinds* of power are necessarily accompanied by certain corresponding constraints. Consider St. Augustine's argument that, prior to eating the fruit—that is, while still operating under the constraint of the divine *should not*—the human exercised a particular kind of power, namely the power not to sin.[33] By exercising another kind of power—the physical power to pluck a fruit and eat it—the human lost the primordial power not to sin, and so became subject to a new set of constraints, symbolized by exclusion from Eden. Now, outside Eden, the biophysical power of twenty-first-century humanity may seem unbounded, human technological ingenuity giving the impression that we can in principle do anything we want. Except that we can no longer enjoy the beatitude for which we were created. That, surely, must qualify as a pretty substantial constraint.

Different kinds of power, and the defining of power by its associated constraints: these themes will crop up time and again in the following chapters and offer insight into why twenty-first-century humanity, unprecedentedly powerful, seems powerless to take its foot off the throttle. And in examining this phenomenon from different angles we will also come to better formulate a question to which Jesus may just be the answer.

33. Augustine, *On Rebuke and Grace* 12. See also Kelly, *Early Christian Doctrines*, 361–66.

IF JESUS IS THE ANSWER, WHAT IS THE QUESTION?

In a book which deals with many of the same ideas which will be covered here, theologian Clayton Crockett, having surveyed our gloomy predicament, asks:

> What is to be done? What can we do? . . . Nothing. There is nothing to be done. Why not? Because it is our nature. We are fulfilling our nature as living beings and we cannot do otherwise. We maximize our resources, we reproduce to fill all available niches, and we emit waste products until our environment is no longer hospitable and we collapse. . . . We cannot change our nature. It is fixed, immutable, a death sentence; just like life. We have to change our nature, but that is impossible. But what if our nature is change? That is the thesis of this book.[34]

Such candor is stark and, in the context of hollow "net zero" platitudes, commendable. The extract ends on an intriguing note though. While I agree with Crockett that change is possible, my aim here is to show (a) why in practice it's so difficult and (b) where to look to find the power, that is, the enabling constraint, to make the right kind of changes. To answer the question of what is to be done in a way which is both hopeful and grounded in the reality of our human condition, we need first to reframe it in a way that brings out certain key facets of our predicament. That's what this book seeks to do.

If, as I've suggested, the human attitude towards power lies at the root of the seemingly suicidal joyride on which our species is embarked, then we need to start by clarifying what we mean by power and how power works. This is the theme of chapter 1, which begins with a brief introduction to the scientific conception of power as the rate of performing useful work. The phenomenon of social power is then explored at greater depth, drawing mainly on the three-dimensional analytical framework provided by sociologist Steven Lukes. The notions of useful work and capacity emerge as common threads uniting the natural sciences and the humanities. Since human work is useful to the extent that it satisfies human desires, this leads to a discussion of desires and interests, and especially the sense in which our desires are "borrowed" from others. Trust figures centrally in the workings of social power, and this prompts a consideration of how money mediates trust, a theme which gets taken up again in later chapters. The mutual entanglement of power and constraint,

34. Crockett, *Energy and Change*, 16–17.

which we've already noticed was apparent in the garden of Eden, is also noted by Lukes: even as we wield power, power is shaping us.[35]

Chapter 2 introduces the idea of *maximum* power for the first time in the form of evolutionary biology's Maximum Power Principle (MPP). This asserts that life is lived on the edge of possibility, with organisms striving to harness energy for useful work at the fastest possible rate. However the way in which this principle gets expressed varies during the life cycles of organisms and ecosystems. The work of ecologists such as Buzz Holling shows how ecological ensembles typically cycle through four stages, which include collapse and some form of eventual reorganization. There are indications that human economies follow similar cycles, with the seemingly good news of increasing efficiency in fact being a sign of approaching senescence. I go on to describe how the recent windfall of fossil fuel energy, in combination with the MPP, has led to the ecological overshoot highlighted by ecologist Bill Rees. All this culminates in a discussion of the MPP's possible implications for human society which draws on anthropologist Leslie White's association of human cultural development with per capita power consumption.

Chapter 3 picks up where the previous one left off, questioning how far the MPP tells the whole story about how natural systems, let alone human ones, work. Here I turn to thermodynamics and introduce the work of Rod Swenson: his proposed Law of Maximum Entropy Production (LMEP) and his account of autocatakinesis, the process of spontaneous ordering which occurs in zones of steep gradients and strong flows. Swenson's ideas show how we can reframe the popular idea of entropy as simple disorder in terms of transformed, or realized, potential. They also allow the MPP to be seen as an emergent phenomenon—an aspect of the optimal expression of the LMEP in a particular kind of context, specifically in biological systems. This leads to a discussion of emergence more generally, as the way in which complexity in nature arises through hierarchical ordering. I illustrate this by turning again to ecology, and show how, during the growth and development of biological and ecological systems, other goals or principles are manifested alongside the MPP, leading to an emergent optimality which varies according to the system's stage of development.

In chapter 4 I look at one particular and fateful instance of how the MPP is expressed. The chapter deals with superorganisms, understood

35. Lukes, *Power*, 169.

as those collective entities which arise when populations of so-called ultrasocial individuals are organized so as to produce (storable) surplus. Superorganisms are emergent forms of life which unambiguously demonstrate the MPP in action, and they've been prone to emerge in human societies whenever settled agriculture has become established. I make connections between the work of several different authors here, including that of economists John Gowdy and Lisi Krall, who see human ultrasociality as being responsible for precipitating the current polycrisis, and that of New Testament scholar Walter Wink in his reading of the biblical Principalities and Powers.

Are organized human societies then doomed to be propelled helplessly towards the edge of the precipice by the MPP? In chapter 5 I return to the theme of power in both its material and social aspects, exploring what they have in common and where they differ. To do this I make use of Gilles Deleuze and Félix Guattari's notions of assembling and its double articulation. These provide a concise and illuminating framework for relating material and social power as two articulations of a common reality. In particular they provide a way of understanding how qualitative social power emerges from quantitative material power, and how this emergence can go wrong. A notable example is the case of money which, though a trust-based social construct, commonly functions as a sublimation of the quantitative brute force associated with material power. I conclude that, crucially, the MPP's expression in human affairs remains underdetermined by its manifestations in biological systems.

Chapter 6 is the point at which sustained attention is given for the first time to the biblical witness regarding power. It offers a reading of the New Testament, and of the Gospels in particular, through the lens of some of the key terms introduced in earlier chapters, allowing the Gospels in turn to cast new light on them. Jesus's power and powerlessness are brought into dialogue with ideas already encountered, namely the difference between material and social power and the always-constrained nature of the latter. Assemblage thinking is deployed so as to both bring out the difference between mere biological fecundity and the abundant life offered by the Jesus of John's Gospel, and in order to illuminate John's presentation of the miracles as signs. The contrast between flesh and spirit in John and Paul underscores how the different stories by which we live can give rise to radically different second articulations of the social assembling. The difference between the church, as the broken body of Christ, and superorganisms generated by the dynamic of ultrasociality is highlighted. Maximum power, understood in a qualitative sense, is expressed in Jesus's death on the cross, and so revealed as the fulfillment of his life and calling.

Finally, in chapter 7, the theme of maximum power is revisited in the light of the various other themes explored in the course of the book. Paul's comments regarding Christ as "the power of God and the wisdom of God" in 1 Corinthians 1:24 provide the basis here. I reflect on the nature of wisdom, both in the biblical tradition and in the writings of theologian Stanley Hauerwas as he discusses what it really means to exercise agency. The chapter closes with a concluding summary of the book's message: maximum power in human affairs is in the end a qualitative, not a quantitative, matter; it is optimal wisdom, and the story of the crucified Christ makes explicit the practical implications of this in a social milieu perversely defaulting to a merely quantitative performance of the MPP. Jesus is the answer, and the only possible one, to the question of how to survive and even thrive through collapse; and mediating God's saving power and wisdom means embracing the constraint of walking the way of the cross.

1

Useful Work? Power, Material and Social

A railway station in an English town, early on a chill winter morning. Last night's wind has now quietened down, but it still whips across the platform, making the assembled would-be passengers shrink into themselves and press hands ever deeper into pockets. Eight people in all with different destinations in view. Who are they, and how did they come to be making these journeys?

Alan doesn't want to be here, but he has no choice. He's wearing handcuffs. Close alongside him is a plain-clothes police officer. These two have the shortest journey, just two stops, to the magistrate's court where Alan's case will be heard for the first time—simply a matter of entering a plea and receiving a bail-application decision. The police officer doesn't want to be here either. Normally they'd have taken Alan in the wagon, but with so many colleagues off sick that's not an option today.[1]

Jake is on his way to Westminster. He's one of the new intake of members of Parliament (MPs): a bright lad, tipped for a bright future. He really isn't looking forward to the day ahead though. There's a big vote coming up on an issue he feels very strongly about, and there's a country mile between where he stands and his party's official position. If he goes with his conscience and defies the party line his ambitions could get seriously thwarted. It might even mean deselection. Deep down he knows he has little choice about which way to vote.

Sarah is another of today's reluctant travelers. Or is she? She's on her way to visit her mom, who lives on the other side of the country.

1. No doubt this is highly irregular, but my intention here is to illustrate how social power works rather than to portray standard police procedure.

Somehow she managed to get a few days off work. It's been manic lately and trying to catch up when she gets back will be a nightmare. But her mom's not well, Sarah hasn't seen her for ages, and their nightly phone calls always end with Sarah feeling guilty about being such a bad daughter. Her husband keeps telling her that her mom's far from death's door and just wants attention. But that doesn't change how Sarah feels: that she has no choice but to carve out the time to go over there.

Nicola is on her way up to London for the demo. She's been to lots before, and each time the police have gotten heavier handed. Last time some people she knows got arrested. This time it could be her, she thinks, as she checks in her bag for the tube of superglue. She's feeling excited, but also a bit scared—she's never glued herself to railings, or in fact to anything, before. Still, what choice has she got? The stakes are so high: we're in a climate emergency, and desperate measures are needed to get people's attention if we're to stand any chance of saving the planet. Her love for the natural world, along with the strength of her friends' convictions, have made it so obvious to her that there's no other way.

Dennis and Lisa are off on holiday. They're on their way to the airport to fly to Madeira. Lisa can't wait. She's been leaving brochures for sunny overseas resorts around the place for months, suggesting options, listing the pros and cons of each destination. Dennis isn't so bothered. If it was just up to him they'd get in the motorhome and head off somewhere in the UK. Lisa's been very persistent though, and careful to let him have the final say about where exactly they go—so long as it's abroad. That's the choice. So: Madeira sounds nice, said Dennis eventually; Madeira it is then, replied a beaming Lisa.

That leaves Hannah, an Anglican priest. She's been in her current post, the first in a parish of her own, for about eighteen months. It's been challenging. The small congregation is used to very traditional ways, and she's been keen to ring the changes. That hasn't gone down well, and a couple of weeks ago she finally lost her temper with a prominent congregation member who'd been hectoring her ever since she arrived. He's not been in church since, and now she's been summoned to see her bishop for a chat about how she's "getting on." Hannah's sure it's because he's had complaints about her. She doesn't want to go to see him today, not a bit. But, as a priest, she has no choice but to accede. He is her bishop, after all.

Eight travelers embarking from the same place but on very different journeys, each with his or her own particular thoughts. But none of these journeys are to be; for just then an announcement on the public address system tells them that train services have been canceled until further notice because of damage caused by the overnight storm-force winds . . .

What is power? This little vignette is an attempt to collect together a range of different answers to that question, illustrating the varied ways in which power is expressed in human life. We shall meet Alan, Sarah, and the rest again in the course of this chapter as we consider their experiences. But the obvious place to begin this discussion is with the *Oxford English Dictionary*. My copy provides no fewer that eighteen different definitions of power. They all relate to either (a) scientific and engineering applications or (b) social contexts.[2] The former are relatively straightforward and are exemplified by the factor which frustrated our travelers' plans that morning: the power of the wind.

MATERIAL POWER: DOING USEFUL WORK

A preliminary definition of power can be found in physics textbooks: "the time rate of (total) energy transfer." Energy is being transferred around us all the time; sometimes as a result of human activity, but more fundamentally as a consistent feature of the world in which humans find themselves. For our world is marked by *gradients* in *fields* of different kinds. Wind, air in motion, blows down gradients in the atmospheric pressure field.[3] Rivers flow only because of gradients in planet Earth's gravitational field. There are many different kinds of fields—gravitational, temperature, electromagnetic, and so forth—and the gradient in any of them creates a propensity for movements or *flows* from zones of high *potential* to zones of low potential.

Power, on its simplest definition, is the rate at which such flows transfer energy. In the *Système Internationale* it's measured in watts, or joules per second. Mathematically, power equals the product of the difference in potential and the rate of flow or motion. The difference in

2. Strictly speaking, the *Dictionary* also offers the following definition of power: "a deity or sixth order of the nine-fold celestial hierarchy." We will encounter Powers of this sort in chapter 4.

3. Actually the direction of wind, and ocean, currents is complicated by the spin of the Earth—the Coriolis effect.

potential in a given field acts as a force on any object interacting with that field; so while an electrically charged particle will respond to a potential difference in an electrical field, an uncharged particle will not. The greater the potential difference, the greater the power associated with the flow. If I drop an object from a height the force associated with the difference in gravitational potential is demonstrated by the acceleration of that object as it falls. The greater the potential difference, the faster the motion, the greater the power associated with that motion.

But that object won't continue accelerating forever. As it falls it will impact with air molecules which exert a force acting to resist its motion; and the faster the motion the greater the resistance. Eventually the force of resistance will balance the force associated with the difference in gravitational potential and the object will stop accelerating, reaching a terminal velocity. If the object is a skydiving human that velocity will be about 118 mph. So the power associated with motion due to a gradient in field potential depends on two factors: (1) the size of the potential difference and (2) the amount of resistance to the motion from the medium in which the motion occurs.

Once we turn from physics to biology or engineering things get more interesting. A new term appears: *work*. And, along with it, a second definition of power as the time rate at which (useful) work is done. How does (useful) work differ from mere energy? Biologist Stanley Salthe offers a simple definition of work as "useful (to some agent) energy degradation."[4] Energy gets degraded in the sense that, as it flows down a gradient, it loses potential for doing work. Just think of a volume of water flowing over, and so turning, a mill wheel: once it has reached the lower level that volume can no longer do work in turning the wheel (though it could of course go on to turn other wheels placed at lower points in the gravitational potential field). Energy can also get degraded when it changes form: burning a piece of wood involves changing the potential energy held in the bonds of the wood's carbon atoms into the kinetic energy (the energy associated with motion) of the air molecules in its vicinity. In the form of heat that energy will disperse rapidly, such that once

4. Salthe, "Natural Philosophy of Work," 85. The idea of useful work is related to that of exergy, defined as "the capacity a system has for performing work over and above what the same system would possess at thermodynamic equilibrium (when the system consists only of inorganic matter in its highest possible oxidation state and contains no gradients)." Ulanowicz et al., "Exergy, Information and Aggradation," 520.

it's briefly warmed your hands it's of no further use. Energy cannot be created or destroyed, but its usefulness depends a lot on what form it's in.

What does Salthe mean by an agent? In biology an agent would be a living organism. Here energy—in forms such as sunlight and food—is put to work in sustaining the functioning of the organs and cells which make up the organism. That work is useful in the sense that it serves the organism's basic goal of staying alive.

In engineering, agents are machines. Here again energy—this time in the form of harnessed flows like rivers or human-generated flows like electricity—is put to work by making human devices function. These devices, in turn, serve human interests within the larger context of the enterprise known as civilization. On this second definition of power, wind can only be regarded as powerful when put to work in this way, for example to drive a turbine or windmill, and not when its unharnessed action brings disruption to railway timetables. It's this second definition of material, or biophysical, power, as the rate of doing (useful) work, which I shall generally use from this point onward.

When energy is harnessed for human use it's helpful to distinguish the energy which actually ends up performing useful work from what are termed primary energy and final energy. An electric light powered by electricity generated through the burning of natural gas at a power station provides an illustration. The efficiency of a simple-cycle natural gas power plant is around 40 percent; that is, only 40 percent of the *primary energy* released when the gas is burned gets converted into electricity, the remainder being dissipated as heat. A further 5–10 percent of the primary energy will get lost overcoming the resistance of the transmission cables conveying the electricity to the consumer. Of the remaining, *final*, energy reaching the consumer, some 90 percent will get converted into light by an LED bulb, and so constitute *useful work*.[5]

5. For a more detailed analysis of the relationship between primary energy, final energy, and useful work, see Grubler et al., *Energy Primer*, 116–19; King, *Economic Superorganism*, 32. Note also that these measures refer to extrasomatic energy, i.e., they do not include the energy contained in food and animal fodder.

FIGURE 3

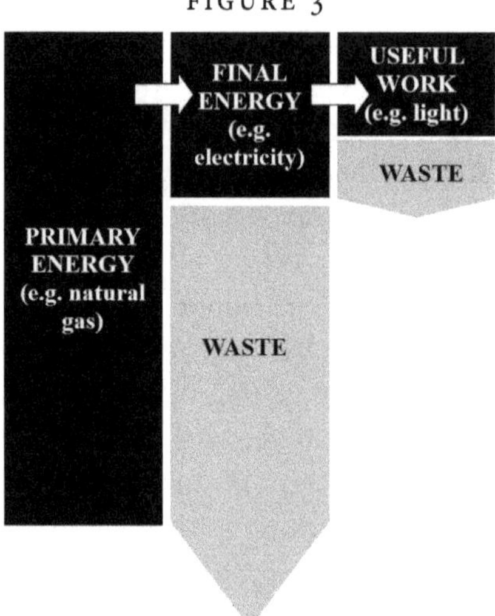

Figure 3: Schematic illustration of the conversion of primary energy to final energy to useful work.

Work, therefore, is energy harnessed for use by some entity or system in order to exercise a function.[6] What about, say, hurricanes and wildfires: these are places where energy gets transferred, but do they do work? Can they be associated with power on this second definition? Salthe concedes that, in some broad sense, they do indeed perform meteorological and ecological functions respectively. Hurricanes are ways in which nature as it were lets off steam, dissipating gradients of temperature and pressure which would otherwise carry on growing indefinitely; and wildfires recycle ecosystems.[7] But they don't *harness* energy to do work in the very specific ways in which, say, a kidney or a microprocessor do. By contrast fire can certainly be said to do work when used to cook, incinerate rubbish, smelt metals, immolate heretics, and so forth, that is to say once it has been harnessed by human beings. And in being harnessed by humans it not only executes a function but also serves a purpose, a purpose animated by desire.

In fact what we should take away from this brief overview of material power as work rate is its essential relation to function and purpose.

6. By definition work must be useful to the entity or system in question but, despite being strictly redundant, the adjective is nonetheless generally retained here simply in order to stress this intrinsic feature of work as such.

7. Salthe, "Natural Philosophy of Work," 85.

An animal's heart—say that of a cat—requires energy in order to do work to keep it alive: that is its *function*. What about the cat itself though; does it have a function? It may happen to exercise some function as part of an ecological ensemble along with other living things, or it might be used by humans to exercise a function such as pest control or companionship. Those uses would be secondary and incidental, though, because inherently the cat is an end in itself. It has no function if it isn't integrated into some larger whole.[8] Its only overarching goal is to stay alive and reproduce. It "works," exercises power, only as it pursues this goal. This basic, instinctive disposition is what the seventeenth-century philosopher Spinoza called *conatus*, a term often translated as *striving*. We shall encounter Spinoza and *conatus* time and again in what follows.

Human beings are animals too. Although they may have jobs and roles within families and organizations, functioning in those roles as parents, bricklayers, and so on, like animals they have no *inherent* function: as Immanuel Kant emphasized, human beings too are ends in themselves. But humans do entertain *purposes*.[9] Unlike the *conatus* of animals and plants, and the functions of machines and biological organs, purposes aren't simply given but are instead often the subject of protracted personal agonizing and intense social debate. "How should I/we use my/our power?" is a question which is always around, if only in the background. Does human life as a whole have an overarching purpose beyond simply staying alive and reproducing, a life plan which gets played out through all the myriad tiny sub-purposes which make up my everyday life? If so, what is it?[10]

Because human purposes aren't simply given but instead have to some degree to be chosen, and because most human life occurs within society, the exercise of power by humans involves a further dimension which sets it apart from the ones considered so far. This is the theme I shall turn to next. But the idea of useful work remains basic to this additional dimension also. And what's deemed useful, however mundane or trivial in itself, must ultimately refer to the overarching purpose of

8. As we shall see in chapter 4, individuals can serve well-defined functions in organized group contexts, notably in the case of ultrasocial animal collectives.

9. In fact human purposing can be seen as "a refinement of more generally occurring tendencies in nature"—the functions of biological entities and the propensities of physical systems: see Salthe, "Purpose in Nature." On teleonomy, the systemic purposiveness of biological systems in general, see, e.g., Corning, *Holistic Darwinism*, 89–121.

10. Sociologist Alfred Schutz has offered a valuable framework for apprehending how life plans are constituted. See, e.g., Schutz, "Some Structures of the Life-World."

the human enterprise as a whole. What counts as social power, therefore, depends on what one takes this overarching purpose to be.

SOCIAL POWER: THREE WAYS TO GET PEOPLE TO DO WHAT YOU WANT

Defining material power is a straightforward matter. Defining social power turns out to be a lot more involved. Sociologist Steven Lukes, who will be our main guide in what follows, is quite candid about this: "There is no agreement about how to define it, how to conceive it, how to study it and, if it can be measured, how to measure it."[11] Consider the following candidate definitions:

1. The POWER of a man [is] his present means to obtain some future apparent good.[12]
2. Power consists in making others act as I choose.[13]
3. Liberty, when men act in bodies, is power.[14]
4. Power is the production of intended effects.[15]
5. Power is getting what one wants.[16]
6. Power is the capacity to get others to do things that otherwise they would not do.[17]

Already here we notice a number of aspects to social power. Most obvious is the idea, expressed in (4) and (5), that power has to do with realizing one's desires. In a social context that typically means affecting the behavior of others so as to achieve that end—hence (2) and (6). (1) suggests that power is in essence something latent, a capacity or facility to realize some goal rather than the exercise of that capacity. Finally (3) identifies social power with the additional freedom deriving from collective action, when the actions of a number of people are united in a common cause.

11. Lukes, *Power*, 66.
12. Thomas Hobbes, quoted in Lukes, "Power and Authority," 85.
13. Voltaire, quoted in Lukes, "Power and Authority," 86.
14. Edmund Burke, quoted in Lukes, *Power*, 67.
15. Bertrand Russell, quoted in Lukes, *Power*, 81.
16. Alvin I. Goldman, quoted in Lukes, *Power*, 81.
17. Mann, *Sources of Social Power*, 5.

There's a case for regarding this last definition (3) as basic to power as a social phenomenon, the collective *power to* achieve a goal which would not be possible for an isolated individual, nor for the same number of individuals acting independently. This can usefully be distinguished from *power over* others (2 and 6), which may or may not be involved when collective action is undertaken. Spinoza long ago made a parallel distinction between *potentia*, the simple power to exist and act so as to cause effects, and *potestas*, the securing of one person's compliance with the will of another.[18]

Let's return to the railway platform and consider how these distinctions help us to understand how power is being expressed through the circumstances of the travelers.

The police officer clearly has *power over* his handcuffed prisoner Alan. However this power isn't exercised simply as an individual but rather, and more consequentially, as a part and representative of a particular social collective, namely the police force. And the police force in turn exercises *power over* the populace in general by virtue of its role as a functional part of organized society. Lukes calls this mode of power *force*, the securing of compliance by the removal of the option not to comply—hence the handcuffs.[19] In this example force is an expression of the state's claim on the monopoly of violence within society, that is, the use of physical, or material, power to achieve its ends. Force, we might say, is power exercised over a body rather than over a person.

Jake, by contrast, is not going to be forced to follow his party's line. The whips aren't going to physically push him down that division lobby.[20] But they can make it very, very clear to him that his career is over if he doesn't toe the line. This is an example of "where A secures B's compliance by the threat of deprivation," termed *coercion* by Lukes. Jake's party wants him to vote one way; Jake doesn't want to; but if he doesn't comply with his party's wishes then there's a risk that he'll be deprived of what he *does* want, namely a long and fruitful political career. In this way his party has *power over* Jake.

18. Baruch Spinoza, quoted in Lukes, *Power*, 78–79.

19. Lukes, *Power*, 26–27, 40–41. With these categorizations Lukes is drawing on the earlier work of Bachrach and Baratz, *Power and Poverty*.

20. Whips are members of Parliament responsible for making sure that their party's MPs vote the way their party wants. MPs vote by walking down one of the two division lobbies in the House of Commons, the Aye Lobby and the No Lobby.

Sarah's mother, likewise, has *power over* her. Except this power is expressed in a more subtle manner. Her mother hasn't asked her to visit as such, but—on her husband's reading, at least—she's deliberately exerted psychological pressure on Sarah so as to get that result. Sarah, for her part, is only aware of a vague but inescapable sense of obligation. This is power as *manipulation*, in which compliance happens without the complier understanding how their action is the result of another's prompting.

Hannah, on the other hand, knows full well why she's going to see her bishop. He asked her to do so, politely but with the power of Hannah's vow of canonical obedience unmistakably in the background. This is *power over* expressed and apprehended as *authority*. Within the shared world of values inhabited by a priest and her bishop there's a recognition of the bishop's entitlement to summon a priest, and of the priest's obligation to obey.

So far these are all examples of what Lukes terms the first dimension of power, in which one person gets another "to do things that otherwise they would not do." What about Dennis and Lisa? Lisa didn't force, coerce, or manipulate Dennis's choice of destination, and neither did she exploit any structure of authority. Madeira was his decision, and his alone. But she was careful to circumscribe his range of options. This illustrates the second of Lukes's dimensions of power, that of agenda-setting. Here *power over* is exercised not by securing compliance with a particular desired outcome but by delimiting the range of issues which are up for discussion, and so the range of possible actions. For Dennis, staying at home was never really on the cards.

Lukes describes the third, final, and most far-reaching of his dimensions of power thus:

> *A* may exercise power over *B* by getting him to do what he does not want to do, but he also exercises power over him by influencing, shaping or determining his very wants. Indeed, is it not the supreme exercise of power to get another or others to have the desires you want them to have—that is, to secure their compliance by controlling their thoughts and desires?[21]

Setting aside more extreme visions conjured by the likes of *1984* and *Brave New World*, this is, after all, how the advertising industry works: by getting us to want what it wants us to want. And in the realm of politics those on the Left, at least since Marx, have inveighed against the deeply

21. Lukes, *Power*, 32.

rooted ideologies which serve to justify, however unconsciously, the arbitrary rule of elites to the masses. But the same processes are at work whenever a particular outlook is cultivated in the mind of another person or whenever an existing set of values is exploited. And, notably, those doing the cultivating and exploiting—presumably unlike advertisers—may indeed believe their own hype.

Nicola's peer group provides an example of this. It's clearly made a huge impression on her and in that sense has exercised *power over* her. She may well not experience this as at all coercive, and if asked would insist that, in going on the demo, she's simply doing what she herself wants to do. Equally, you could argue that her response simply reflects the success of the peer group members' efforts in recruiting Nicola to their cause. To point this out isn't necessarily to impugn their sincerity or question their motives. Her peer group is no doubt made up of true believers, and it would be a mistake to see this is as an instance of manipulation, a mode of the first dimension of power. Rather the third dimension goes beyond the deliberate eliciting of certain specific actions to the possibly unconscious nurturing of a general disposition.[22] This dynamic will feature again below when we touch on René Girard's theory of mimetic desire.

SOCIAL POWER: STRONGER TOGETHER

Lukes's three dimensions are examples of what he calls asymmetric power, the power of one party over another, Spinoza's *potestas*. But this is secondary to social power in its most basic form, which is *power to* or *potentia*. People acting together collaboratively can achieve more than the aggregation of the same people acting independently; the group is more powerful than the totality of its individual members; the whole is greater than the sum of its parts; together, we are empowered. In practice this may well involve an element of some people exercising *power over* others; but, by being harnessed into a collective effort, each individual has a share in the enhanced collective power of the whole. That said, the cost of this may be a loss of individual agency, or identity even, with the individual reduced to being little more than a cog in a machine. Slavery represents an extreme instance of individuals having to endure *power*

22. "To focus on 'manipulation' by defining the concept of power as deliberate intervention is unduly to narrow its scope. Power can be at work, inducing compliance by influencing desires and beliefs, without being 'intelligent and intentional.'" Lukes, *Power*, 141.

over while being alienated from the *power to* arising from their collective effort. As we shall see in a later chapter, the changes in social organization following the Neolithic agrarian revolution, even when they've stopped short of outright slavery, illustrate this well.

Yet human life is always already social and, in some measure, collaborative. From infancy a person can only exist as part of some larger social whole—the family, followed by school and the workplace. And, from infancy, the power relations in which a person is immersed assume two related forms: trust and authority.

Social relationships wholly devoid of *trust* are scarcely imaginable. That I venture out each morning without wearing a stab vest implies that I trust those strangers whom I will meet *not* to come at me with a knife. That trust may not always prove justified, but even in areas blighted by high rates of knife crime actually getting stabbed is the exception that proves the rule of justified trust. This is before we even begin to think about the levels of trust required in the simplest cooperative task or commercial exchange: people may occasionally let me down or swindle me, and I may become more wary as a result, but in general I'll likely continue to trust my colleagues and business partners, at least up to a point. This is because trust is imbued with such "extraordinary creative potential," *potentia*, *power to*.[23] To live in society at all is to trust.

Trust can exist as a purely "horizontal" phenomenon. That is, it doesn't presuppose any social hierarchy, but instead spontaneously occurs as a feature of peer relationships. Sometimes trust is formally expressed through making a *promise*. If I make a promise I grant someone else *power over* me—that is, I constrain myself to act in a certain way. Equally I exercise *power over* the other person via the risk that I might renege on my promise and so leave them in a compromised position.[24] Promises can be coerced—"promise me this or else"—but need not be. However they always presuppose *desire* on the part of both parties entering into a formal relationship of trust.

Imagine you've lent me some money. Maybe I've agreed to pay you interest; maybe you just want to feel good about having done someone a favor. My IOU states that I'll settle up on payday. You wouldn't accept the

23. Philip Goodchild makes a central distinction between credit—the extension of creative, informal trust—and debt, as expressed in formal, quantitative promises to repay. Defined in this way, God's power is the power to grant credit. See Goodchild, *Credit and Faith*.

24. Consider bailed-out banks regarded "too big to fail" by governments.

IOU if you didn't trust me (assuming the sum involved is nontrivial to you). However there's one particular kind of IOU which enables strangers, even enemies, to do business with each other. An example of that kind of IOU is the £20 note you gave me. On it is written: "I promise to pay the bearer on demand the sum of twenty pounds." It's another IOU, this time from a third party, namely the Chief Cashier of the Bank of England. Do either of us know and trust her? The question is irrelevant to our transaction. What matters is that we both trust the social institution represented by the Chief Cashier. This trust is different to the trust you and I have in each other because this isn't a relationship between peers. It's "vertical"—that is, it represents some kind of social hierarchy, and so an additional facet of power. Such vertical trust is a form of *authority*.

Authority in this example is institutional, and so impersonal. However it can also be expressed in personal ways, as when someone asserts authority simply by the way they speak, their physical appearance, or their general demeanor. What personal and institutional authority share is the element of social hierarchy: we defer to them, that is, we acknowledge by our actions that they are in some respect senior or superior to us (though we may resent it).[25]

Why do people living, as I do, in the UK trust the Bank of England's IOUs? Because they know that everyone in the UK wants them. Why do they want them? There are two related reasons. First, if I want something you have—that apple, for example—it's likely that you'll satisfy my desire in return for enough of the Bank's IOUs; and you in turn can be confident that you'll be able to swap those IOUs for something you want from someone else. The second and more basic reason is that the Bank's IOUs are required in order to avoid incarceration. How come? Because the government asserts its authority, and so its *power over* us via coercion and force if necessary, by demanding that we pay taxes. And that tax liability can only be met by handing over enough of the Bank's IOUs to the government. So in accepting a Bank of England IOU what I'm actually trusting isn't that the Chief Cashier of the Bank will swap it for something else (she won't), but rather that the UK government will accept it in settlement of £20 of my (government assessed) tax liability.[26]

25. One kind, or instance, of authority may trump another: "The crowds were astounded by Jesus's teaching for he taught as one having authority, and not as their scribes." Matt 7:28–29.

26. Ryan-Collins et al., *Where Does Money Come From?*, 35–37.

Authority in general certainly represents a form of *power over*. It has its sanctions; and these, depending on the authority in question, can be exercised by means of force, coercion, or manipulation. But, as Lukes notes, authority can't be reduced to these expressions of power. No one is going to put a gun to Hannah's head if she declines to visit her bishop, though there would be considerable disciplinary consequences. However that's not why she set out to see him. Disciplinary contingencies are there as a backstop in the (unusual) event of noncompliance. It's of the nature of authority that when it elicits assent it does so primarily because one feels one *should* obey, not because of the consequences if one does not. Lukes describes those commands deemed authoritative as seeming "reasonable" within the value system shared by both parties.[27] This suggests that it's the third dimension of power which is chiefly at work in the case of authority, even when acquiescence is reluctant as in the case of Hannah and indeed that of Alan had he conceded, on being arrested, "it's a fair cop."

Trust and authority, then, grant *power over*. They also *empower*. Being highly social and political creatures, *power to*, Spinoza's *potentia*, arises when humans act "in concert."[28] It was the authority of the Church of England, as an institution and as embodied in its bishops, which empowered Hannah at her ordination and licensing to minister in the first place. Without that she'd lack the general social recognition which enables her, as a vicar, to have an impact on the lives of innumerable others, congregation members and strangers alike. When we exchanged the £20 note and the IOU it was the conjoined authorities of the Bank of England and the UK government, along with your "horizontal" trust in me, which empowered us by a single act to achieve different goals which otherwise wouldn't have been possible.

Collective action may then require that I permit a larger social whole, and so certain representative figures within the hierarchy of that whole, to exercise *power over* me. In doing so I forfeit some of my individual freedom to act as I choose, and so also the prima facie power at my individual disposal, in order to conform to my role within the whole. However in that role I may experience new freedoms and exercise new kinds of power unavailable to me as an individual. It seems that enabling and constraint can be, and often are, mutually entangled, as Lukes puts it.

27. Lukes, *Power*, 26, following Bachrach and Baratz, *Power and Poverty*.

28. Arendt, *On Violence*, 44.

These reflections lead us to question whether social power should be regarded after all, as it commonly is, as a thing possessed by some but not by others. Might it not better be seen as belonging to the web of relationships which makes up life in society, a web generating a field of potential which individuals inhabit, in the same way that charged particles together generate an electrical field which then affects their motion? Indeed, insofar as I "am" my role, or the complex of roles I play on the various stages which make up my life, some would even go so far as to argue that my very identity is forged by these power relationships. Such a radical view, that power "makes up people,"[29] is to be found in the dense writings of Michel Foucault (1926–84). Lukes quotes a pithy summary of Foucault's hallmark concept of subjectification:

> Individuals are both *subject to* the constraints of social relations of power, that is, *subject to* a power that is being exercised over them, and simultaneously enabled to take up the position of a *subject* in and through these constraints or operations of power.[30]

Some suggest expanding Lukes's analysis by including Foucault's account of subjectification as a fourth dimension of power.[31] Each person operates within a particular social ontology, some account, shared with others, of what "we" consider real and therefore also of who "I" am. As such it goes beyond Lukes's third dimension by underpinning a fundamental sense of right and wrong conduct that goes much deeper than anything that could be suggested by an advertising agency. Social ontologies are not of our own making but are rather, like the railway network, inherited from largely anonymous past actors. Nonetheless they provide the conditions of possibility for how we act in the present, so enveloping us in always-prior fields of power.[32] The subtle interplay of *power over* and *power to* noted above does indeed lend support to the idea that human actors should be seen as vehicles of power at least as much as agents straightforwardly deploying power as they would a tool. This realization may seem disconcerting, but it need not dismay us as its implications can also prove liberating.

29. As per Hacking, "Making Up People."

30. Hamilton, "Power, Domination and Human Needs," 51, quoted in Lukes, *Power*, 168, emphasis in original.

31. Haugaard, "Rethinking the Four Dimensions of Power."

32. Haugaard and Pettit, "Conversation on Power and Republicanism."

How so? Let's use the scenario presented in the earlier vignette as an analogy. If I want to get somewhere on the other side of the country the rail network in principle empowers me to do so much more quickly and easily than if I were to trudge there under my own steam. In order to gain *power to* travel I must accept the train companies' *power over* me. For in traveling by train I'm constrained by two basic factors which are outside my control: the routes and the timetable. The rail network doesn't extend everywhere so some destinations are simply out of bounds. As a rail passenger I have no power to reach those destinations. Those which *are* served by the network may be connected indirectly in such a way that in order to get to my destination I have to undertake a long and tortuous journey. Similarly, the timetable constrains when I can travel. And, once aboard and underway, if the train breaks down or is otherwise delayed I and my fellow passengers will be deprived of the promised *power to* proceed to our destinations in a timely manner, and left wholly at the mercy of the train companies' and the elements' combined *power over* us. In all these ways *my identity as a rail passenger is "made up" by these various power relations.*

Notice also how the rail routes represent, in varying degrees, historical artifacts of social power. Possibilities for travel today reflect exercises of power which occurred decades ago when train companies were formed, sought investment, and competed for revenue; and when, over the course of time, decisions were made regarding which lines were viable and which had to close. Decisions made back then continue to exercise *power over* travelers today, irrespective of the intentions of those who made those decisions. This illustrates how social power can remain inscribed in the material fabric of societies for generations. Likewise, inherited cultural traditions enable particular ways of interacting with others. They provide friends and strangers with the *power to* live alongside each other to generally common advantage without having to reinvent protocols of interaction all the time. Typically these traditions involve asymmetric relationships such that in any given interaction one party may exercise some kind of *power over* another; though, as the above example of the loan of money demonstrates, complex reciprocal forms of *power over* may obtain between the parties also.

SOCIAL POWER: BORROWED DESIRES

> Humankind is that creature who lost a part of its animal instinct in order to gain access to "desire," as it is called. Once their natural needs are satisfied, humans desire intensely, but they don't know exactly what they desire, for no instinct guides them. . . . The essence of desire is to have no essential goal. Truly to desire, we must have recourse to people about us; we have to borrow their desires.[33]

Desire has been mentioned a few times in the foregoing. Lukes's three dimensions of social power are all about realizing one's desires, getting what I want, in a social context. The way in which desire shapes power relations was illustrated back on the railway platform. Jake's party's *power over* him depended on Jake's desire to succeed as an MP. Sarah's mother's *power over* her depended on Sarah's desire to be regarded as a good daughter. Nicola's peer group's *power over* her leveraged her prior love of nature into a desire to do whatever was needed to save the world. *Had those desires waned the power deriving from them would have evaporated.* Understanding social power therefore requires giving some attention to how desires in general arise.

René Girard (1923–2015) developed a distinctive thesis concerning desire on the basis of wide reading in literary criticism, psychology, anthropology, history, and theology. Drawing on this diversity of sources, he made the claim that human desire at root is *mimetic* in nature. When I want something it's because I'm aware, however unconsciously, that this thing or state of affairs is already the object of another's desire, a desire which I find myself spontaneously mimicking. My basic appetites—my physical needs for food, shelter, and so on—are of course simply given, but the ways in which even they get satisfied are informed by how others around me meet such needs. How much more so desires for specifically cultural objects such as status, acceptance, and gratitude. Desires, claims Girard, originate neither in me nor in the objects of desire but in other people who unwittingly model desire for me. Moreover they're learned via the examples of particular others, not of society in general; they are "interdividual" in origin. In fact you could go so far as to say that the object of desire, whatever it may be, is secondary to the primary social dynamic of *mimesis*.[34]

33. Girard, *I See Satan Fall Like Lightning*, 15.

34. "Desiring mimesis engenders its objects." Girard, *"To Double Business Bound,"*

If my desires are mediated by the conduct and attitudes of others—that is, if we end up wanting the same things—it follows that desire has a dual aspect. On the one hand it may promote conformity to established social norms of desire and so a collaborative ethos. On the other hand it's always latently rivalrous, and not only when the object of desire is in some way scarce. Girard sees the phenomenon of mimetic desire, in its rivalrous mode, at the root of violence in human communities. Such violence characteristically culminates, on his understanding, in the identification and elimination of scapegoats, actions which may become culturally preserved in the form of mythologies and rituals.

My desires, then, are "borrowed" from others. So on the face of it these various others would seem to exercise *power over* me, the imitator. Yet these others—models or mediators, in Girard's terms—need not be aware of the effect they're having. No deliberate exercise of power is taking place. Indeed the roles of model and imitator are endlessly interchangeable. And whether mimetic desire issues in concerted *power to* would seem to depend on whether it takes on a conforming or a rivalrous aspect.[35] Here Girard distinguishes between what he terms externally and internally mediated desires.

With *externally* mediated desires there is enough distance between model and imitator to preclude rivalry emerging. This distance could be literal: think of a social media influencer living on the other side of the world, or of a celebrated historical figure. Or it could be symbolic, relating to social status among proximate peers: think of the convention "Women and children first" when a lifeboat is filling with passengers on a sinking ship. Desire in this latter instance is externally mediated in the sense that how each person acts is scripted by their defined social identity, in this case as either a man, a woman, or a child. As a result mimetic desire issues in behavior conforming to shared social norms. If there are clear, if perhaps implicit, rules about how different people relate to each other then concerted effort (*power to* evacuate the ship in an orderly manner in this example) is to be expected, even in situations of scarcity.

However in the absence of role-defining conventions—for example when, on a narrow road, two mutually anonymous motorists approach

---

91. Indeed the object can "disappear" in the pure rivalry of conflictual, internal mimesis, as described below.

35. Market competition provides an example of where rivalry can issue in the collective *power to* operate a functioning economy, albeit not without both winners and losers.

each other from opposite directions—rivalrous competition may be expected. This is an example of what Girard terms *internally* mediated desire. Commenting on this, Mark R. Anspach writes that "the erosion of traditional social barriers favors the rise of internal mediation, and this in turn leads to a loss of distinctions between mediator and imitator, who are destined to end up as symmetrical rivals."[36]

To reiterate, desire does not belong to the model any more than it does to the imitator. In fact, rather as per Foucault, there *is* no subject prior to the interdividual relationship: "The 'self' [is] a convergence point in an indeterminate field of mimetic desire . . . which is constituted, at base, by its interactions with others."[37] Girard's understanding of desire therefore seems very congruent with the mooted fourth dimension of power: desire, like power, "makes up people."

Some would argue that Girard over-eggs the pudding of mimetic desire, yet his position is in some ways not so far from that of mainstream social psychology. Although Girard's interest was mainly in rivalrous interactions, the link between mimetic desire and social conformity is confirmed in this review of literature about social norms:

> What other group members do, approve of, and care about are vastly important determinants of human behavior. The most reliable way of getting people to do something is to make others around them do it. Telling people that their neighbors are conserving energy is a better way of getting them to conserve energy than appealing to their sense of social responsibility, desire to save money, or hope to safeguard the Earth for future generations. What people will and will not do closely mirrors what they think others do and do not do.[38]

We should note that, in line with Girard's definition of non-rivalrous external mediation, conformity requires the metaphorical distance generated by symbolically coded social roles, in this case social peers. The key word in the above extract is "neighbor"; that is, more generally, "people like me" or "my tribe."

Back on the railway platform it isn't hard to see examples of how power is playing out according to Girard's account of mimetic desire. Jake has long wanted to be in politics because of his admiration for great

36. Anspach, "Imitating Oedipus," xxxiv; see also Fleming, *René Girard*, 29–30.

37. Fleming, *René Girard*, 36.

38. Kesebir, "Superorganism Account of Human Sociality," 243.

statesmen of the past, but equally this creates rivalry between him and similarly motivated MPs. Sarah's desire to be a good daughter will no doubt have been unconsciously sown by past examples of daughterly duty offered by family members and friends. By setting off for the demo armed with her tube of superglue Nicola is very clearly imitating the members of her peer group; without them and the precedent of similar groups, would a simple love of nature and awareness of humanmade climate change have prompted her to contemplate this act? Hannah meanwhile is part of an institution in which imitating saintly role models is actively commended and pursued, and she need not have any specific examples of a good priest consciously in mind as she enacts, albeit reluctantly, a desire "borrowed" from the cultural norms of her religious tradition.

POWER, SOCIAL AND MATERIAL: OF POTENTIALS AND FLOWS

Between the first and second editions of *Power: A Radical View* Lukes revised his understanding of power to refer to a *capacity* rather than the exercise of that capacity: "Power is the capacity to secure compliance and can be at its most effective when it doesn't need to be exercised."[39] In this section I want to explore points of similarity between social and material power based on Lukes's insight regarding power as capacity. I will argue that the same underlying dynamic is at work in both biophysical and social settings, and that in order to adequately grasp how they differ (which will be explored in a later chapter) we need first to be clear about what they share in common.

Imagine a reservoir of water housed behind a dam. The reservoir holds a given volume of water in the same way that a battery holds a quantity of electrical charge. In both cases this capacity, or stock, generates flows which can be deployed in a number of ways. Water flows from a reservoir can be used to supply homes and businesses in a city; to operate a hydroelectric power plant; to lower the level of water in the reservoir in order to facilitate maintenance work; to provide a leisure facility for canoeists . . . All these represent *potential uses* of the stored water, and wholly depend on *gradients in gravitational potential.*

In the same way, while the electrical charge remains isolated at one pole of the battery its use remains latent, a capacity or stock which could

39. Lukes, *Power*, 3.

be used in a variety of ways. When the two poles are placed in circuit, the power associated with the resulting flow of current will depend on two factors: the difference in electrical potential between the poles (the battery's voltage rating) and the impedance, or resistance, encountered by the flow of current through the circuit.

As we have seen, social power is an expression of human desire. The magnitude of that power will depend on the intensity of desire as it occurs in individuals and on its social organization. The common desire of a multitude can achieve more than that of an isolated individual. Equally, the desire of a single individual occupying a particular social role could achieve more again (consider the political leader with access to nuclear weapon launch codes). On the other hand resistance from those objecting to a given use of power may diminish, or even negate, its effect.

We can imagine desire as a difference, or gradient, in potential. Without a difference in potential there can be no flow and so no material power; likewise without desire there can be no intentional human action, and so no social power. Desire on this analogy appears as a latency or capacity, like the stock of water in a reservoir, and so represents what we might term a *conative potential*. Like the water in the reservoir, conative potential can be realized in many different ways.

This way of understanding desire is explored by Gilles Deleuze and Félix Guattari in their book *Anti-Oedipus*. As they put it, with typical color, "It is a matter of flows, of stocks, of breaks in and fluctuations of flows; desire is present wherever something flows and runs, carrying along with it interested subjects—but also drunken or slumbering subjects—toward lethal destinations."[40] Stocks "interrupt" flows in the same way that a reservoir interrupts the otherwise continuous flow of water as mountain runoff into streams and rivers. Stocks are secondary to flows in the sense that, for Deleuze and Guattari, flows are the true stuff of life as a process of becoming. By the same token, flows can only occur and persist in the presence of a stock, understood in a dynamic sense as a maintained potential gradient which enables continuing flows: "Desire causes the current to flow, itself flows in turn, and breaks the flows."[41] In the case of water flows from a reservoir the potential gradient is maintained by the hydrological cycle, the circular flow of water through the biosphere. This flow is powered by flows of radiant energy from the sun, which is itself

40. Deleuze and Guattari, *Anti-Oedipus*, 115.

41. Deleuze and Guattari, *Anti-Oedipus*, 6.

made up of a finite stock of nuclear-fusible material. In the case of conative potential the gradient is maintained at root by the *conatus* of life itself though, as we shall see, this process may get sabotaged by life-denying social organization.

Flows can take different forms—they are "coded," in Deleuze and Guattari's terms, such that "it is impossible to grasp a flow other than by and through the operation that codes it."[42] Flows from a reservoir's stock are variously coded, that is, ordered and quantified, as potable water, fuel for a power plant, and so forth. Flows associated with desire are human actions, and these may be coded in multifarious ways, such as a caress, a command, the tapping of keys on a computer keyboard which in turn can encode the flow of desire in myriad ways . . . the possibilities are endless.

We saw above that, for Girard, desire is *not* essentially associated with a prior lack or want for a particular thing. Deleuze and Guattari agree, though for different reasons: a "satisfied" desire represents nothing more than a temporary break in flow. Neither should desire be seen as a discrete event or "discharge." Rather it is continuous and productive, retaining a latency of object—where it is going—and trajectory—how it gets there. To pursue the hydrological analogy, consider a rivulet of water flowing down the gradient of a hillside during a shower of rain, tracing the topography, exploring the degrees of freedom afforded to it, in unprescribed ways; dividing, perhaps, on encountering a random stone along the way, part of it then going on to connect and merge temporarily with another stream encountered as a result of its unplanned change in direction. As they flow these rivulets modify the terrain, eroding and leaving their mark so as to influence the trajectory of subsequent flows. There is no predetermined route and no predetermined terminus. Nonetheless there is, at any given moment, a specific direction of travel within an overall downhill trajectory. This, rather than the engineered and enforced channeling of dammed flows to specific destinations, represents the authentic outworking of desire for Deleuze and Guattari.

Transposed into a social context, desire as the ever-renewed gradient in conative potential connects what is and what might be, the actual and the possible. In the same way that geophysical processes are responsible for both the orogenies that create mountains and the erosive forces which weather them away, so also desire is associated with both the generation of conative gradients and their attrition. Likewise physical

42. Smith, "Flow, Code and Stock," 44.

potentials resemble desires in that they are many and various in kind. Gravitational, electrical, and temperature potentials are not interchangeable, and in the same way wanting to scratch my nose and wanting to rule the world are two very different, incommensurable desires, even if both feel equally strong.

Desire à la Deleuze, writes Alison Ross, is "a social force . . . able to form connections and enhance the power of bodies in their connection."[43] In terms of the discussion in this chapter, desire is that which enables *power to*, the ability of human beings in association to leverage the aggregate power of individuals to extraordinary degrees. The figure behind this conception of desire is someone we have already encountered, namely Spinoza. His notion of *conatus* was defined above as the basic urge to persist in being and reproduce. With humans things are rather more complicated though. Human *conatus* is expressed through desire and, as René Girard stressed, there is more to desire than merely animal appetite. *Conatus*, as desire, "should be thought of as entering into combinations with other modes such that our ability to affect and be affected is increased rather than diminished,"[44] "ability" here being Spinoza's *potentia* as discussed above.

If desire underpins *potentia*, *power to*, what about *potestas*, *power over*? As we shall see in a later chapter, the enhanced collective *power to* enabled by collaborative endeavor has historically been achieved through the often exploitative and brutal exercise of *power over* some by others. More than that, it has led to large sections of whole populations ending up enduring a worse quality of life than would have been the case otherwise. That is to say, desire has issued in connections which have enhanced *collective* abilities to affect, but not always the abilities of many *individual members* of that collective. What stops them from disengaging from such exploitative structures, in part, is the exercise of *power over* them in the various dimensions discussed above. But they are also typically impeded by having become locked into roles within that social structure and so dependent upon it, such that a relatively autonomous life in an alternative social structure is hard to even imagine let alone realize. As we have already noted, in the exercise of power, constraint and enabling go hand in hand.

43. Ross, "Desire."

44. Adkins, *Deleuze and Guattari's* A Thousand Plateaus, 96.

Relevant here is Deleuze and Guattari's prominent concept of a *body without organs*. In an organism each organ has a well-defined role. This role is essential for the functioning of the organism as a whole. Equally, each organ is wholly dependent on the way it's connected to the rest of the organism in order to survive: a heart removed from a body won't survive long; neither will a kidney or liver whose anatomical locations are swapped. Deleuze and Guattari's project is centrally about alerting readers to the extent to which they, as members of society, are in this sense organ-ized, trapped in a moribund stasis, unfree to experiment with new, life-giving connections. They want life in society to increasingly resemble what they term a body without organs, a limit-condition in which people are able to affect and be affected, that is, mediate power, to a full extent.[45] The theme of the organ-ization of people, and its underlying dynamic, will be developed further from a different perspective in chapter 4.

Finally in this section a word is in order regarding the native context of the language of stocks and flows deployed by Deleuze and Guattari in expounding the nature of desire. Deleuze's use of this language derives from John Maynard Keynes's analysis of the economy, in which money or economic value, coded via accountancy conventions, exchange rates, and so forth, flows through and accumulates in bank accounts, which act as stocks, or stores, of value.[46] Money could in fact be said to embody bare, unqualified desire. This is clear from the first of the three functions which it's generally taken to discharge, namely as a unit of account, whereby it represents sheer quantity, a general equivalent which reduces the qualitative differences between goods and services to numerical ones. In this respect it resembles material power as wattage, a simple scalar measure of magnitude. Secondly, as a store of value money represents a stock or potential, a capacity for the future exercise of social power. Thirdly, as a means of exchange it represents the flow, that is the actual exercise, of social power. Insightfully, James Buchan entitled his very readable inquiry into the meaning of money *Frozen Desire*.[47]

To take the monetary metaphor a step further, consider a stock of money. It only has value because it ultimately represents spending power, yet it can be deployed in one of three basic ways. First it can simply be spent, that is made to flow in such a way that the stock is depleted at the

45. This central but typically elusive deleuzoguattarian idea is discussed helpfully by Adkins, *Deleuze and Guattari's* A Thousand Plateaus, 96–107.

46. Smith, "Flow, Code and Stock," 44.

47. Buchan, *Frozen Desire*.

discretion of the owner according to her desires—the consumer's option. Second, it can be hoarded, left in its "frozen" state, safely under the mattress, to be supplemented from time to time by further additions to stock in readiness for the endlessly deferred rainy day—the miser's option. Finally, it can be made to flow as investment in a speculative venture, that is, treated as capital, in the hope that it will increase in quantity; as Marx expressed it, MONEY → COMMODITY → MORE MONEY—the capitalist's option.[48]

From Deleuze and Guattari's point of view, the first option represents mere "discharge," desire speciously expressed as the (temporary) satisfaction of a particular want. The second option represents the open-ended interruption of desire, the refusal to make life-giving connections and so, ultimately, death. This leaves the third, capitalist, option as the one which most closely resembles their ideal of a powerful life, in which money is plowed back into investment, manufacture, and selling time and again, each time making new connections such that the capitalist's abilities to affect and be affected are ever enhanced.[49] Here capital represents potential for profit, capacity for increased financial power, and has surely become the major way in which social power is expressed in the modern world.

POWER: TO WHAT END?

In his small book *The Passions and the Interests* Albert Hirschman provides an illuminating and relevant account of the cultural process by which the ascendancy of financial power came to be.[50] By the seventeenth century there was widespread doubt about whether the classical virtues were equal to sustaining civility in a society unsettled by increasing commercialization and the associated waning of traditional mores. Machiavelli had already argued a century before for a revised politics based on a "realistic" account of human nature which fully acknowledged the strength of the various vices to which the human lot is subject. From the ensuing debates the idea emerged that the most destructive passions—gluttony, lust, anger, and so on—could best be managed by subordinating

48. Marx, *Capital*, 247–57.

49. "Ultimately, capitalism is a collective investment of trust in this [capitalist] machine itself: capitalism is trust in capitalism, a religion which worships itself." Goodchild, *Credit and Faith*, 169.

50. Hirschman, *Passions and the Interests*.

them to a single countervailing passion bearing a more socially constructive aspect. David Hume identified this "obstinate passion" or "interested affection" as avarice, or acquisitiveness, the love of gain. Around the same time Helvétius applied the term "interest" to it, a more neutral and therefore acceptable term for a proclivity which up until then had been seen as a vice. With this rebranding, a concern for one's interests came to be accepted as the best check on vice in general, and was conveniently consonant with the burgeoning capitalist spirit as described famously by Max Weber.[51] And the effect of successfully applying the obstinate passion was and is ever-growing financial capacity, potential for yet further investment. Simply put: more power.

Unwelcome as the suggestion would have been to Deleuze and Guattari as Marxists, Hume's obstinate passion seems to do duty for ensuring the continuous flow of desire rather well.[52] And Keynes, from whom the metaphors of stocks and flows were taken, was scarcely a Marxist. Capitalist practices are all about maintaining, indeed increasing, the potential gradient down which money flows so as to accelerate these flows. "Enough" potential, "enough" gain, are oxymoronic notions in a world organized according to the obstinate passion. And since, in society as much as in the natural sciences, the stronger the flows the greater the *power to* affect the world and the human lot within it, identifying interest with acquisitiveness generates a positive feedback loop resulting in more and more power.

Lukes too discusses the relationship between power and interests. In the first edition of *Power: A Radical View*, he defined *power over* as entailing a conflict of interests between the parties concerned. He was later to regard that as a mistake, admitting in the introduction to the second edition that "you can be powerful by satisfying and advancing others' interests."[53] Having noted one possible conception of interests—as desire oriented towards the increase of financial power—how else could, indeed should, they be understood? Is it in Nicola's interests, as distinct from

51. Weber, *Protestant Ethic*.

52. The standard deleuzoguattarian rejoinder to this objection would be that capitalism subsumes desire within a set of axioms which specify that everything be interchangeable via the purely quantitative medium of money, while Deleuze and Guattari's commended schizoid practice avoids the application of any axioms. Against this, John Milbank has argued that capitalism already represents an optimal outworking of Deleuze and Guattari's univocal ontology. Milbank, *Theology and Social Theory*, 273–74, 315–16.

53. Lukes, *Power*, 17.

those of the climate emergency movement, to glue herself to the railings? Is it in Sarah's interests to visit her mother? Is it in Dennis's interests to go on holiday to Madeira? And so on. What exactly do we mean by *interests*, anyway?

Lukes outlines three possible ways of understanding interests:[54]

- first as *subjective preference*, what I myself (currently) want, regardless of whether that's consciously articulated or suppressed;
- second as *human welfare*, which involves basic physical requirements for leading a healthy life such as food, water, shelter and security;
- third as *well-being*, all that goes with leading a worthwhile life.

Consider our travelers again. In terms of the second definition, human welfare, it's fair to say that no one's interests are threatened by the use of power over them. So far as the first definition, subjective preference, goes, Alan, Hannah, and maybe Sarah would see their prospective journeys as contrary to their interests; Nicola certainly wants to go on the demo but is nonetheless apprehensive; while the situations of the rest are unclear since their preferences are all in different ways ambivalent. Even when subjective preference at this point in time suggests a clash of interests, who can say how our travelers will feel years from now? Perhaps Alan will emerge from a custodial sentence a reformed character. Perhaps Hannah will come away from her bishop having picked up some useful tips about coping with awkward customers. Perhaps Jake will come to see this rare compromise of his principles as a price worth paying for being able to go on to make a real difference for good in people's lives. Perhaps all our travelers, looking back, will be glad they had power exercised over them in these various ways on that cold winter morning, and would admit that their well-being was ultimately enhanced by their being denied their subjective preferences at that point.

If we settle instead on the third definition, that interests are indeed to do with well-being, "all that goes with leading a worthwhile life," then we have to recognize that "what counts as worthwhile or valuable and what counts as worthless and wasteful remains a deep, central and controversial ethical question."[55] Beyond merely animal survival and reproduction, what is the meaning of human life, its ultimate purpose? My

54. Lukes, *Power*, 86–88.

55. Lukes, *Power*, 87.

answer to that question may not tally with my own subjective preferences at any given moment (I might believe that ultimate well-being consists in divine union through ascetic discipline but, right now, I could murder a beer). And interests understood in terms of well-being may clash directly with those understood in terms of welfare as defined here (I might embark on a hunger strike in support of a cause dear to my heart, but this is not likely to serve my physical welfare).

The modern identification of interests with the desire for financial gain, Hume's obstinate passion, offers one particular vision of human well-being, one particular answer to questions like "Who am I and why am I here?" This leads us inevitably into the territory of the fourth dimension of power: the constituting of people as subjects, their formation within the "indeterminate field of mimetic desire." What is the story of human life *about*, in the end? If it's not about making money, if it's not about striving to achieve more and more *power over* others, then what is it about? And if "I" can't elude being caught up in flows within fields of power which are always already there, what agency remains to "me" to position myself within these fields?

SUMMING UP

We've come a long way since we started on that railway platform. Following Steven Lukes, we discovered that social power can be seen as three dimensional. I exercise power by getting others "to do things that otherwise they would not do," by circumscribing the range of options available to them, and by shaping their underlying desires. These are all examples of how I can exercise *power over* others, which implies imagining power as an instrument or tool which, in a given situation, some people possess and others don't.

Social power always depends on relationships of trust, and on a special, hierarchical form of trust, namely authority. Through these relationships we can not only exercise *power over* each other but also, collectively, exercise *power to* achieve common goals which would otherwise be beyond us. These relationships therefore enable or empower us collectively, but equally they constrain by requiring us to enact the particular roles which they set out. Noticing this leads us to wonder whether power, after all, isn't something which one can possess, but might better be imagined as a network or field of varying intensities which we all inhabit. We play the parts we play by virtue of where we sit within that network of relationships. In this sense we don't so much exercise power as mediate it. And since power is mediated in order to realize desires, we can further imagine ourselves as nodes in the network, junction points through which desires flow and intermingle.

Which raises the question: whose desires are these, anyway? As highly social beings, the expression of our basic physical appetites is hugely conditioned by the attitudes of those around us; we live by the borrowed desires of others, as René Girard puts it (which underscores the significance of Lukes's third dimension of power). Prominent among these is the desire for financial gain, the so-called obstinate passion. If we want to understand the workings of social power we can scarcely underestimate the significance of money, that mode of social power which most strongly resembles its material counterpart because of its essentially quantitative nature.

It's a commonplace to observe that we desire according to what we take our interests to be, and for much of the modern period the term "interest" has been identified with financial gain. But how otherwise might I understand that term? As what I happen to want right now? Or as what will best serve my long-term physical health and survival? Or do my interests lie in my well-being, my flourishing as a person in the fullest sense? If it's the latter then that would seem to imply some conception of the ultimate purpose of life, a vision of what it really means to be human—an unavoidably philosophical or even religious question.

Only humans entertain purposes, in the strongest sense of that word. Animals and plants have much simpler lives. What animates them is *conatus*, the basic striving to stay alive and reproduce. What they have in common with humans, and with human devices, is the idea of useful work: all these harness energy from their environments and put it to work in order to achieve whatever their goals might be. To do so they exploit gradients in various biophysical fields, harnessing the currents which flow spontaneously from zones of high potential to zones of low potential. And the time rate at which they harness this energy for work useful to attaining their goals is also called power—material power.

Social power, then, depends upon material power. Our would-be train passengers, caught up within different networks of social power, had this in common: they were depending on the material power of a diesel locomotive in order to attain their various goals, and were likewise frustrated in this regard by the wind. That wind, though certainly powerful according to the common usage of the term, doesn't qualify as an instance of material power as defined here since it performed no useful work on that occasion—quite the contrary. Like material power, social power involves the performance of useful work; but it differs in that it embodies the pursuit of human purposes, which are many and various, and go beyond a simple lust for survival. These purposes give expression, under particular circumstances, to a person's overarching purpose or life plan (however unconscious). It therefore follows that what counts as social power, the performance of useful work in society, depends on what one takes the overarching purpose of the human project to be.

So much for power, material and social. The exercise of power in living things is in the service of *conatus*, the striving to survive and reproduce and, in the case of humans, a further striving to enact purposes which may—or may not—be aligned with those more basic ends. Is the exercise of power in service to something even deeper, though? Something which not only conditions the evolution of plants and animals but, ineluctably, constrains human purposes too? The next chapter will begin an exploration of these questions.

2

Life on the Edge: Maximum Power

HOMER: Kids, there's three ways to do things. The right way, the wrong way and the Max Power way!

BART: Isn't that the wrong way?

HOMER: Yeah, but faster![1]

It's 1975. The last day of March. A car draws into the dusty little township of Lone Pine, Inyo County, California. Back in 1872 an earthquake leveled the place. These days it's in better shape: movies like *How the West Was Won*, *High Sierra*, and *Hop-Along Cassidy* were filmed around these parts and, with several national parks on the doorstep, it's become a popular tourist destination.

The car pulls up outside a motel, and out step two such tourists. He's a seventy-five-year-old retired academic, she—well, we don't know much about her except that she looks a lot younger than him. He's not a well man: he's survived prostate cancer, a heart attack, and a series of minor strokes in recent years, and it shows. It's been a sad and lonely time for him ever since his first wife, Mary, died sixteen years ago. Sure, he hadn't exactly been a faithful husband, but she had put up with that and he, for his part, had completely depended on her. He's not been the same since. He did remarry, but that was a mistake. They quarreled violently and eventually divorced, acrimoniously enough. But then the drinking hadn't

1. "Homer to the Max," *The Simpsons*, season 10, episode 13, February 7, 1999, on Fox.

helped. According to friends—who became fewer and fewer in number as time passed—he spent much of the seven years immediately following Mary's death in an alcoholic haze. One day he crashed his car into a tree, police got involved, and he turned to Alcoholics Anonymous. To his credit, he hasn't touched a drop since.

Still, the damage was done. So it was that today, just a few hours after checking into that motel, he suffered another heart attack and died, albeit "in a manner that would make most men jealous were it not for its finality," as his biographer discreetly put it.[2]

Lone Pine, Inyo County, California proved to be the setting for the final scene in the life of maverick anthropologist Leslie Alvin White. He courted controversy throughout his forty years at the University of Michigan. White was "feisty, opinionated . . . a difficult man, prone to attacking those whom he perceived were not supportive of his work."[3] Even though, towards the end of his career, he attained the distinguished position of president of the American Anthropological Association, there were times when he was too drunk to deliver the annual presidential address. His socialist sympathies, along with his contempt for organized religion and for most of his professional colleagues, provoked hostility from churches, the FBI, and university administrators alike. So why mention him here? Because, in 1943, he first set down what is still known as White's law of cultural development: "Culture develops as (1) the amount of energy harnessed and put to work per capita per unit of time increases, and (2) as the efficiency of the means with which this energy is expended increases."[4]

Energy harnessed per unit time: power, in other words. And, by association, the theme of this book and of this chapter in particular, namely the Maximum Power Principle, the tendency for systems which deploy the most power, or perform useful work at the fastest rate, to prevail over time. White was a materialist, in this respect at least, and his "culturalism" sought to reintroduce general, evolutionary themes into a field of study which had lately become focused on the particular at the expense of a comparative perspective and the big picture. If a culture is to advance materially then it has no option other than to work faster and faster.

While White's scholarship was concerned with the impact of material power on human culture, his story provides a fascinating, if tragic,

2. Peace, *Leslie A. White*, 231.

3. Peace, *Leslie A. White*, xiii–xiv.

4. White, "Energy and the Evolution of Culture," 345.

account of the workings of social power too. Throughout much of his adult life he was buffeted by political intrigues, both professionally within the American anthropological community and, in the context of McCarthyism and the Cold War, off campus also. Just as significant for him was his personal powerlessness when it came to resisting the temptations presented by impressionable female students and the bottle.

We'll return to Leslie White and his eponymous law at the end of this chapter, when I shall link it to human society's rocketing energy consumption rates and its seeming inability to do much about that. There are clear parallels between White's biography and the collective story of an unsustainable nineteen-terawatt society. But in order to lay the groundwork for this we need first to look further at material power, specifically the Maximum Power Principle as exhibited in the workings of biological systems. This will lead on to an account of how power consumption varies throughout the ultimately finite lifetimes of both biological systems and human economies, and will be followed by reflections on the role that Charles Darwin's notion of natural selection plays in framing our sense of future possibilities.

THE TORTOISE AND THE HARE

As every driver trying to overtake another vehicle knows, a car will initially accelerate rapidly as the engine rev rate increases. But beyond a certain optimal rev count the ability of the engine to accelerate further starts to decline, even though you put your foot to the floor. The rev counter will continue to climb, the car will continue to accelerate, but ever more slowly. More and more fuel, and so energy, is being expended, but less and less of that additional energy is performing useful work in moving the car. If I put my foot to the floor I'll get to my destination more quickly than if I'd been in less of a hurry. I'll also run down the tank more quickly, since fuel will be injected into the engine at a faster rate than the machinery can efficiently process, so that the excess, unburned fuel will simply get expelled through the exhaust pipe along with the various combustion products. Of course the unburned fuel doesn't produce useful work and is instead simply wasted.

In fact, whenever work is done in any system, not all of the energy consumed can be put to effective use by the organism or machine involved. This is because—as we saw in chapter 1—all work involves overcoming some kind of resistance, such that some energy is inevitably lost, or wasted, ultimately as heat. So, when work is done, the total energy consumed is always the sum of (a) the energy actually involved in performing useful work and (b) the energy wasted. Moreover, the ratio of wasted energy to total energy consumed varies according to the rate at which work is done, so that faster work rates are associated with greater inefficiencies: "The hastier the work, the less complete the dissipation."[5]

FIGURE 4

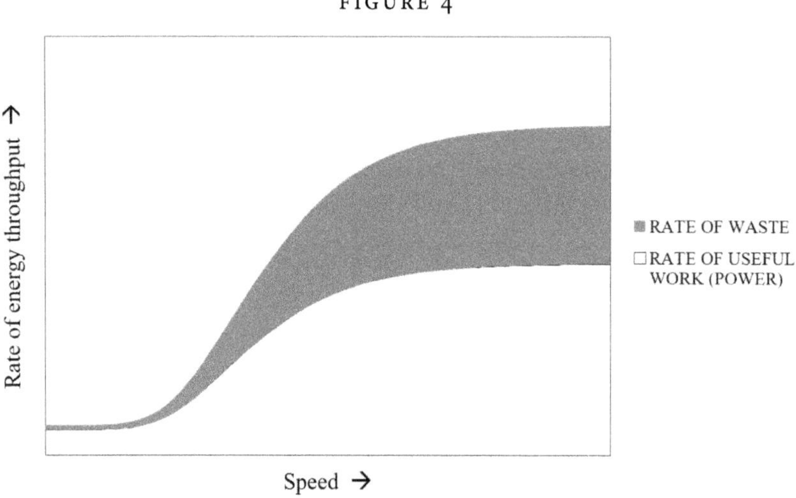

Figure 4: Schematic illustration of engine efficiency as a function of vehicle speed.

How I drive will therefore tend to reflect the size of my fuel budget. If money is no object I can cheerfully zoom around with my foot to the floor; but if I'm counting the pennies I won't exceed the optimal, that is, the most fuel-efficient, speed. This simple analogy helps us to understand a key insight contained in a 1922 paper by Polish American chemist and statistician Alfred J. Lotka.[6] Lotka's interest lay not in driving but rather in the operation of Darwinian natural selection in living systems:

> In every instance considered, natural selection will so operate as to increase the total mass of the organic system, to increase the rate of circulation of matter through the system, and to increase

5. Salthe, "Maximum Power and Maximum Entropy Production," 118. Cf. Sextus Empiricus (third century CE): "The mills of the gods grind slowly, but they grind exceeding fine." *The Free Dictionary*, "Mills of the Gods."

6. Lotka, "Contribution."

> the total energy flux through the system, so long as there is presented an unutilized residue of matter and available energy. This may be expressed by saying that natural selection tends to make the energy flux through the system a maximum, so far as compatible with the constraints to which the system is subject.[7]

In other words, the effects of natural selection on organisms include favoring growth in size and increased rates of nutrient and energy consumption. This last point is the one to which we need to attend, along with the caveat "compatible with the constraints," as Lotka explained:

> Where the supply of available energy is limited, the advantage will go to that organism which is most efficient, most economical, in applying to preservative uses such energy as it captures. Where the energy supply is capable of expansion, efficiency or economy, though still an advantage, is only one way of meeting the situation, and, so long as there remains an unutilized margin of available energy, sooner or later the battle, presumably, will be between two groups or species equally efficient, equally economical, but the one more apt than the other in tapping previously unutilized sources of available energy.[8]

Put otherwise, *in—and only in—a competitive environment of constrained energy resources*, evolution will favor those organisms which can tap that energy most efficiently—the equivalent of driving at the optimal speed; whereas, *when energy is plentiful*, efficiency becomes less important since evolution will favor those organisms which can tap gross energy at the fastest rate—the equivalent of putting your foot to the floor. Pursuing the analogy, the evolutionary contest can be imagined as a multistage race in which, at the end of each stage, the slowest competitors are eliminated, but with the added restriction of finite fuel supplies. The winner will therefore be that competitor which (a) makes it to the finishing line and (b) crosses the line before the others. There's a trade-off here between, on the one hand, putting your foot down and, on the other, ensuring that you have enough left in the tank to get to the finish. The hare may zoom ahead at the start of the race, but if it collapses exhausted short of the finish then the winner will be the slower, more energy-efficient tortoise.

This is Lotka's Principle of Maximum Energy Flux and, as this chapter will show, its implications are considerable. Better known these days is the similar—though importantly different—Maximum Power Principle

7. Lotka, "Contribution," 148.

8. Lotka, "Contribution," 150.

(MPP), which originally featured in an influential 1955 paper by ecologist Howard T. Odum and physicist Richard Pinkerton.[9] Odum had been intrigued by measurements indicating that the efficiency of photosynthesis, the foundational process underpinning complex life, is surprisingly low. The authors concluded that this is because, in order for a system to operate at maximum power, its efficiency should be about 50 percent only; or, as Odum later put it, "whenever it is necessary to transform and restore the greatest amount of energy at the fastest possible rate, 50% of it must go into the drain."[10] Maximum power is the supreme altar at which efficiency, and by implication everything else, must be sacrificed.

It turns out that this version of the MPP won't quite do. There are questions about the validity of the analysis presented by Odum and Pinkerton, and evidence shows that the efficiency of operation of actual biological systems is rather variable.[11] One significant omission in this statement when compared with Lotka's argument is the "compatible with the constraints" clause. Efficiency *does* become a critical consideration in situations where there is competition for scarce resources. This is the caveat which Lotka's earlier formulation, with its explicit reference to natural selection, captures nicely.[12]

Positively, Odum and Pinkerton's contribution was twofold: first by making explicit the link between efficiency and speed (the faster the activity, the greater the resistance, the lower the efficiency); and second by dividing Lotka's maximum total energy flux through a system into two parts: useful energy (work) and wasted energy. As per Lotka, the total energy flux will always be maximized relative to relevant constraints, and the ratio of useful work to wasted energy will depend on the prevalence of competitive pressures. High competition for resources promotes low wastage, that is, high efficiency, and vice versa. And so, recalling that power is the rate at which a system performs useful work, we could synthesize Lotka and Odum's arguments in this way: *Evolution by natural selection favors the most powerful under prevailing circumstances.* Unsurprising perhaps, baldly stated, but by no means trivial. In any event, with Lotka's caveat incorporated, this is the version of the MPP which will be used hereafter in this book.

9. Odum and Pinkerton, "Time's Speed Regulator."

10. Odum, *Environment, Power, and Society*, 37.

11. Mansson and McGlade, "Ecology." A more affirming retrospective on Odum's work can be found in Hall and McWhirter, "Maximum Power."

12. Sciubba, "What Did Lotka Really Say?"

CYCLES OF LIFE

How the MPP gets expressed depends on circumstances, then, and these include competitive pressures. In an ecosystem organisms of many different kinds interact in a variety of ways, some competitive, some cooperative, and the competitive pressures will vary according to the ecosystem's stage of development. As this story unfolds two different sorts of actors play out characteristic roles.

In an ecosystem which is starting from scratch, so-called r-strategists are the first to appear on the scene. Imagine a wheat field, abandoned and left to its own devices. Over the course of time it will revert to a meadow, featuring a diversity of plants previously excluded through the application of weedkillers. Eventually the odd bush will appear here and there and, finally, trees will emerge and take over, completing the transition from a field to a forest—a model example of ecological succession.

In this simple example the r-strategists are the grasses and other erstwhile weeds which are the first to colonize the newly available territory. These are pioneers which, in pursuing their own ends (growth and reproduction), also generate niches suitable for later colonization by other species—the so-called K-strategists, the prime example of which here are the trees. The actors' unwieldy names derive from a theory of ecological succession which relates the number of individuals in a population to the rate of population growth (r) and the carrying capacity of the environment (K), that is, the maximum number of individuals which the environment can support.[13] At immature stages, systems are dominated by small, opportunistic, fast-growing species—r-strategists—while later, at the climax stage of development when systems are approaching their carrying capacities, they become dominated by relatively large, slow-growing species—K-strategists. During this development process the number and intricacy of connections between system components increase, as do their interdependencies.

Both r- and K-strategists demonstrate the MPP but in different ways. The former are the boy-racers of the ecological world, exploiting relatively abundant virgin resources with scant regard for efficiency given the relative absence of competition at this early stage in succession. Later

13. The original analysis of population growth was due to Pierre-FrançoisVerhulst (1804–49). Lotka himself was to develop this theorization via the Lotka-Volterra equations which describe the dynamics of an interactive predator-prey system. See Holland, *Complexity*, 59–62.

on, in a more crowded landscape with scarcer resources, efficiency begins to confer a competitive advantage on the more sedate drivers, those organisms which dissipate energy at the slowest rate per unit mass. This pattern of succession is summarized in the following schematic figure.

FIGURE 5

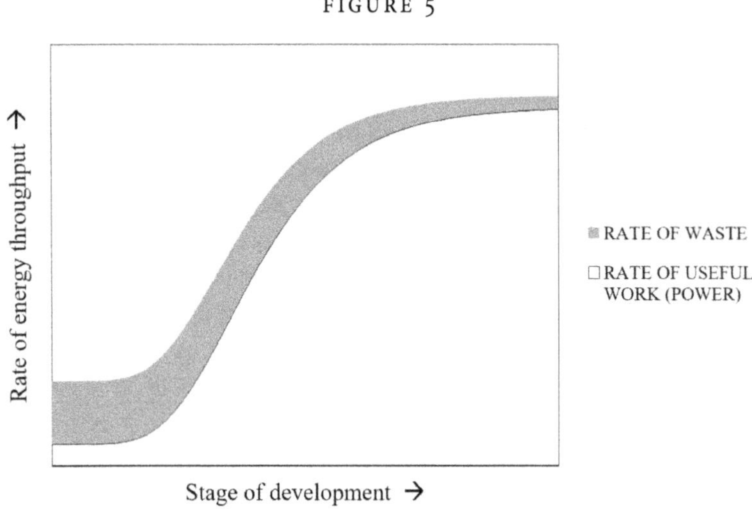

Figure 5: Schematic illustration of ecosystem efficiency as a function of stage of development.

During its lifetime, then, an ecosystem will both *grow* in volume and mass and also *develop* in the sense of multiplying interconnections between its components, with the result that the system comes to function more and more as an efficient, organized whole. In that respect it can start to resemble the highly coordinated functioning of an organism. And organisms exhibit variations on a pattern known as Kleiber's law.

It was in the 1930s that Swiss-born chemist and biologist Max Kleiber came up with the observation that the basal metabolic rate of an animal—the rate at which it burns up energy while at rest—depends on its mass raised to the power of three-quarters.[14] Technically speaking, this is an example of a sublinear relationship. So while a 5,000-kilogram African elephant is 200,000 times heavier that a twenty-five-gram mouse, its required calorie intake rate is only around 9,500 ($200{,}000^{3/4}$) times larger. In other words, on a weight-for-weight basis, elephants make more

14. Kleiber, "Body Size and Metabolic Rate." See also Von Bertalanffy, "Quantitative Laws."

efficient use of the food they eat, much as a mature ecosystem dominated by K-strategists is characterized by a relatively slow dissipation of energy per unit mass. Why is this? Again, mature ecosystems provide a clue in that they have developed efficient networks for the exchange of energy and matter. Similarly, the sheer size of larger organisms allows the deployment of more elaborate internal circulation networks which minimize resistance to the flow of blood around the body, so leaving more energy available for useful work.

Kleiber's law doesn't apply uniformly to all organisms. In particular the weight-metabolism scaling can vary according to the maturity of the organism. The basal metabolic rates of saplings and fish embryos, for example, show superlinear scaling, that is, they vary according to mass raised to a power greater than one.[15] In other words a growing fish embryo which doubles in size will more than double its energy consumption. This accords with conditions in which efficient internal networks have yet to form, and parallels the maximizing of energy dissipation in the early, r-strategist-dominated stages of ecosystem development.

Remarkably, perhaps, there are grounds for believing that human economies too obey something like Kleiber's law. In 2011 a group of scientists published a study entitled "Energetic Limits to Economic Growth."[16] They plotted per capita gross domestic product (GDP) against per capita annual energy consumption for each of 220 countries over a twenty-four-year period (1980–2003). They found that energy consumption rates varied with GDP to the power of 0.76, strikingly close to Kleiber's ¾ power scaling relationship. The authors note that this may not be just a coincidence since both animals and economies can be said to possess metabolisms—that is, they both harness and dissipate energy in order to operate—with larger national economies being able to take advantage of new technologies and economies of scale in order to deploy energy more efficiently.

15. King, *Economic Superorganism*, 216–19.

16. Brown et al., "Energetic Limits to Economic Growth."

Of course GDP and mass are very different measures. To begin with, and drawing on terms we encountered in the previous chapter, GDP per annum represents a rate of *flow* of money through an economy while mass represents an accumulated *stock* of matter. However, as researcher Carey King has pointed out, energy in industrial societies is consumed by various physical machines which, economically, represent physical capital; and the greater the combined mass of such machines, the greater the GDP. So the Kleiber-like behavior of national economies may indeed be more than coincidence.

In fact King and coauthor Andrew Jarvis have gone a step further, plotting total global energy consumption rates for the years 1900–2018 against global GDP, or gross world product (GWP). The slope of the resulting curve turns out *not* to be straight; but it does lend itself to being divided into straightish sections for each of the following time periods: between 1900 and 1920 the relationship of energy consumption rate to GWP was superlinear; between 1920 and 1970 it was roughly linear; since 1970 it has been sublinear.[17]

On the face of it we might be inclined to cheer this news: since 1970 we've been getting richer more efficiently, that is, without having to expend as much energy doing so! But it's a more complicated tale than that, and potentially more worrying.[18] Remember those saplings and fish embryos, and how their power consumption grew more quickly with increasing size than that of their mature fellows? What if human systems resemble biological systems at least inasmuch as increasing efficiencies reflect the approach of old age? What if, in economic historian Fernand Braudel's charming turn of phrase, efficiency is a sign of autumn?[19]

17. King, *Economic Superorganism*, 220–27.

18. GDP presents another complication. GDP values, especially when compared across time and space, are not reliable measures of prosperity. For example, King notes that the exact definition of GDP has varied, changing in 1993 to include interest payments on loans. A large portion of GDP may also be comprised of so-called imputations such as benefits in kind provided by employers and the merely notional income represented by owning a home outright, so not having to pay rent or mortgage interest. And, notoriously, GDP indiscriminately counts "bads," like the expenditure required to clean up an oil spill, alongside genuine goods. See King, *Economic Superorganism*, 33–35; Morgan, *Perfect Storm*, 50.

19. Braudel, *Perspective of the World*, 246, 266–67.

We've already seen how this is a feature of ecological succession, with energy dissipation per unit mass becoming minimized during latter stages of development. A 2016 paper coauthored by an economist, a biologist, and an ecologist argued that OECD economies have indeed entered the mature stage of capitalist development, and that unless steps are taken to avoid this, maturity will inevitably lead on to senescence—"informationally overburdened, committed to old habits, rigid, brittle," and so vulnerable to destabilizing disruptions.[20] Getting old is no fun.

Nothing lasts forever. Every organism inevitably grows old and dies. The same goes for an ecosystem. Having reached its climax stage in due course it will start to become senescent, in the sense of being increasingly prone to systemically damaging disruptions, and so eventually unravel. For example, a chance forest fire might destroy an ecosystem dominated by mature trees (plenty of tinder around), so setting the stage for reversion to a simpler system comprising, once again, r-strategist grasses. This observation gave rise to the highly fruitful notion of the *adaptive cycle* introduced by C. S. "Buzz" Holling (1930–2019), one of the most influential ecologists of his generation, credited with defining ecological resilience as the capacity of a system to bounce back when disturbed.

Drawing on his fieldwork in the coniferous forests of the Pacific Northwest, Holling proposed that ecosystems in general exhibit cycles consisting of four developmental stages: exploitation, conservation (or climax), release (or collapse), and reorganization.[21] This "lazy eight" pattern has been widely taken up, adapted, and applied both within and beyond the field of ecology. A modified version is reproduced in the following diagram, which stylistically illustrates how the values of various ecosystem indicators—such as usable energy storage and biodiversity—vary in relation to the total number of internal connections between system components and external connections to the outside world.[22]

20. Matutinović et al., "Mature Stage of Capitalist Development."
21. Holling, "Resilience of Terrestrial Ecosystems."
22. Burkhard et al., "Adapting the Adaptive Cycle."

FIGURE 6

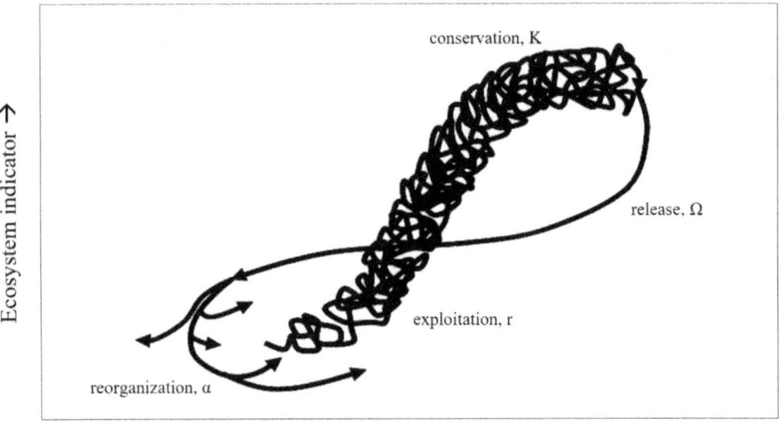

Figure 6: Schematic illustration of the adaptive cycle. Adapted from Burkhard et al., "Adapting the Adaptive Cycle."

We've already come across the exploitation phase of the cycle, characterized by the prevalence of opportunistic r-strategists, and the conservation phase, in which K-strategists emerge and dominate. Holling qualifies the simple succession-to-climax model of ecosystem development by positing that during the highly interconnected conservation phase systems lose their room for maneuver and so become less resilient if subjected to some kind of disruptive event. Since all ecosystems are prone to disruptions, both exogenous and endogenous, some combination of these will eventually overwhelm the resilience of a given system and precipitate a relatively rapid simplification, or collapse, in the course of which connections between components are lost. This is the release, or Ω, phase. Eventually the disconnected components will begin to reconnect and the process of system development starts afresh—the reorganization, or α, phase. Note the left-pointing arrow in the diagram at this point: this represents how, depending on prevailing circumstances, reorganization may lead to the development of an ecosystem configuration quite different to its predecessor.

Holling's work on the adaptive cycle therefore suggests that all ecosystems have a finite lifespan. Eventually a large-enough perturbation will come along which overcomes the system's resilience, pushing it beyond conservation into release. Indeed, any attempts to artificially extend the conservation, or climax, phase must prove self-defeating in the end.

> Because systems are moving constantly through adaptive cycles on numerous linked temporal and spatial scales, every conservation phase will ultimately end. The longer a system remains in the conservation phase (or is kept artificially there by management measures, e.g., by nature conservation or subsidies paid for certain economies), the smaller are the external or internal shocks needed to end this phase and to initiate a release phase.[23]

The work of ecologists such as Holling and biologists like Stanley Salthe[24] has proved highly suggestive for those wanting to make sense of the human predicament during the early years of the twenty-first century. Underpinning all these, however implicitly, is the MPP, the natural selection of those organisms and systems which maximize the rate at which energy is harnessed for useful work within prevailing constraints. What this implies is that, as systems mature and perforce become more efficient, the scope for further efficiencies—the buffer of spare capacity represented by immature systems' wastefulness—declines, as illustrated in figure 5. A mature system's energy dissipation rate per unit mass is already minimized, leaving little or no scope for further economies. At earlier stages of development challenges or shocks to the system can be managed by reconfigurations which make use of previously unutilized energy in order to address the challenge and so maintain system stability. But in later stages enhanced interdependencies between system components mean that the capacity for such saving reconfigurations declines too. Eventually some shock comes along which exceeds the by now senescent system's capacity to adjust and we enter Holling's euphemistically named release phase. If this applies to organisms and ecosystems, so the argument goes, it must apply also to systems which include, and indeed are dominated by, humans.

Few have been more vocal in sounding the alarm than Canadian ecologist Bill Rees. Rees, the co-originator of Ecological Footprint analysis, has authored several pieces in recent years in which he sets out his outspoken views clearly. Most vivid perhaps are a couple of papers published in the wake of the COVID-19 pandemic in which he speaks provocatively of "humanity's plague phase." In one of these he compares the current situation of the human race to that of the reindeer introduced onto the hitherto reindeer-free Pribilof Islands off the coast of Alaska in

23. Burkhard et al., "Adapting the Adaptive Cycle," 2879.

24. See, e.g., Salthe, "Natural Philosophy of Work," 87.

1911.[25] On one island the original herd of twenty-five had mushroomed to more than two thousand by 1938 before summarily collapsing to a tiny remnant by 1950. Although originally introduced to provide local people with a supply of fresh meat, hunting pressure was modest; and the environment was free of nonhuman predators. So why did the population plummet so dramatically given such apparently favorable circumstances? The study on which Rees draws concluded that it was down to overgrazing in combination with a series of unusually cold winters.

Rees's point is this. With the advent of fossil-fueled industrial society the human race has found itself in a position akin to that of reindeer parachuted into a previously unexploited, lichen-rich environment. As per the MPP the reindeer got busy harnessing energy at the fastest possible rate; and humans have done the same by exploiting coal, oil and natural gas to drive their machines and expand their economies. Like the reindeer, the human population has mushroomed, from less than half a billion at the time of Christ to a billion in 1800 to more than eight billion in 2025. But already the long-term viability of maintaining, let alone further increasing, this level of population is very uncertain, to say the least.

Quite apart from the threats posed by the various consequences of ecological overshoot, there are also grounds for believing that humanity has overgrazed its environment, in the sense that we seem to be struggling to maintain our rate of energy consumption relative to population. Figure 7 shows global per capita primary energy consumption from 1820 to 2023.[26] Notice how the rapid rise in consumption was arrested in the 1970s following the energy shocks of that decade, only to revive again from around the start of the new millennium after China had joined the World Trade Organization and begun its coal-powered ascendancy. Notice too how per capita consumption has stalled again since the Great Financial Crash of 2008.

25. Rees, "Fractal Biology of Plague."

26. Energy Institute, "Statistical Review of World Energy"; Smil, *Energy Transitions* (with major processing by Our World in Data); Our World in Data, "Global Direct Primary Energy Consumption."

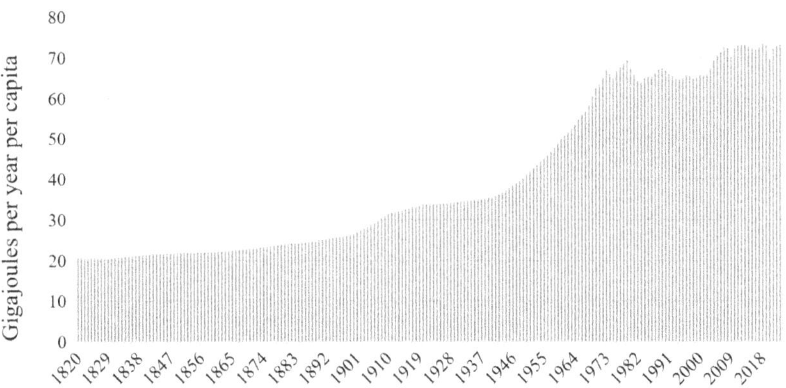

Figure 7: Global per capita primary energy consumption, 1820–2023. Source: See footnote.

Of course this is primary energy and, as we saw in chapter 1, what matters is actually the energy available for useful work. A plateau in primary energy consumption would not be such bad news if our ability to do useful work with that energy was increasing. However, take a look at figure 8.[27] Based on a study of data from between 1900 and 2014 it shows that the percentage of global primary energy converted to useful work did indeed grow from the low twenties before the Second World War to around 35 percent by 1970—but has stayed stuck at that level ever since. Within the current fossil fuel regime efficiency seems to have reached its limits. Where do we go from here? As with the reindeer on the Pribilof Islands whose numbers had bumped up against the carrying capacity of the once-abundant vegetation, all it needs to reset the human population is the equivalent of a couple of bad winters.

27. Author's calculations based on data in De Stercke, "Dynamics of Energy Systems."

FIGURE 8

Figure 8: Useful work performed as percentage of global primary energy consumption, 1900–2014. Source: See footnote.

Humans, claims Rees, are very much exemplars of the MPP. That's how it comes to be that, as a biological species, *Homo sapiens* is currently in the plague phase of a global population cycle. But what makes humans different from reindeer—in principle—is that they can see ahead and understand the implications of the imminent limits presented by terrestrial carrying capacity. We *should* be able to adjust our way of life in minimally destructive ways so as to acknowledge the impossibility of continuing growth before the reality hits us in the face and sends us spiraling down into Holling's Ω-phase. Rees therefore argues for a managed contraction of the human enterprise, involving drastically rationed use of remaining fossil fuel stocks and a planned contraction of the human population to around one quarter of its current level.[28]

We *should* be able to do this. But we're not doing it. And, at the time of writing, it doesn't look much like we will. It's as if something is compelling us to live life on the edge, straining to the extremes of what's possible. An established, mature ecosystem reflects a balance of power between different organisms, knit together in a sophisticated bromance of competition and cooperation. Ecosocial systems, that is, ecosystems dominated by humans, are different.[29] Even before the advent of industrial-scale fossil fuel usage humans consistently disrupted existing ecological balances by their technological innovations, as we shall see further in chapter 4. But since then any putative balance has been knocked sideways. If people

28. Rees, "Ecological Economics for Humanity's Plague Phase."

29. *Ecosocial* is a term coined by Stanley Salthe: Salthe, "Infodynamics," 10.

like Holling and Rees are correct, the unabated lust for maximum power can have only one outcome, and it's not pretty.

NATURE, RED IN TOOTH AND CLAW

Some readers may be bridling at the idea that just because the MPP determines the behavior of biological systems it must apply to human societies too, and possibly to such dark effect. Rees is no stranger to such objections and, unabashed, urges his readers to reject the doctrine of human exceptionalism. Like it or not, he says, we share with all other species predispositions to expand into all accessible habitats and to use all available resources. This is the so-called fecundity principle, and it's a basic axiom of Darwinian evolution:

> In looking at Nature, it is most necessary to keep the foregoing considerations always in mind—never to forget that every single organic being may be said to be striving to the utmost to increase in numbers; that each lives by a struggle at some period of its life; that heavy destruction inevitably falls either on the young or old, during each generation or at recurrent intervals. Lighten any check, mitigate the destruction ever so little, and the number of the species will almost instantaneously increase to any amount.[30]

And increasing numbers entail an associated expansion of territory: "All organic beings are striving to increase at a high ratio and to seize on every unoccupied or less well occupied place in the economy of nature."[31] *Homo sapiens* like every other species given the slightest opportunity will spontaneously expand into and press against every corner of the *Lebensraum*, living space, available to it, and will only retreat when forced to do so by circumstances. So argues Rees.[32] Life as such is always, in this respect, life on the edge.

Natural selection is commonly seen as Charles Darwin's trademark idea, and it derives from the fecundity principle in combination with two further axioms.[33] First, the finitude of resources. Every living space,

30. Darwin, *On the Origin of Species*, 52–53.

31. Darwin, *On the Origin of Species*, 98.

32. Rees, "Ecological Economics for Humanity's Plague Phase."

33. In fact a number of contemporaries of Darwin, including Patrick Matthew and Robert Chambers, had already identified and remarked on the fecundity principle prior to the publication of *On the Origin of Species*. Neither was the idea of natural selection

however initially abundant with food and all else needed for the thriving of a species, is ultimately limited. If those resources get depleted at a rate faster than that at which they can be renewed then there's a problem. That's what the reindeer on the Pribilof Islands found, and it's an observation which is central to Rees's ecological footprint analysis. Consequently life is a struggle between both individuals and collectives to gain and retain as much *Lebensraum* as possible.

The final axiom states that the winners in this struggle prevail not only here and now but over the long term also. This is the idea of the heritability of differences: those distinctive traits which enabled the winners to win are passed on genetically to their descendants such that, over time, those traits become characteristic of the species as a whole.

If these three axioms hold, then the process of natural selection is the logical outcome. And, as we have seen, natural selection is essential to Lotka's version of the MPP. So, do these three axioms apply to the workings of human societies?

Jem Bendell thinks not—or, at least, they need not apply. Humans are not algae in a pond, he urges (nor indeed Rees's reindeer), doomed to unsustainable population explosions whenever an extra helping of food turns up. We encountered Bendell in the introduction as, among other things, the author of a book which explains why our current global civilization is on the verge of collapse. He's insistent though that this unhappy situation was not predestined; Bendell cites several examples of past societies which have managed to live in a sustainable balance with their environments and energy flows. Neither is it the case, historically, that the sporadic use of fossil fuels around the globe has automatically spawned a bonanza of extraction and consumption akin to the one through which we're now living. This time something is different.

In like manner he takes issue with Andrew Schmookler's "parable of the tribes," which describes how arms races between human groups become inevitable once one of them decides to follow a path of aggressive expansionism.[34] Those tribes which don't follow suit will surely get weeded out through a process of natural selection, says Schmookler. Such a Darwinian logic, of "nature, red in tooth and claw," may indeed seem very natural, as much because of what we read in human history as because of what we observe in the animal world. But Bendell points

original to Darwin. See, e.g., Swenson, "Evolutionary Theory Developing."

34. Schmookler, *Parable of the Tribes*.

out that this dynamic does not typify the behavior of all human groups everywhere, any more than does environmental devastation.

> Whereas some ancient people did indeed trash their environments, they then learned from their experience to change their ways. . . . Therefore something must have happened in the last few hundred years not only to engender the massive destruction, but also to prevent people from recognising and feeling it properly. . . . The systems of money power provided an illusion of power and progress that masked our relationship with nature.[35]

By referring to "systems of money power" I believe that Bendell has put his finger on something crucially important. Human overshoot isn't simply a biophysical phenomenon. There's a cultural, historically contingent element involved here too, and this can make all the difference between—well, life and death. A symbolic episode in this cultural story took place in 1694, and it's worth taking a moment here to reflect on it and its consequences.

In that year a group of wealthy merchants lent King William III of England (William of Orange) £1.2 million to spend on war against France at 8 percent per annum interest, to be funded from taxation. This marked a momentous turning point in the history of how money works. Although the shadow of financial power had hung over great and small alike for centuries, this event marked the formal establishment of a *credit money* system because, having made this interest-bearing loan, the investors used it as an asset to set up the Bank of England. The bank

> received a royal monopoly on the issuance of banknotes. What this meant in practice was they had the right to advance IOUs for a portion of the money the King now owed them to any inhabitant of the kingdom willing to borrow from them, or willing to deposit their own money in the bank—in effect, to circulate or "monetize" the newly created royal debt.[36]

Following this "integration of the state and its creditor class" both central banks like the Bank of England and commercial high street banks came to adopt the *ex nihilo* creation of interest-bearing debt—money as bookkeeping entry conjured from thin air—as their business model.[37]

35. Bendell, *Breaking Together*, 335.
36. Graeber, *Debt*, 49.
37. Ryan-Collins et al., *Where Does Money Come From?*, 37–42.

This is fractional reserve banking, and Bendell is only one of many who have noted how this practice amounts to an act of faith in a constantly growing economy, since in order to pay back a debt with interest there needs to be more money sloshing around tomorrow than there is today. And, since money is a claim on wealth that means that we, collectively, need to be getting wealthier all the time. And forever.

For quite a while during the heyday of competitive colonial expansion and the early industrial era that act of faith held up tolerably well, despite major economic recessions and even depressions along the way, at least for the countries of what became known as the Global North. Nowadays, burdened by chronically sluggish growth rates, things don't look so rosy, but mainstream economic talk still takes this model entirely for granted. In the light of the ground covered in this chapter, it isn't hard to see this seventeenth-century innovation as an expression of the fecundity principle. Credit money necessarily involves a built-in drive to expand, so that the financial system we have inherited resembles the fecundity principle turbocharged and sublimated into the governing principle of human relations.

Via the money system, therefore, it looks like the first of the MPP's axioms is well embedded in contemporary human society. What of the finitude of resources? There's no limit to the amount of money that can be printed, of course; but if money is a claim on wealth and, as we noted in the introduction, generating wealth requires the expenditure of energy, then the plateauing of global per capita primary energy consumption since around 2008 suggests that the MPP's second condition also is satisfied.

Heritability, the final condition, is trickier to assess. Naturally there's no question of genetic inheritance here; but in a competitive environment, insofar as effective business and macroeconomic practices get noticed and copied, it's not unreasonable to assume that something approximating to heritability also typically obtains. Success breeds success, after all.

So it doesn't take too much imagination to make out the contours of the MPP here, albeit with profit and growth rates substituted for watts. As Bendell suggests, the nature of modern money takes us to the heart of our predicament, though the predicament itself is bigger than just money. The adoption of a credit money system was not fated but, once established, has proved very hard to shrug off. Although past human societies have exhibited a variety of patterns of economic behavior, we seem to have gotten stuck with a system based on a biophysically nonsensical premise, one amounting to a commitment to endless exponential growth; and, as someone once memorably said, "Anyone who believes that exponential growth can go on forever in a finite world is either a madman or an economist."[38]

Support for Bendell's position comes from a 2023 study of female fertility and infant mortality rates.[39] Drawing on data from sixty-four low- and middle-income countries, it found that these two factors are strongly correlated: the higher the death rates among children, the more children women bore. This suggests that, with humans at least, the fecundity principle and the Malthusian principle of scarce resources are not independent, with the former kicking into action only when the results of the latter become apparent. In other words, in humans the outworking of the fecundity principle seems to depend on future expectations. If the story by which I understand my life, based on recent experience, tells me that there's a fair chance that my children will die in infancy then, consciously or otherwise, that will encourage me to go on getting pregnant. My fertility therefore reflects in part the story by which I live. This general issue—the relationship between human sense-making and the expression of biophysical processes—will get further explored in chapter 5.

Importantly, Bendell reminds us that prior to the invention of modern credit money human societies showed themselves quite capable of adapting constructively to hitting environmental and energetic limits. This shouldn't surprise us. As we saw earlier, ecosystems spontaneously adjust from the prodigality of r-strategies to the frugality of K-strategies as they mature. Earlier societies may indeed have been able to learn from their mistakes, but given that the material power available to humanity today is so much greater than in the past, the stakes this time around are correspondingly higher too. We may not get a chance to learn this time.

Be that as it may, if we look under the hood of the MPP we will unavoidably find Darwin peeping back at us. More specifically, we can't avoid the fecundity principle and the axiom of finite resources which, if we take both as valid and in combination, can make for a turbulent mix. Darwinian ideas have gripped the popular imagination since they first emerged, and have acquired the status of common-sense truisms in many

38. Boulding, "Comment to the US Congress Hearing." See Jackson, *Post-Growth Challenge*, 2.

39. Bradshaw et al., "Lower Infant Mortality."

circles. But even among their advocates they can leave a sense of disquiet when applied to the workings of human societies. Darwin himself wasn't immune to having qualms, however much he attempted to stress how apparent altruism among nonhuman animals provides a platform for human moral progress.[40] These days the phrase "social Darwinism" is seldom used in a complimentary way.

This is a good point to reengage with the character introduced at the start of this chapter, namely anthropologist Leslie White. White's proposed law of cultural development seems to present an altogether sunnier application of the MPP to human life: "Culture develops as (1) the amount of energy harnessed and put to work per capita per unit of time increases, and (2) as the efficiency of the means with which this energy is expended increases." Looking back at it from the deepening shadows of the 2020s, White's law seems to express the blithe optimism of the middle years of the twentieth century, before we became increasingly aware of the darker sides of material progress. Writing in 1943 White, the socialist visionary, was clear about this.

> The key to the future, in any event, lies in the energy situation. If we can continue to harness as much energy per capita per year in the future as we are doing now, there is little doubt but that our old social system will give way to a new one, a new era of civilization. Should, however, the amount of energy that we are able to harness diminish materially, then culture would cease to advance or even recede.[41]

As mentioned previously, White's understanding of culture is essentially materialistic. For him, cultural advance seems to consist in more and more labor-saving devices, progressively relieving the common man and woman from the drudgery of acting as cogs in the capitalist machine.[42] Eighty-plus years later this outlook may seem more than a little starry-eyed. In fact, as we saw in the introduction, quality of life doesn't necessarily improve beyond a particular, relatively modest, threshold of power consumption. Yet White wasn't stupid. Historically, material quality of life and power consumption have generally gone hand in hand, so

40. Wilson, "Darwin and Nietzsche," 363–64.

41. White, "Energy and the Evolution of Culture," 350.

42. A more recent version of this vision is explored in Bastani, *Fully Automated Luxury Communism.*

that just to question the need for ever more power is to evoke the specter of culture going backwards, to gaze into the abyss.

The abyss was to yawn before White in a personal way following the death of his wife in 1959, but not before he had further expounded his thesis in a book, *The Evolution of Culture: The Development of Civilization to the Fall of Rome*, where he cites some of the other authors and concepts with which we're concerned here.[43] Alfred Lotka's Principle of Maximum Energy Flux is referenced. The fecundity principle and victory in the struggle for existence are presented in terms of the ability to capture energy at the fastest rate. With victory in this struggle come both growth in population size and a higher stage of evolution in which human cultures become "more differentiated structurally and more specialized functionally."[44] And, to anticipate the next chapter, the second law of thermodynamics makes an appearance as that which underpins not only biological life but human culture too; on that basis life itself is characterized as a process of self-augmentation which happens through the progressive degrading of external potentials.

In viewing culture as animated by the same impetus as biological evolution, White was very much treading in Lotka's footsteps. In his 1922 paper Lotka concludes that human beings act as unwitting vehicles for processes of natural selection, having already entertained this possibility in an earlier publication when he observed that

> the influence of man, as the most successful species in the competitive struggle, seems to have been to accelerate the circulation of matter through the life cycle, both by "enlarging the wheel," and by causing it to "spin faster." The question was raised whether, in this, man has been unconsciously fulfilling a law of nature, according to which some physical quantity in the system tends toward a maximum. This is now made to appear probable; and it is found that the physical quantity in question is of the dimensions of power, or energy per unit time.[45]

Not least since the industrial harnessing of fossil energy human cultures have been adept, as Lotka put it, at both enlarging the wheel and making it spin faster, seemingly "unconsciously fulfilling a law of nature," specifically the MPP. We shall explore the relevance of the MPP

43. White, *Evolution of Culture*, 33–40.
44. White, *Evolution of Culture*, 40.
45. Lotka, "Contribution," 149.

for human beings further in the following chapter. For now this provisional conclusion demands to be taken seriously: that our fossil-fueled global economy has reached a stage of advanced maturity if not senescence, and that some form of release as per Buzz Holling's adaptive cycle is inevitable. Continuing cultural advance consequent on ever-increasing power consumption, as envisaged by White, might have seemed credible while the global economy was at the exploitation stage of the adaptive cycle. But with the onset of the conservation stage, as resources deplete and rates of waste production exceed the rates at which the nonhuman environment can process that waste, White's law now appears defunct on a species level.[46]

Nonetheless the possibility of cultural advance remains real, indeed urgent, provided we understand culture in more than simply material terms. Getting to grips with a world in which taken for granted, material comforts are receding will require the fostering of a culture fully as elaborate as anything conjured by abundant fossil fuels. But this culture, unlike the one celebrated by White, will need to be animated by a regard for *better* rather than *more*. And *better* only has meaning in a context where qualitative values have pride of place, and the reign of mere quantity has been overthrown.[47]

SUMMING UP

This chapter has been freighted with a plethora of laws and principles: White's law of cultural advance; Lotka's Principle of Maximum Energy Flux and Odum's related Maximum Power Principle; Kleiber's law of mass and metabolic rate; Holling's adaptive cycle. With the exception of the first they all derive from the natural sciences and so share a common deterministic thrust: under such-and-such circumstances *this* must follow. So, applied to the human predicament as we now find it, they together paint a picture of a world of extremes, of life lived on the very edge of possibility. And if we take seriously the warnings of ecologists like Bill Rees regarding ecological overshoot then it would seem that we find ourselves already poised above the abyss.

46. Though White's law may well still apply to global South societies where power consumption remains inadequate to ensure a decent quality of life.

47. The phrase "reign of quantity" (though not the accompanying thesis) is taken from Guénon, *Reign of Quantity*.

Lotka's work, as channeled by Odum, set the scene for what followed: natural selection favors those systems which can harness available energy for performing useful work at the fastest rate given environmental constraints. Efficiency only becomes an issue when these constraints manifest as limited resources. In ecosystems this is a feature of maturity, when carrying capacities have been reached and so-called K-strategists hold sway. The adaptive cycle charts a journey from opportunistic exploitation through the conservation phase of maturity ultimately to release, the disassembling of the system, and beyond that to the prospect of reorganization.

The life of Leslie White, the anthropologist who attributed cultural advance to increasing material power, offers something of a parallel to our twenty-first-century predicament. In a sad irony, the social power which he ostensibly attained as his career progressed was accompanied by a corresponding powerlessness, both professionally and personally. The human race, White's chosen object of study, seems to be following a similar trajectory. Since White first enunciated his law in 1943 the average human has become twice as materially powerful,[48] yet this has happened in tandem with an apparent collective powerlessness to avoid an imminent global car crash of some kind or other—scarcely a sign of cultural advance.

Significantly, natural selection features at the very foundation of this unfolding tale, and raises disquieting questions about how we got here and how we might proceed. Must our future, like nature in Tennyson's poem, be red in tooth and claw? Is natural selection *really* fundamental to how the world works? What other factors may lie at the root of the struggle, the striving which natural selection embodies? In the next chapter we shall see that the MPP is not where the story starts after all, nor where it ends. Rather it's a curious in-between manifestation of something deeper which, with the appearance of humans on the scene, may yet be expressible in ways which don't issue in a terminal outcome. In fully realizing its manifold potential, the human race need not also live life on the edge.

48. Based on per capita global primary energy consumption: 1943—37 gigajoules; 2023—73 gigajoules. See Our World in Data, "Global Direct Primary Energy Consumption."

3

Life on the Edge? Emergent Optimality

Drop Thy still dews of quietness,
Till all our strivings cease;
Take from our souls the strain and stress,
And let our ordered lives confess
The beauty of Thy peace.[1]

Nightfall in Philadelphia on May 17, 1838. An angry mob, bearing torches, is gathering outside Pennsylvania Hall. A figure, disguised, manages to sneak into the building undetected. He's a tall, slight young man in his early thirties. If you'd met him under normal circumstances you'd have thought him rather shy. These are not normal circumstances, however, under which he makes his way to the basement and into the office of an abolitionist journal called the *Pennsylvania Freeman*. Hurriedly he gathers together the plates of the following day's edition and then, the plates concealed about his person, exits the building as furtively as he had entered. He has accomplished his mission not a moment too soon; the building is already ablaze. The young man's heart is heavy, for this is not an arsonist or a thief, but rather the journal's editor. He's used to setbacks though, for his convictions, and his courage in expressing them, mean that he's no stranger to hostility. His name is John Greenleaf Whittier, and he's a fighter.[2]

1. Whittier, "Brewing of Soma."

2. Tomek, "Pennsylvania Hall"; O'Donnell, "John Greenleaf Whittier"; Poetry Foundation, "John Greenleaf Whittier."

Churchgoers will likely recognize the verse with which this chapter began as part of the well-known hymn "Dear Lord and Father of Mankind." In fact the hymn itself is an extract from a longer poem, "The Brewing of Soma," composed by Whittier (1807–92) later in life. He was a lifelong member of the Society of Friends and, with its soothing vocabulary of peace, quietness, and sabbath rest, the words of the hymn are redolent of the popular image of Quakerism.

But there was more to Whittier's spirituality than a longing for inner serenity. Born into a simple life on a family farm in northern Massachusetts, much of his career involved active struggle: as a boy working on the farm (his health was never good); as a young man trying to make a living; as a poet seeking to establish a name for himself; and, not least, as a vocal and persistent protagonist for what was, prior to the Civil War, an unpopular cause—the abolition of slavery. None of these came easy. In taking a stand against slavery he faced ostracism and was threatened with violence. And, with the outbreak of war, his Quaker pacifism did not get in the way of his support for the Union cause. Whittier, then, was no retiring quietist. On the contrary, he was quite prepared to embrace the striving, the strain, and the stress which the words of the hymn seem to repudiate.

In fact, the striving deplored in the original poem is a quite different animal, namely the vain attempt to stir up religious ecstasy. "As in that child-world's early year, / Each after age has striven / By music, incense, vigils drear, / And trance, to bring the skies more near, / Or lift men up to heaven!"[3] Rather than chase after intense religious experience, true piety is a matter of "simple trust" and a willingness to follow where God leads. The object of the struggle makes all the difference in the world, and Whittier's poem draws attention to the woes of striving after the wrong object. His life, on the other hand, witnessed to an altogether more constructive and laudable endeavor.

The notion of striving has already cropped up several times in this book. In chapter 2 we saw how Charles Darwin's fecundity principle—the claim that all organisms everywhere are always striving to multiply and expand to the limits—is basic to the idea of evolution by natural selection and so to the Maximum Power Principle (MPP). And in chapter 1 the striving for physical survival and progeny made an appearance in the form of Spinoza's *conatus*. Equally, in the same chapter we noticed how

3. Whittier, "Brewing of Soma."

the striving for mere existence which is characteristic of life in general gets complicated once human beings appear on the scene, and the part striving played in Whittier's life illustrates this well: rather than prioritize propagating his genes (he never married) he embraced instead the risky controversy of a cause which he could safely have ignored. Whittier's striving calls to mind the words of an imprisoned St. Paul: "Forgetting what lies behind and straining forward to what lies ahead, I press on towards the goal for the prize of the heavenly call of God in Christ Jesus."[4]

In this chapter I will review the MPP, and the striving which underpins it, from two angles. First from underneath as it were, by exploring the suggestion that the MPP is in fact only the expression in the realm of living things of a more fundamental principle; and, second, from above, by considering the principles governing the development of living things operating together as systems—ecological ensembles. Placed in these contexts, it turns out that the MPP's apparent thrusting of life to the edge of possibility doesn't represent the first or the last word on what makes the universe tick. Rather, the MPP is best seen as one among a hierarchy of principles emerging at different levels of reality, culminating at the level of the human struggles exemplified by Whittier's life. In order to see why, we'll need to start with a contemporary of Whittier's who, in his case, strove to better understand the workings of his age's most emblematic invention.

STRIVING TO REALIZE POTENTIAL

That invention was the steam engine, and the person in question was the German physicist Rudolf Clausius (1822–88). Clausius is celebrated as the author of the second law of thermodynamics whereby, simply stated, "the universe strives to increase its entropy to a maximum."[5] These days entropy is commonly taken to be synonymous with disorder, so that the second law is assumed to imply that the world is going inexorably downhill, doomed to an eventual heat death (a term coined by Clausius). However, as ecologist Rod Swenson has argued for many years, the identification of entropy with disorder—specifically the random microscale distribution of velocities among gas molecules in a closed box—is due

4. Phil 3:13–14.

5. More sophisticated formulations are possible; e.g., Yen et al., "Thermodynamic Extremization Principles," 620–21, provide summary statements of the zeroth, first, second, and third laws of thermodynamics.

to the later work of Ludwig Boltzmann (1844–1906).[6] Clausius's original definition had instead been inspired by the macroscale conversion process of thermal energy into mechanical energy in a steam engine. His law is based on the simple yet profound observation that the cooled water emitted from the engine no longer has potential for doing useful work. On the scale of this phenomenon talking about order and disorder adds nothing and may only serve to confuse matters. The second law could equally—better—be rendered as "the universe strives to decrease its potentials to a minimum."

Swenson insists that the German word *strebt*, "strives," in Clausius's account of how the universe operates has often been unhelpfully translated as "tends." Contrary to the common view of the nonliving world as essentially inert, Swenson interprets its striving literally, as an expression of its basic nature. There is, in his view, no fundamental dichotomy between the living and nonliving worlds, between biology and physics. In the same way that all "organic beings" strive to grow and expand, as per Darwin, so also the inorganic universe strives to degrade, to cancel out, physical potential differences of various kinds. All systems, living and otherwise, are in some sense drawn to the limits, to the edge, of what is possible. In fact Swenson goes beyond the second law by advancing a thesis that could be considered his personal trademark, namely, the Law of Maximum Entropy Production (LMEP), which he regards as a fourth law of thermodynamics. The LMEP states that "a system will select the path or assembly of paths out of available paths that minimizes the potential or maximizes the entropy at the fastest possible rate given the constraints."[7] As with the MPP the time rate of a process is maximized, this time one which includes nonliving physical processes.

By way of illustration, in figure 9 below the LMEP would select path A over path B since it exhibits a faster potential minimization rate: 5 units per unit time (a reduction from 10 to 5 over one time unit) compared to 1 unit per unit time (a reduction from 10 to 0 over ten time units). This is despite the fact that, in this example, path B's slower rate leads to a more complete degrading of potential, so reflecting the adage "the hastier the work, the less complete the dissipation."

6. Swenson, "Grand Unified Theory," 4–5.

7. Swenson, "Grand Unified Theory," 10.

FIGURE 9

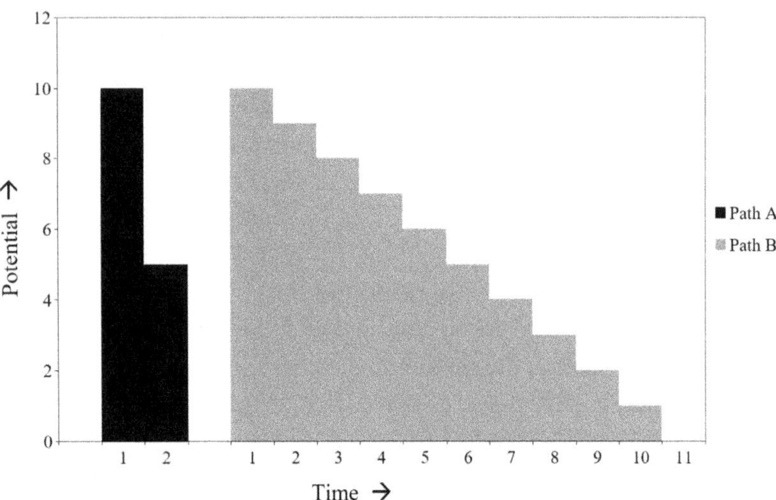

Figure 9: Illustrative potential minimization rates. Other factors being equal the LMEP would select path A.

To see the link between these two strivings—that of living things to expand and that of the universe to minimize potentials—a further piece of the jigsaw needs to be added. This is the remarkable though utterly commonplace phenomenon variously named by different authors as self-organization, dissipative structuring and, by Swenson, autocatakinesis.[8] Imagine a non-isolated system which is in disequilibrium—that is, one in which there's a gradient in the potential of some intensive property, such as temperature, pressure, or electrical potential.[9] As per the second law of thermodynamics, flows—of heat, air, electric current, etc.—will occur

8. See Swenson, "Grand Unified Theory," 7–9. Peter Corning argues that "self-ordering" is a better term for this general phenomenon, with self-organization applying only to a subset characterized by "functional design—adaptations (and structures) that are either directly or indirectly products of natural selection." See Corning, *Holistic Darwinism*, 113. With that caveat I shall continue to use the common term "self-organization" in what follows.

9. Physicists talk about three kinds of systems: isolated, with no flows of matter or energy across their boundaries (think the perfect thermos flask); closed, with flows of energy only (think the planet Earth, excepting the odd meteorite and spacecraft); and open, with flows of energy and matter (think your own body, or human society). Autocatakinesis can only occur in a non-isolated system which is far from thermodynamic equilibrium, that is, one which is traversed by strong flows of energy and/or matter, which are caused in turn by steep gradients. See Fieguth, *Introduction to Complex Systems*, 14–23.

which "strive" to flatten the gradient and restore the system to equilibrium. However if the gradient is sufficiently steep, that is, if the system is far from equilibrium, something else, and entirely counterintuitive, happens: autocatakinesis. This is the process by which strong flows lead to potentials becoming locally *enhanced* in such a way that flow structures of various kinds are generated. Locally, entropy works *backwards*, and we get "order for free."[10]

These flow structures are generated and maintained precisely through the degrading of the potentials in their environment. Indeed they are, in Swenson's words, inherently "selfish": "Through the circular relations that define them they are self-amplifying sinks, or 'deviation-amplifying systems' acting back on themselves to pull environmental resources into themselves in their own space-time extension."[11] Although, globally and over the long term, the second law of thermodynamics is obeyed—that is, the rate of potential degradation exceeds that of enhancement—this process is as much about *transforming* potentials, or realizing them in new ways, as it is about minimizing them.[12]

The etymology of Swenson's rather clunky term elucidates how the process works. *Auto*, "self," signifies that structure arises spontaneously from within the system rather than being imposed from outside. *Cata*, "down," stresses the top-down, ordering action of the emerging structure on its component parts. *Kinēsis*, "motion," points to the essential role of strong flows in causing this phenomenon. Autocatakinesis happens in both living and certain nonliving systems maintained sufficiently far from equilibrium, and examples of self-organizing entities include "all living systems from cells to ecosystems at whatever scale (including the planet itself) . . . [and] abiotic systems such as dust devils, tornadoes and experimental systems like Bénard cells."[13]

10. Kauffman, *Origins of Order*, 120.

11. Swenson, "Selection Is Entailed by Self-Organization," 170.

12. Those fearing that the universe is therefore doomed, in Clausius's phrase, to an eventual "heat death" should be reassured by Stanley Salthe's observation that "the universe is way out of equilibrium and getting even more so all the time." Salthe, "Infodynamics." That is to say that, on the cosmic scale, potential gradients are forever getting steeper since the universe is expanding, as it has been ever since the Big Bang. And this expansion shows no signs of slowing down—to the contrary, the expansion is accelerating. See, e.g., Davis, "Relax." This means that, on the macro-scale, the universe is departing further and further from thermodynamic equilibrium.

13. Swenson, "Grand Unified Theory," 8. Bénard cells are geometrically ordered convection patterns which can arise when a fluid is heated from below, and are described further later in this chapter. Another well-known example of self-organization

Swenson locates his insights in a tradition of thought going back to Aristotle's so-called "principle of plenitude," that is, his contention that nature has an innate tendency to make actual all its potentials.[14] Not irrelevantly, the English word "entropy" derives from the original Greek *entropia*, which could be rendered as "inward transformation."[15] During the twentieth century thermodynamic theory developed considerably, and in unexpected directions. Precursors to Swenson's ideas include Erwin Schrödinger's notion of what he termed negentropy in living things,[16] Ludwig von Bertalanffy's distinction between closed and open systems,[17] and Nobel-Prize-winner Ilya Prigogine's analysis of dissipative structures.[18] So, although Swenson's thesis may seem surprising to those who assume that the second law of thermodynamics is only about ever-increasing disorder, in fact it stands in a solid tradition. What distinguishes it is the way in which his notions of the LMEP and autocatakinesis represent possibly the most worked-out and doggedly advocated variation on this theme.[19]

A simple example of autocatakinesis from the realm of ecology has been provided by Robert E. Ulanowicz. He invites us to dip our toes into a subtropical freshwater lake.[20] Here we find three actors whose cooperation leads to the formation of a simple ecological ensemble. First the bladderwort, an insectivorous plant anchored to the lake floor. Second the microscopic water flea, one of the species on which the bladderwort

in chemical systems is the Belousov-Zhabotinsky, or BZ, reaction: see, e.g., CLEAPSS, "Oscillating Reactions."

14. Aristotle, *Metaphysics* 9. Cf. Swenson, "Evolutionary Theory Developing," 58.

15. From *en-*, in, and *tropē*, a turning or transformation. "Clausius invented the word entropy as a suitable name for what he had been calling 'the transformational content of the body.'" Klein, "Scientific Style of Josiah Willard Gibbs," 102.

16. Schrödinger, *What Is Life?*

17. Von Bertalanffy, *Problems of Life*.

18. Prigogine, "Time, Structure and Fluctuations."

19. While I focus on Swenson's account of autocatakinesis here, several recent variations and elaborations on this theme can be found in, e.g., Prigogine and Stengers, *Order Out of Chaos*; Varela et al., *Embodied Mind*; Kauffman, *Origins of Order*; Kauffman, *World Beyond Physics*; England, *Every Life Is On Fire*; Deacon, *Incomplete Nature*; Chaisson, *Cosmic Evolution*. I don't propose to enter the debate on the (lack of) relationship between thermodynamic and informational entropy, and restrict my attention here to the former. For a variety of views on this issue, see, e.g., Swenson, "Fourth Law of Thermodynamics"; Salthe, "Infodynamics"; Nielsen and Ulanowicz, "On the Consistency"; Bawden and Robinson, "Few Exciting Words"; Corning, *Holistic Darwinism*, 313–33.

20. Ulanowicz, *Ecology, the Ascendent Perspective*.

feeds. Third the blue-green algae which exploit the bladderwort's leaves as a growth substrate, and on which the water fleas graze.[21] In this simple ecosystem, each component has its own individual identity and acts as an agent in its own right. In principle, each can live quite independently of the others. But, together, they can also form a new, emergent structure which works like this.

The fleas are drawn to the bladderwort because it hosts the algae on which the fleas graze. In the vicinity of the bladderwort they can easily end up getting sucked into one of its bladders and consumed. This promotes the growth of the plant, which in turn means more plant surface for the algae to colonize, which in turn means more algae, which in turn means more water fleas, and so on.

This is an example of a positive feedback, or autocatakinetic, loop.[22] The bottom-up interaction of the components issues in a structure of mutual dependence which then exerts a top-down influence on those same patterns of interaction. Such mutualism is commonplace not only in ecology but in complex systems generally and is key to the arising of new, higher-order structures.

In an ecosystem such as the one just described *a particular autocatakinetic structure can become so well established that it can be regarded as an emergent entity in its own right*. This is shown by the way in which the structure can survive the change of one or more of its components. Imagine that a new insectivorous plant species is introduced into the lake, functionally similar to the bladderwort but with a more elaborate, crenulated surface which can host a greater density of algae. Exactly the same autocatakinetic process will therefore mean that it will tend to outcompete the bladderwort by attracting more fleas. Eventually the bladderwort might die out through lack of food—but the threefold structure would survive, albeit with different components.

Why on earth should such structures come about, thermodynamically speaking? The clue is in one of the names by which they are known: *dissipative* structures. They have the property of dissipating energy, or degrading energy potentials, *at a more rapid rate* than would their components were they simply jumbled together in an unstructured way, and

21. More accurately, the fleas feed on a film comprising algae, bacteria, and diatoms.

22. Ulanowicz uses the term autocatalytic, to which Swenson would object on the grounds that this is a term proper to chemistry only. I shall follow Swenson's convention here.

so they get selected by the LMEP. The potential degradation rate is enhanced because the flows which comprise these structures are *constrained* in ways which expedite the rate of dissipation.

How does this work? The emergence of Bénard cells in heated liquids and gases illustrates this constraint well. Imagine heating a pan of water on the stove. As the liquid is heated from underneath the transfer of thermal energy from the bottom of the pan to the top is initially entirely down to *diffusion*: the thermal energy of the heat source is converted into the kinetic energy of the molecules of the liquid nearest the source of heat. These therefore move faster and further, so transferring energy via collision to molecules higher up the pan. If the rate of heat transfer by diffusion is slower than the rate at which energy is being supplied at the base, this will result in an increasing temperature gradient between the top and bottom of the pan. Once this gradient exceeds a threshold value, a new, *convective* process of heat transfer is triggered, with liquid molecules now moving en masse in vertically circular flows. If the layer of liquid is relatively thin, and the bottom of the pan is smooth enough, the convection cells will be hexagonal in cross section—so-called Bénard cells.[23]

Convection cells are a simple example of a dissipative structure in that they have the property of being able to transfer heat energy, and so dissipate it at the surface, at a much faster rate than the previous molecular diffusion regime. The liquid in the pan self-organizes by means of these structures in order to minimize the vertical temperature (potential) gradient at the fastest possible rate, as required by the LMEP.

As in the example of the bladderwort-algae-water flea ensemble, each convection cell is a higher-order structure than the parts—in this case, the molecules—which comprise it. In moving from a diffusive to a convective regime there are accompanying increases in scale in both time and space. And this regime change requires that the micromovements of previously "free" molecules now be constrained, as the molecules' motion becomes entrained in the ordered macro-flow of the convection cells. Autocatakinetic regime change entirely depends on molecules becoming constrained to act as parts of larger wholes in this way.

Evolution in its by-now-familiar Darwinian guise has become all but synonymous with the mechanism of natural selection. But, for Swenson, natural selection is only one special case of the fundamental metaprocess

23. See, e.g., Chang, "Rayleigh-Bénard Convection"; National Oceanic and Atmospheric Administration (NOAA), "Rayleigh-Benard Convection Cells."

which is autocatakinesis, one in which the structuring mechanism is replicative. In his view evolution is simply the unfolding over time of autocatakinetic processes, and the fecundity principle underlying the Darwinian system only one particular manifestation of the striving of the universe as a whole towards an increasingly differentiated and structured arrangement. As Swenson admits, he's here aligning himself with an understanding of evolution more in keeping with that of Herbert Spencer (1820–1903) than that of Darwin.[24]

Likewise the second law of thermodynamics as classically formulated in terms of the universal striving to minimize potentials, while correct so far as it goes, draws attention to one aspect only of this larger evolutionary process, its shadow side as it were. This shouldn't surprise us, as the second law was originally formulated on the basis of how machines—specifically, steam engines—behave, and machines are *not* self-organizing dissipative structures. Rather, machines wholly depend on one particular kind of self-organizing dissipative structure in order to exist at all: human beings. By the same token human beings, augmented by their machinic prostheses, have the capacity to severely disrupt the self-organizing structures of the nonhuman world on whose functioning they in turn wholly depend.

From Swenson's perspective the MPP is simply the expression in biological systems of the more fundamental LMEP. Organisms and ecosystems are living kinds of dissipative structures and, as such, are selected to exist by the LMEP because they effect the degradation of environmental potentials at a faster rate than would otherwise be the case.[25] Life, on this understanding, is made up of structures of high internal potential, the price the universe pays *locally* in order to maximize the *overall* rate of potential degradation.[26] The LMEP therefore favors the existence of living things since they have the ability to both (1) persist in being while all the while degrading potentials and (2) seed other similar structures to compensate for their own inevitable decline over time due to wear and

24. Swenson, "Evolutionary Theory Developing."

25. A trivial example: each year there are around 1,000 tornadoes in the US, dissipating a median of around 60 gigajoules of energy each—60,000 gigajoules in total. This is equivalent to the amount of energy dissipated over the same period by only 6,000 hunter-gatherers consuming 10 gigajoules per annum each. In 2024 the US population dissipated 92 billion gigajoules of primary energy—a million times the amount dissipated by tornadoes. See Fricker and Elsner, "Kinetic Energy," and Energy Institute, "Statistical Review of World Energy."

26. Schneider and Kay, "Life as a Manifestation."

tear.[27] Biological *conatus* and the fecundity principle are simply down to that. By extension the MPP—the tendency of a living system to maximize energy flows through itself for the purposes of work which is useful to that system—follows because, in the end, work is useful to the extent that it furthers (1) and (2).

The ultimate selection criterion on this view is the LMEP, and dissipative structures, living and otherwise, are functional to the extent that they promote potential degradation rates. Animals, plants, and even tornadoes make use of energy sequestered from the environment, degrading potentials in the process; but this is only because they themselves are in harness to the LMEP, used as means to the end of realizing other, increasingly complex potentials. Those other, more complex potentials *are* the animals, plants, tornadoes themselves—and, further, in the case of those dissipative structures known as human beings, the sociotechnological constructions which they build.

The reader may have been struck by how dissipative structures only arise through the imposition of *constraints* on their parts. There's a sense therefore in which constraints can function in creative ways, making possible the appearance of new things, new orders of things, which otherwise could not exist. This might seem surprising since the word generally carries the negative connotation of inhibition or suppression. Yet it's appeared consistently throughout these three chapters in connection with the enhancement of power. Philosopher Alicia Juarrero, who has written extensively on the role of constraints in complex systems, defines them in this way:

> Constraints are entities, processes, events, relations, or conditions that raise or lower barriers to energy flow without directly transferring kinetic energy. Constraints bring about effects by making available, structuring, channeling, facilitating, or

27. The significance of the persistence in time of living dissipative structures is borne out in a study of ecosystem development in the Amazon. Maximum entropy production (MEP) during the course of ecosystem development is achieved in three ways: "The first maximizes the rate at which entropy production increases through successional time (dEP/dt), which, initially at least, is achieved via rapid colonization and increases in leaf area and biomass (i.e. r-selected species with fast individual/population growth rates). The second selection component of MEP is for maximum sustained entropy production during maturity (EP_{mature}). This is achieved via maximizing biomass and structural complexity and necessarily involves longer-lived, larger, slower-growing organisms (i.e. K-selected species). The third selection component is for stress-tolerating species extending the effective mature phase and postponing retrogression." Holdaway et al., "Trends in Entropy Production," 1444–45.

> impeding energy flow. Gradients and polarities, for example, are constraints; others include catalysts and feedback loops, recursion, iteration, buffers, affordances, schedules, codes, rules and regulations, heuristics, conceptual frameworks, ethical values and cultural norms, scaffolds, isolation, sedimentation and entrenchment, and bias and noise, among many others.[28]

Notice how constraints can "bring about effects" by adopting a great variety of forms which extend beyond the biophysical to include human phenomena such as ethical values and cultural norms. This point will get taken up again and explored at greater depth in the following chapters. But in concluding the present section it's worth asking: if the LMEP applies to living systems in general, what does it imply for human societies specifically?

Prior to the first Industrial Revolution humans generally operated near environmental carrying capacities, depending largely on the steady, or regularly fluctuating, energy inputs of solar radiation, mediated via biomass and the motions of wind and water. Wastes produced by humans were either already highly degraded, or were produced at rates sufficiently slow to allow timely and thorough degradation by nonhuman processes. This approximates to path B in figure 9, and corresponds to the way the MPP is expressed in mature biological systems, as described in the last chapter. Importantly, it also illustrates how, *in living systems, the LMEP may get expressed in counterintuitive ways*—a point which will be taken up again below.

Since then our ecosocial system[29] has self-organized so as to dissipate a huge (if finite) one-off subsidy of unprecedentedly energy-dense fossil fuels. The outputs from these processes include a set of deleterious wastes—carbon dioxide, plastics, nitrous oxide, for example—which tend to accumulate within the terrestrial environment, since their rates of production exceed those at which they can be broken down by nonhuman processes. In the wake of a sudden resource cornucopia, this behavior is consistent with the MPP's expression in immature systems: the rate at which energy sources are degraded, rather than the thoroughness of that degradation, gets maximized—path A in figure 9.

28. Juarrero, *Context Changes Everything*, 40. Juarrero distinguishes between enabling constraints, which take systems away from equilibrium, and constitutive or governing constraints, which bring about higher-order structures.

29. As defined in chapter 2, an ecosocial system is an ecosystem dominated by human activity: see Salthe, "Infodynamics," 10.

Our current ecosocial system, then, is behaving rather like a boy-racer who has just passed his driving test. As resources become more scarce, natural selection pressures are already favoring more efficient processes in some areas. But efficiencies won't suffice to compensate for the exhaustion of finite, nonrenewable resources. How much longer will global humanity enjoy "order for free" as energy flows stall and, in due course, start to decline?[30]

HIERARCHY AND EMERGENCE

So, according to Swenson at least, the striving of living things is just the expression of a more fundamental process. This process acts according to the LMEP, which preferentially selects dissipative structures because their increased space-time scales enable more ordered flows and so the erosion of potential gradients at faster rates. Increased scales of operation in both space and time mean that, as we noted when looking at the bladderwort-algae-water flea ensemble, there's a sense in which these structures can be regarded as entities in their own right, entities of a higher order than their components. In this respect Swenson's analysis coheres with, and reinforces, a hierarchical vision of how the world in general works.

Notable proponents of this hierarchical vision have included the American complexity scientist Herbert A. Simon (1916–2001) and the Hungarian-British chemist and philosopher Michael Polanyi (1891–1976). In a seminal 1968 paper entitled "Life's Irreducible Structure," Polanyi sketched the hierarchical operation of living systems in the following way.

> Processes at the lowest level are caused by the forces of inanimate nature, and the higher levels control, throughout, the boundary conditions left open by the laws of inanimate nature. The lowest functions of life are those called vegetative. These vegetative functions, sustaining life at its lowest level, leave open—both in plants and in animals—the higher functions of growth and in animals also leave open the operations of muscular actions. Next, in turn, the principles governing muscular actions in animals leave open the integration of such actions to innate patterns of behaviour; and, again, such patterns are open in their turn to be shaped by intelligence, while intelligence itself can be

30. Recall figures 7 and 8 in chapter 2.

> made to serve in man the still higher principles of a responsible choice.[31]

Polanyi stresses how the functioning of a given hierarchical level wholly depends on that of lower levels and, equally, applies constraints upon them through the imposition of various boundary conditions: "Each reduces the scope of the one immediately below it by imposing on it a boundary that harnesses it to the service of the next-higher level, and this control is transmitted stage by stage, down to the basic inanimate level."[32] Although this is a hierarchical arrangement, it clearly exhibits a kind of two-way traffic; for example the viral infection of a cell can affect the host organism by causing illness and death and, by the same token, the death of the organism from some other cause will lead to the breakdown of the cell.

Thinking in these terms allows us to express the relationship between different classes of phenomena as a so-called specification hierarchy: {physical processes {chemical affinities {biological forms {societal organizations}}}}. That is, chemical affinities represent a subclass of physical processes, and so on. Biologist Stanley Salthe comments: "Levels in the specification hierarchy mark the qualitative differences of different realms of being, as in 'physical realm' versus 'biological realm.' It is an intensional construct, open at the top (the innermost level is unbounded above, and so free to give rise to ever higher levels)."[33]

Notice the *qualitative* nature of differences between the "realms of being" represented by the classes in this hierarchy. This contrasts with the *quantitative* increases in space-time scales associated with autocatakinesis within a given class of phenomena. For example a physical entity such as a tornado (which is just a glorified convection cell with added horizontal rotation) exists over space-time scales orders of magnitude greater than the motions of its constituent air molecules; whereas a simple biological organism such as the single-celled amoeba, though so much more complex than a tornado that it belongs to a different class of phenomena, is tiny by comparison. Climbing the ladder of phenomena subclasses therefore need not mean quantitative increases in physical size or duration; rather what distinguish the levels are particular qualitative

31. Polanyi, "Life's Irreducible Structure," 1311.

32. Polanyi, "Life's Irreducible Structure," 1311. See also Salthe, *Evolving Hierarchical Systems*, 75–113, on the basic triadic structure of hierarchical systems.

33. Salthe, "Summary of the Principles," 14.

differences, a point which will attract our attention again in what follows in this and later chapters.

Hierarchies in nature exist alongside heterarchies, a notable example of the latter being the workings of the brain.[34] In a heterarchy "the relation of elements to one another . . . are unranked or . . . possess the potential for being ranked in a number of different ways, depending on systemic requirements."[35] A soccer team provides an instance of a social heterarchy, where the role of the team captain is largely nominal and each player, though assigned a particular position, is free to either attack or defend—indeed even a goalkeeper may charge up the pitch and score a goal. Although hierarchical and heterarchical arrangements might seem in principle as unlike as chalk and cheese, in real processes they often relate to each other in a dialectical manner.[36] This is worth noting, as it chimes with the process of assembling which will be described in chapter 5.[37]

Hierarchy theory provides a helpful steppingstone to talking about the phenomenon of *emergence*. Bénard cells and ecological ensembles were both described above as emergent, but what exactly does that mean? The term was first used in this way by George Henry Lewes (1817–78). Lewes was a man of many parts: an actor, a novelist, a literary critic, a philosopher, and someone who took a keen interest in physiology and psychology. In his multivolume *Problems of Life and Mind* (1874–79) he defined emergence as a "cooperation of things of unlike kinds" which generates an outcome qualitatively different from its component parts.[38]

As an example of an emergent phenomenon we need look no further than what comes out of the tap. The emergent wetness of water, H_2O, can't be predicted from the properties of hydrogen and oxygen molecules in isolation. Biological systems likewise: your body contains some ten trillion cells of around 250 different types, which have to be organized within certain tolerances in order to go on producing you. Or what about stainless steel, an alloy of iron, carbon, nickel, and chromium

34. McCulloch, "Heterarchy of Values."

35. Crumley, "Heterarchy," 2.

36. Crumley, "Heterarchy," 2.

37. An accessible general introduction to hierarchy theory is provided in Wu, "Hierarchy Theory: An Overview."

38. Lewes, *Problems of Life and Mind*, 413. See also Clayton, "Conceptual Foundations of Emergence Theory"; Elder-Vass, *Causal Power of Social Structures.*

which exhibits the emergent properties of not rusting or tarnishing?[39] Or a car, which could be considered an emergent product of its thousands of varied parts, inasmuch as the parts must be arranged to "cooperate" in a very specific way in order to produce a working automobile? A car is also qualitatively different to its components inasmuch as it can move around, play music, regulate the internal temperature and so on, which its parts in isolation cannot.

However, whereas cars and stainless steel are the results of deliberate design and production, the term "emergent" is more commonly reserved for self-organizing phenomena. The bladderwort-algae-water flea ensemble provides such an instance of spontaneous emergence. The ensemble's components are all organisms, of course, though of different species—indeed different kingdoms, when you consider that it includes both plants and animals. Although the ensemble, like its components, is a biological entity, it exhibits a distinctive pattern of behavior which sets it apart from the behavior of any of its components in isolation. This shows how emergence need not produce a physically contiguous whole (like a car) but only a novel configuration and pattern of operation of its parts.

If we loosen Lewes's "things of unlike kinds" stricture then many other phenomena qualify as emergent. A starling murmuration, for instance: even an expert ornithologist can't predict the next move of a murmuration. Likewise the workings of human society defy prediction on the basis of even the most comprehensive study of individual psychologies. Things can get really interesting though if you do mix together components as unlike as humans, viruses, and advanced pharmaceuticals: as the events of 2020 showed this mix can give rise to emergent outcomes as varied as economic recessions, reduced CO_2 emissions, population lockdowns, and mass vaccination mandates. Here a highly heterogeneous combination resulted in a highly novel set of consequences. We'll reflect further on the COVID-19 phenomenon in chapter 5.

I said above that the bladderwort-algae-water flea ensemble, once constituted, exercises top-down influence on its members. However some would argue that top-down causation properly speaking, or *strong* emergence, only applies to systems in which lower-level components are so thoroughly adapted to specific higher level contextual niches that they become nonviable apart from those niches. Compare, for example, a starling murmuration and a single starling. The sight of a flock of densely

39. Corning, *Holistic Darwinism*, 52, 133.

packed starlings swooping and pulsating in the fading light of a winter dusk irresistibly suggests the dance of a single being, or at least the directing hand of a single unseen conductor. Of course there is no such conductor. The behavior of the flock is an emergent product of each bird's survival instinct (*conatus* again) as it seeks to minimize the risk of being targeted by predators. In fact the extraordinary changes in the shape and trajectory of a swarming flock can be simulated computationally in a bottom-up manner by applying three simple rules to the behavior of each individual computational agent (starling):

- avoid collisions with nearby birds;
- attempt to match velocity with nearby birds;
- fly towards the center of the flock.[40]

The murmuration is thus an emergent, bottom-up product of the interaction of individual starlings. Other complex systems which display bottom-up emergent behaviors include phenomena as commonplace as avalanching sand piles, along with the above-mentioned Bénard cells and various ecological ensembles.[41]

In contrast, the interaction of the parts of a single starling—that is, its organs—can't be captured in this way since the starling, as a biological whole, exercises top-down causation in a strong sense by imposing a definite, fixed context upon its organs. Organisms in general "organise and shape the interactions of lower-level 'sub-systems' (downward causation), just as genes, organelles, tissues and organs shape the behaviour of the system as a whole (upward causation)."[42] An individual starling therefore possesses an ontological identity which eludes the starling murmuration. In crude terms, a starling is a "thing" and the murmuration isn't. The starling's component parts are also things, and are so in a descending, nested hierarchy—a starling is made up of organs, an organ

40. Reynolds, "Flocks, Herds, and Schools." Note that Rod Swenson would insist that such numerical simulations of self-organization, and rule-based computational systems in general, are not examples of autocatakinetic systems since they "bracket the whole environment or relational ontology out of the term, which from the point of view argued here is nearly everything. All rule-based systems . . . sit internal to autocatakinetic systems which account not only for the selection of the rules, but the requisite reading, writing and translation of them to function or have a reason for doing so." Swenson, "Grand Unified Theory," 14.

41. See Fieguth, *Introduction to Complex Systems*, 253–57.

42. Corning, *Holistic Darwinism*, 138.

is made up of cells, a cell is made up of organelles, and so on.[43] But they only remain *living* things thanks to the unconscious top-down causation of the living thing next above them in the hierarchy.

Top-down causation defined in this narrower sense is definitive of what is known as strong emergence, and biological systems in general are examples of this. Strong emergence requires that all four of the following conditions obtain, while weak emergence requires only the first three:

1. Ontological monism: reality is fundamentally composed of just one kind of "stuff."[44]
2. Genuinely novel properties can emerge when certain objects interact in sufficiently complex ways.
3. Such novel properties are irreducible to, and unpredictable from, the lower-level components from which they arise.
4. The emergent whole exhibiting these novel properties constrains the operation of its parts by imposing particular functions on them.[45]

The difference between strong and weak emergence is no mere academic quibble. It becomes a crucial issue when discussing the nature of those ensembles which have been described as superorganisms, as we shall see in the next chapter. For now we need only note that both strong and weak forms have their thermodynamic basis in the phenomenon of dissipative structuring or autocatakinesis which Swenson argues is universally selected by the LMEP.

Writing in 2023, Swenson claimed that the LMEP "meets the most rigorous standard possible in science, namely, [it is] stated in a way that subjects it to falsifiability with simple physical experiments, and like the first and second laws, the fourth law has never, in the three and half decades since it was formulated, been falsified."[46] He may well be right. In fact, Swenson's is only the most theoretically rigorous and comprehensive version of several maximum entropy principles which have been formulated over the years in the wake of physicist and engineer Hans Ziegler's seminal work in the 1960s. Several different kinds of system have been

43. Ellis, "Top-Down Causation and Emergence."

44. This is not necessarily to claim that this is the stuff with which physics—or any other scientific discipline—concerns itself.

45. Clayton, "Conceptual Foundations of Emergence Theory," 2–4.

46. Swenson, "Grand Unified Theory," 11.

shown to demonstrate maximum entropy production—in climatology, oceanography, biology, and so on.[47]

Set in this context the MPP can be viewed as an emergent expression of the LMEP, relevant to dissipative structures in which the ideas of useful work, and therefore of power as the rate of performing useful work, make sense. Such structures, living and otherwise, exhibit what Swenson calls "identity through flow." Importantly, in order for a dissipative structure to emerge the flows which constitute it must be constrained in certain ways. This coheres with the observation made in chapter 1 regarding social power, namely that constraint and enabling go hand in hand. But, having now been introduced to the idea of dissipative structures, we can speak in more general terms and say that *to be (an agent of some kind) is to be a locus of power (of some kind)—and to be subject to corresponding constraints*. With this understanding in mind we can return to the question of the *human* mediation of power.

BEYOND MAXIMUM POWER

Given the apparently fundamental nature of the LMEP, might it—or the MPP as its emergent expression—explain why human societies behave as they do? Ecology provides important clues for answering this question, as it offers a helpful bridge between the worlds of thermodynamics and biology on the one hand and that of human societies on the other. Two points in particular are relevant and stand out: the multiplicity of ecological goals, and their variable expression across a system's lifetime; and the notion of an optimal degree of ordering consistent with a system's longevity.

Let's start with the multiplicity of ecological goals. When introducing the MPP in chapter 2 I quoted Alfred Lotka: "Natural selection will so operate as to increase the total mass of the organic system, to increase the rate of circulation of matter through the system, and to increase the total energy flux through the system."[48] Observant readers will have noticed that the maximizing of energy flux is not the only outcome of the workings of natural selection. Other principles, or goals, are identified, namely maximizing mass and the matter circulation rate. More recent ecological studies bear this out. It transpires that *at each stage in ecosystem growth*

47. See Court, "Energy Capture, Technological Change," 7–8 for an overview.

48. Lotka, "Contribution," 148.

and development several different goals get expressed in particular combinations. For example, though power consumption increases throughout a system's lifetime, it does so at progressively slower rates during later stages, while energy dissipation rates level off completely during these stages simply because the system has stopped growing in size and so is no longer able to capture greater amounts of solar energy.[49]

In fact this was already implied in chapter 2's description of how the MPP's mode of operation changes as an ecosystem nears its carrying capacity and becomes dominated by K-strategists. Although a system may have stopped growing in size it can still continue to develop, in the sense of multiplying connections between its parts. Under these circumstances path B in figure 9 ends up getting selected over path A: energy is degraded more thoroughly as it trickles slowly down through the multiple trophic levels in a complex ecosystem, with soil minerals absorbed by plants, plants eaten by herbivores, herbivores eaten by carnivores . . . This pattern of slow trickling tends to minimize waste, and we see it replicated in the metabolism of individual organisms—consider the convoluted process by which the energy contained in the food you eat eventually gets to your muscles. As a result, the MPP and the LMEP get expressed through the multilevel richness and longevity of a hierarchical potential-realizing system, and not only by the instantaneous rate of potential degradation.

The thing to note is that ecosystems have to juggle a number of different ecological goals, and that these goals' pattern of expression will reflect the system's stage of development. Neither the MPP nor the LMEP in isolation represents the last word here. In fact what these studies suggest is that, rather than view a system as tending to maximize (or minimize) a particular metric, we should instead think in terms of an *optimal* functioning which is the upshot of several factors in combination, and which may vary across time. If we're dealing with an ecosystem then these factors are the various ecological goals. More generally, we can make use of a term with which we're already familiar, namely *constraint*, and conclude that, *at any given stage in a system's development, there exists*

49. Fath et al., "Ecosystem Growth and Development," examine the following ecological goals: energy throughflow rate (power), energy dissipation rate (entropy), energy retention time, energy storage, and energy dissipation rate per unit mass. These are by no means exhaustive: Yen et al., "Thermodynamic Extremization Principles," identify no fewer than thirteen possible ecological goals. See also Fath, "Systems Ecology."

an optimum mode of functioning which involves the co-application of a particular set of constraints.

This has major implications for human systems. We've seen how a nonliving emergent structure like a Bénard cell or a tornado, subject simply to the LMEP, necessarily reflects the particular physical constraints applied to the lower-level micro-flows from which it emerges. At the other end of the specification hierarchy given by {physical processes {chemical affinities {biological forms {societal organizations}}}}, we find human beings. In chapter 1 we noted that humans are distinct by virtue of entertaining purposes, constraints on behavior which go beyond instincts for survival and reproduction. Extending the class/subclass notation, we can link purpose to biological *conatus* and underlying thermodynamic principles by writing {propensity {function {purpose}}}.[50] This is a concise way of expressing purpose as an emergent property, one arising from prior biophysical factors: purposes provide constraints on the behavior of human individuals and societies in the same way that functions and propensities constrain the behavior of biological and physical systems respectively. As emergent, purpose represents a qualitative novelty, so it can't be reduced to the sum of a set of maximized (or minimized) biological and thermodynamic goals. And, as history shows, purposes can also vary a lot, thus giving rise to the remarkable diversity of human cultural expression. Optimal realization of potential for humans is therefore all tied up with *which* prevailing purposes constrain the operations of a given culture.

Optimality, this time in relation to a system's degree of order, also appears in the very suggestive work of another ecologist whom we've already encountered, namely Robert E. Ulanowicz. Unlike some others in his discipline, Ulanowicz has embraced the tools of information theory in order to better understand interactions between ecosystem components, and so the development of ecosystems as a whole. For we'd be mistaken if we took Buzz Holling's adaptive cycle to imply that all mature ecosystems are forever poised on the edge of an imminent Ω-phase, or collapse. Whereas some, like the spruce-budworm systems of the Pacific Northwest studied by Holling, do demonstrate a certain proneness in this direction, others, such as the mesophyte forests of the East Coast of North America, appear to be far more robust, exhibiting climax, or

50. Salthe, "Purpose in Nature," 54.

K-, phases which persisted for centuries prior to the advent of human interference.[51]

Ulanowicz has largely pioneered an approach which quantifies the degree of interconnectedness of an ecosystem's components by measuring the relative rates of nutrient flow between them. This enables him to define an overall *degree of order* for the system as a whole, on a scale of 0 (minimally interconnected or ordered) to 1 (maximally interconnected or ordered). Theoretical considerations lead him to make predictions about how a system's *robustness*—that is, its sustainability, or fitness for change while still retaining a measure of structural identity—varies according to its degree of order. This relationship is summarized in the following figure.

FIGURE 10

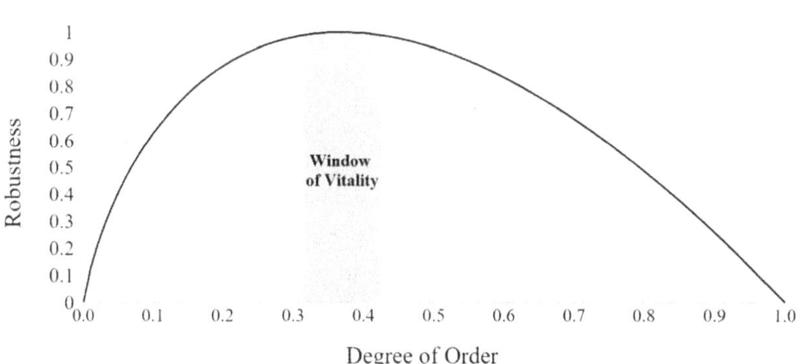

Figure 10: Ecosystem robustness as a function of degree of order. Source: Ulanowicz, "Increasing Entropy."

Intriguingly, peak robustness occurs at an order degree value not of 0.5 as one might simplistically assume, but of 0.37;[52] in other words, with a bias towards relatively unordered systems. Since the components of more ordered systems are more interdependent, connection-damaging shocks make these systems more vulnerable to "avalanches," sudden and drastic losses of order. Beyond a value of 0.37 systems become

51. Ulanowicz, "Widening the Third Window," 281–82.

52. 0.37 = 1/e, where e is the base of the natural logarithm and exponential function, a mathematical constant with a value of roughly 2.71828, sometimes called Euler's number or Napier's number. See Stewart, "e."

increasingly brittle in this sense. Less ordered systems can cope better with the breakdown of linkages between components since the prevailing autocatakinetic propensity will tend to quickly foster new linkages. Exactly the same propensity will however hasten the breakdown of a stressed system which is already highly ordered. Being highly ordered means being highly efficient, and so highly adapted to a given environment. That's fine while the environment stays the same, but if it changes then relatively inefficient though adaptable systems are better placed to survive and prosper.

This leads Ulanowicz to define a *window of vitality*, or optimal order, around the value corresponding to maximum robustness. In the language of complexity science, this acts as an attractor for actually existing ecosystems of all kinds, such that less ordered systems tend to progress rapidly towards it, and more ordered systems which have developed beyond it tend not to last so long, given that their direction of travel, according to the logic of natural succession, is towards increasing interconnection and so brittleness.

Ulanowicz echoes Swenson when he says, "It no longer becomes necessary to view the production of entropy as a hell-bent rush into nothingness. Increasing entropy also displays a distinctly obverse behavior. Whenever [the degree of order] of a complex dissipative system plots between 1/e [0.37] and 1, the conventional second law pull toward disorganization will prevail. By strict contrast, if the degree of order in a system falls between 0 and 1/e and it has access to additional energy and resources, increasing entropy will result in augmenting system organization."[53] Empirical studies confirm that actual ecological ensembles do indeed tend to cluster around order degrees of 0.37, the point of maximal robustness, with the clustering becoming even more pronounced once very small systems lacking richness and detail are omitted. Other factors being equal, ecosystems can persist for extended periods within windows of vitality without thereby violating the MPP or the LMEP.

If anything Ulanowicz goes beyond Swenson in affirming the positive consequences of the second law of thermodynamics in non-isolated systems far from equilibrium. Systems like these are in the business of creating order every bit as much as that of destroying it. There is a "yin and yang" on display in any dissipative structure, "two countervailing tendencies": on the one hand, "a continuous stream of perturbations

53. Ulanowicz, "Increasing Entropy," 93.

[working] to erode any existing structure and coherence"; on the other, "the workings of autocatalytic configurations, which drive growth and development and provide repair to the system."[54] This reinforces the claim made earlier in this chapter, namely that increasing entropy in systems far from equilibrium is, as much as anything, a matter of realizing potentials, their transformation into new kinds of things.

The implications of Ulanowicz's work for ecosocial systems are intriguing. At this stage, we can at least infer that there's no reason why they too can't inhabit windows of vitality marked by a sufficient degree of flexibility in socioeconomic relations, such that when disruptions arise connections can be reconfigured without the complete loss of the ecosocial system's identity. True, given where we've got to, this might well require some unwelcome socioeconomic simplifications, but there's no *biophysical* reason why this is impossible. Certainly, the LMEP and/or the MPP don't in themselves amount to a death warrant. If there is a force dragging humanity out of its window of vitality then, although it may have some basis in these principles, it can't be reduced to them. The nature of this mysterious force has already been hinted at, and will get examined further over the coming chapters.

To sum up this section: if the ways in which living systems operate can't be predicted straightforwardly on the basis of the MPP and/or the LMEP, perhaps a more felicitous way of expressing their effect in an ecosocial setting might be as *the optimal purposed realization of potential*. There's much more to entropy than just waste, and not only because my waste may become someone else's fuel. During the growth and development trajectory of ecosocial systems, therefore, it's reasonable to suggest that the LMEP may get expressed not only via a crudely material MPP but also via a range of other specifically *ecosocial* goals. And ecosocial goals will inevitably embody and reflect prevailing human purposes, purposes which are underdetermined by the MPP/LMEP and act instead as constraints on their expression.

This point is worth stressing because it's not obvious to everyone. If all you had to go on was the LMEP, you might naively assume that the exclusive goal of life, human and otherwise, is to degrade biophysical potentials at the fastest rate and at the largest scale. That would indeed seem to be the position of some transhumanists who advocate what they

54. Ulanowicz, "Dual Nature of Ecosystem Dynamics," 1889. Again, Swenson would correct "autocatalytic" to read "autocatakinetic."

call effective accelerationism (e/acc).[55] Drawing in part on the work of physicist Jeremy England who, like Swenson, interprets the emergence of life thermodynamically, they argue for endless material expansion leading to a posthuman colonization of the stars.[56] "Effective accelerationism aims to follow the 'will of the universe': leaning into the thermodynamic bias towards futures with greater and smarter civilizations that are more effective at finding/extracting free energy from the universe and converting it to utility at grander and grander scales."[57] The reference to utility is significant, since for the author it denotes not usefulness in promoting some vision of human flourishing but rather the quantitative measure derived by neoclassical economists from the ethical theory of utilitarianism.[58] Essentially their program boils down to the transformation of the qualitatively diverse material world into greater and greater amounts of an abstract quantity, money, all in the service of a libertarian economic model.

As one critic points out, e/acc is all about maximization—of energy consumption harnessed to utility production.[59] With this goal e/acc's proponents dream of ascending the Kardashev gradient, which ranks civilizations according to their power consumption: stage 1, capturing all the energy available on the planet; stage 2, capturing all the energy produced by the sun; stage 3, capturing all the energy available within the galaxy.[60] Ascending this gradient is taken for granted as desirable, if not destined, "the will of the universe": Leslie White's law of cultural development as *Star Trek* storyline. What's missing is any understanding of emergence, specifically the way in which, as we have just seen, the LMEP's expression gets modified with the onset of living systems. A host of specifically biological and ecological goals arise such that system development can no longer be defined by a simple maximization criterion. And this is before human beings turn up to complicate things

55. On e/acc see Thomas, *Politics and Ethics of Transhumanism*, 178–81. Transhumanism more generally has been defined as "the intellectual and cultural movement that affirms the possibility and desirability of fundamentally improving the human condition through applied reason, especially by developing and making widely available technologies to eliminate aging and to greatly enhance human intellectual, physical, and psychological capacities." Humanity Plus, "Philosophy."

56. England, *Every Life Is On Fire*.

57. Jezos, "Notes on E/acc Principles and Tenets."

58. See, e.g., Heilbroner, *Teachings from the Worldly Philosophy*, 199–244.

59. Torres, "'Effective Accelerationism.'"

60. Zhang et al., "Forecasting the Progression of Human Civilization."

still further. Key to the selection of living systems by the LMEP is their persistence in time. This isn't irrelevant given that e/acc urges the single-minded acceleration of entropy production, regardless of ecological costs and the associated risk (trumpeted by others within the transhumanist movement) of human self-termination.

Taking emergence seriously—the chemical emerging from the physical, the biological from the chemical, the human from the biological—allows us to reframe the expression of the LMEP/MPP in terms of *an emergent optimality under constraints*, so creating a space to realistically imagine an ecosocial system which remains within its window of vitality and so avoids self-termination.[61] If dissipative structures arise only through the application of constraints then, in human systems, the kinds of social structure which emerge will greatly depend not only on material factors such as humanity's gross wattage, but also on the balance of those specifically human constraints—cultural, moral, spiritual—which are in play and end up conferring identity on the emerging structure. For Leslie White, cultural advance meant increasing material sophistication based on increasing wattage. For the twenty-first century it likely means exactly the opposite.

SUMMING UP

The notion of striving featured prominently in the first two chapters, and it's done so again in chapter 3. Taking his cue from Rudolf Clausius's original choice of words for the second law of thermodynamics, Rod Swenson extends the province of striving beyond the biological realm to the material world in its entirety. This striving isn't at root about the race to increase the extent and duration of my kind. Neither is it about the simple destruction of order, despite the popular understanding of entropy. Rather it's about the realization of potentials at the fastest rate permitted by the conditions, their transformation into increasingly complex and sophisticated structures, drawing as it does so on the ever-bountiful provision of an expanding universe. Here we have Swenson's Law of Maximum Entropy Production and mechanism of autocatakinesis in a nutshell, his "grand unified theory for the unification of physics, life, information and cognition."

61. The phrase "emergent optimality under constraints" is borrowed from Court, "Energy Capture, Technological Change," 8–9.

This has major implications for how we understand the Maximum Power Principle. Alfred Lotka's version of the MPP, as we saw in chapter 2, is predicated on the process of natural selection. Swenson's reading of evolution, standing as it does in the tradition of Spencer rather than that of Darwin, has the substantial merit of not being similarly predicated. For Swenson natural selection, as the outcome of agonistic struggle by always incipiently excess populations for finite resources, is only one possible, emergent mode of expression of the more fundamental LMEP.

The story of autocatakinesis is the story of emergence, the interactions between dissimilar things giving rise to new and unpredictable dynamical forms at ever larger scales. This requires that the components of emergent wholes submit to constraints on the possibilities otherwise available to them. Component species in an ecological ensemble, for example, become constrained through their interdependencies. Living systems are therefore inherently hierarchical, composed of multiple strata each one of which operates according to specific principles irreducible to those of lower levels, with each stratum serving as a constraint upon those lower down. This ultimately enables a form of purpose to emerge, a "self" capable of exercising some measure of autonomy with respect to the lower-level processes which give rise to it.

A human group, in this sense, is a self of sorts; and, especially since the first Industrial Revolution, global humanity as a whole has been shaped by a particular set of autocatakinetic constraints. Their effect has been to organize societies so as to accelerate the rate of energy consumption—that is, to maximize material power. But the ground covered in this chapter raises the possibility that this need not be so. There can be no bypassing the LMEP or MPP for humans but, as studies of ecosystem growth and development illustrate, their expression may change at higher levels. Within living systems the MPP expresses the LMEP alongside a number of other goals in such a way that the simple metric of energy dissipation rate no longer exclusively defines the trajectory of the system's development. With the emergence among living things of the human we can therefore, by analogy, expect that the expression of the MPP in turn may be modulated and supplemented by other goals which become meaningful only at the human level, that is, in ecosocial systems. For example, might power itself acquire a new dimension such that it gets expressed diversely as different *kinds* of power, each with its own enabling constraints? Mediating each kind of power would then naturally mean submitting to those constraints proper to it—socioeconomic, cultural, and so on. There's no biophysical reason why human societies, like ecosystems, can't persist within widows of vitality; all that's needed is the adoption of the right set of constraints.

The preamble to this chapter gave us a glimpse into the life of John Greenleaf Whittier, and in so doing introduced the idea that, on the human level, the striving which Swenson sees at the heart of all things can be expressed in many different *kinds* of ways. Striving for survival at all costs; for religious ecstasy; for the liberation of one's fellow humans; these are all very different projects. Which of these, if any, counts as useful work will depend on one's overarching life plan. The link between power and that for which we strive is all too apparent and reinforces the conclusion that, in human life, what's at stake is *which* constraints get adopted rather than whether constraints get adopted at all.

However it's the particular constraints associated with the emergence of society as we know it which have foisted our current predicament upon us. What exactly are these constraints, anyway? How did they arise? Are they inevitable? And what is their underlying animus? Exploring these questions leads us into the territory of the superorganism, which will be the subject of the next chapter.

4

Enough Is Too Little: The Superorganism Emerges

Go to the ant, O sluggard; consider her ways, and be wise. Without having any chief, officer or ruler, she prepares her food in summer, and gathers her sustenance in harvest.[1]

Social insects fascinate us: ants, termites, and many species of wasps and bees. Their capacity to spontaneously collaborate as functionally diverse parts of a single whole was a source of marvel to the author of the book of Proverbs, as it has been for countless others throughout human history. Among the most remarkable of social insects are leafcutter ants, genus *atta*, found in the American tropics. They are farmers, the life of a millions-strong colony being exclusively dedicated to the cultivation of a fungus of the *Leucocoprineae* family on which the ant larvae feed.[2] To this end the ants scour the floor of the rainforest, cutting and processing fresh vegetation to feed the fungus. The leafcutter has been so successful that, over the course of the last eight to twelve million years, it has become the dominant herbivore in that part of the world.

A rigorous division of labor is the secret of this success. The ant colony comprises four castes, named according to their relative sizes: foraging is undertaken by the Mediae, care of the young by the Minims, patrol

1. Prov 6:6–8.

2. Actually this is a strongly symbiotic relationship, such that one could even claim that, in a sense, the fungus farms the ants: see Kooij et al., "*Leucoagaricus gongylophorus*." See also Arthur, "Leaf-Cutter Ants."

and first-line defense of the foraging trails by the Minors, and responses to concerted attacks on the nest by the Majors. The net effect of these joint endeavors is to render a mature colony "the ecological equivalent of a large mammalian herbivore in terms of collective biomass, lifespan and quantity of plant material consumed."[3]

Likewise, a single honeybee colony—comprising cleaners, builders, brood carers, guards, and foragers—can be regarded as "a mammal in many bodies."[4] All this is down to what celebrated sociobiologist Edward O. Wilson called the eusocial nature of insects such as these, those whose way of life wholly depends on elaborate patterns of strict role-based collaboration.[5]

Strange as it may seem, in certain important respects humans have more in common with these social insects than they have with their nearest primate relatives.[6] Perhaps even more remarkably it turns out that fungus-growing ants and termites have more in common with contemporary humans than with honeybees, inasmuch as they share an *ultrasocial* mode of life: that is, their societies are organized for the single purpose of surplus resource production. The phenomenon of human ultrasociality is the focus of this chapter, but before being addressed directly it needs first to be located in the context of another phenomenon, one we have already come across, namely emergence.

SUPERORGANISMS EMERGING

Whether we consider humans, bees, or ants, we're dealing with acutely interdependent collections of individuals. In fact the use of the word "mammal" as a metaphor to describe a single bee colony brings out the way in which it can be regarded without hyperbole as a single organism, the social whole exercising primacy over its individual parts. What that means is that in order to adequately understand the behavior of an individual bee you have to set the behavior in the context of the operation of the colony as a whole. Indeed colonies of social insects were described as

3. Schultz and Brady, "Major Evolutionary Transitions in Ant Agriculture."
4. Tautz, *Buzz About Bees*, 3.
5. Wilson, *Social Conquest of Earth.*
6. Kesebir, "Superorganism Account of Human Sociality."

superorganisms as long ago as 1911 by American entomologist William Morton Wheeler.[7] But what exactly does this imply?

By definition an organism is a living thing made up of various interconnected organs. Each organ has a distinctive function, so making a particular contribution to the life of the organism. In fact the organism remains alive only as long as the operation of its vital organs remains healthy and coordinated. As per its etymology (the Greek *organon*), each organ is essentially a tool, an instrument of the organismic whole. In other words, the being of an organ is exclusively defined by its function with respect to that whole. Consider the human body. Some organs (for example, the appendix, the spleen, even a kidney) are less essential for the functioning of the organism than others (for example, the heart or the brain), and so are relatively expendable. But no organ can survive on its own in isolation from the organism of which it is a part.

A superorganism can be defined as a behavioral or social system in which the independent actions of its parts, at least some of which are themselves organisms, are organized so as to pursue a collective goal.[8] This entails two crucial requirements: a specific division of labor between the parts of the system; and feedback mechanisms which ensure coordination of the parts towards the goal. In a superorganism, the low-level interactions of the constituent organisms give rise to higher-level operational structures. These then reinforce certain underlying interactions between organisms which in turn reinforce those higher-level structures, so setting up a positive feedback loop—a process which, as we saw in the last chapter, has been termed autocatakinesis by ecologist Rod Swenson. So, while an individual ant or termite qualifies as an organism in its own right, it can only survive in a natural setting by functioning as an organ of a superorganismic colony. The colony as superorganism is no mere metaphor.

Of course, the lower-level organisms could interact variously so as to generate a range of possible higher level structures (a bottom-up process); which, if any, structure comes to prevail may be the result of chance but, once it has emerged, this structure can become self-reinforcing, locking in one particular organization of the lower-level components (a top-down process). To adapt a formula of biologist Stanley Salthe's: the lower level proposes, the higher level disposes.[9] In this sense the higher-level

7. Wheeler, "Ant Colony as an Organism."

8. Following the definition offered by Corning, *Holistic Darwinism*, 192–93.

9. Salthe, "Summary of the Principles," 16.

whole exceeds the sum of its lower-level parts. The former is an *emergent* product of the latter in the sense introduced in the previous chapter.

In the case of the leafcutter ant the superorganismic emergent whole is not the ant colony in isolation but rather the ecological ensemble comprising the colony and its farmed fungus. But it was not always thus. It's been argued that such organized foraging may have evolved within prior groups which practiced cooperative hunting.[10] If so, then this can be seen as an example of a major evolutionary transition.[11] Transitions of this kind can occur at all levels in a hierarchical fashion, again as previously outlined:

> Self-replicating molecules have given way to self-replicating complexes (e.g. chromosomes). The eukaryotic cell is a symbiotic community of previously autonomous bacteria, some of which have given up their reproductive independence to join the eukaryotic cell. Multicellular organisms are collections of individual eukaryotic cells that work together as a highly cooperative unit. And finally, such multicellular organisms as ants, termites, honeybees, and naked mole rats transitioned from groups of solitary individuals to colonies that act much like one organism: a superorganism.[12]

These are all examples of emergent phenomena, the cell emerging from the interaction of bacteria, organisms emerging from the interaction of cells, and so on.[13] In each case the emerging whole exercises top-down control over its component parts. A superorganism in turn can be viewed as an emergent social phenomenon.

Ecological ensembles such as the bladderwort-algae-water flea complex encountered in the last chapter share with superorganisms the distinguishing emergent property of the whole exceeding the sum of its parts, in the sense that the emergent whole transcends its components. Equally, ensembles and superorganisms also differ in important ways. Like the organs of an organism, the components of a superorganism are defined by their function within the whole of which they are parts; they exhibit a systemic purposiveness, or teleonomy.[14] So, while the compo-

10. O'Donnell et al., "Extraordinary Predation."

11. Maynard Smith and Szathmáry, *Major Transitions in Evolution*.

12. Kesebir, "Superorganism Account of Human Sociality," 236.

13. See further Baum and Baum, "Inside-Out Origin"; Brunet and King, "Origin of Animal Multicellularity."

14. Corning, *Holistic Darwinism*, 114–17.

nents of an ecological ensemble may happily survive the dissolution of the ensemble, the viability of a superorganism's components would typically be compromised if the superorganism breaks apart: an organ divorced from its native organism does not thrive. Ecological ensembles are therefore examples of so-called *weak* emergence while superorganisms arguably qualify as examples of *strong* emergence, a term which, as we saw in the previous chapter, only applies strictly speaking to systems in which lower-level components are thoroughly adapted to specific higher-level contextual niches such that they cannot function independently of those niches.[15]

The distinction between strong and weak emergence is important to bear in mind as we now move on to examine the suggestion that human societies have evolved to become superorganisms in this sense.

A HUMAN SUPERORGANISM?

The vision of human society as an organic unity comprising a functionally interdependent citizenry can be traced back at least as far as Plato.[16] It's also been a staple of sociological theory since the time of Victorian polymath Herbert Spencer.[17] However the term "superorganism" has been used to novel effect more recently in a series of articles by ecological economists John Gowdy and Lisi Krall to describe the development of human societies since the agrarian revolution of the current Holocene epoch. This challenging account of the current human predicament merits close attention, and what follows is a summary of their arguments.

Between around eight thousand years ago and the start of the Common Era the global human population grew rapidly from some six million

15. Does the ant superorganism represent an instance of strong emergence? In his discussion of top-down causation George F. R. Ellis, for one, says no. But this is surely questionable. All the ants in a given colony share the same genome, all being the offspring of the same mother. Caste differentiation occurs in the course of embryo development as a result of various environmental factors. These determine which genes get expressed as the embryo develops, leading eventually to the birth of a member of a specific caste. The context in which the embryo developed is therefore coded into each individual ant, so rendering it functionally specific within the context of its colony. The colony can therefore be said to exercise a primary top-down influence over each individual as it goes about exercising its epigenetically prescribed function. See Ellis, "Top-Down Causation and Emergence," 127; Chittka et al., "Epigenetics: The Making of Ant Castes."

16. Plato, *Republic* 2.

17. Spencer, *Principles of Sociology*.

to 200 million. This was the Neolithic Demographic Transition, and it was made possible by the rise of large-scale agrarian societies. Prior to the start of the Holocene around 11,700 years ago human beings existed exclusively as hunter-gatherers: small itinerant bands, highly egalitarian in ethos and exhibiting little or no division of labor except by age and sex.[18] Theirs was usually a subsistence existence involving the extensive exploitation of plants and animals for food. The impact of such a small population on the nonhuman world was comparatively modest, though there's evidence that fire was used to modify environments from perhaps as long as two hundred thousand years ago, not long after the time *Homo sapiens* emerged;[19] and debates continue regarding the human contribution to the extinction of large animals such as mammoths at the start of the Holocene.[20]

Members of *Homo sapiens* have always been "uniquely social mammals,"[21] "unique in their manipulation of cultural symbols, language, and their ability to cooperate with non-kin."[22] However, with the widespread adoption of agriculture, this preexisting sociability was transformed into a phenomenon already exhibited by some social insects: ultrasociality. Gowdy and Krall define the term thus:

> The active harnessing of the inputs to food production and a reconfiguration of the group in order to do so. Ultrasocial species are configured to actively produce and expand their food supply rather than wait for nature to provide it.[23]

Gowdy and Krall consider the advent of ultrasociality to be a major evolutionary transition, comparable to the emergence of DNA from RNA. From this point onward human populations came to resemble ultrasocial insects in the following key respects:

- explosive population growth;
- domination of ecosystems;

18. This simplified account requires some qualification, as we shall see in chapter 5.

19. Gowlett, "Discovery of Fire by Humans."

20. Meltzer, "Overkill."

21. Gowdy and Krall, "Ultrasocial Origin of the Anthropocene," 138.

22. Gowdy and Krall, "Agriculture as a Major Evolutionary Transition," 182.

23. Gowdy and Krall, "Economic Origins of Ultrasociality," 3. The authors admit that there is no consensus regarding the definition of this widely used term. Compare, e.g., Tomasello, "Ultra-Social Animal."

- extensive and intensive exploitation of natural resources in order to maximize agricultural surplus;
- complex and hierarchical division of labor;
- prioritization of group interests over those of individuals.[24]

The cause of this fateful transition was a step-change in *group dynamic* to one optimized for the production of agricultural surplus, the equivalent of the epigenetic developments in social insects which give rise to particular phenotypic expressions (the castes mentioned above). It's not difficult to imagine such a step-change as the congealing of a perennial wont to have something "put by for a rainy day."[25] However it came about, humans disengaged from dependence on the unpredictable resource flows supplied by nonhuman nature—sun, rain, the fluctuating availability of prey—and came instead to rely on stocks of surplus grain production accumulated at harvest. As well as being available at any time, all year round, stocks also had the advantage of being convertible to flows at any required rate, so acting as a source of greater power than that afforded by contingent seasonal flows.[26]

For Gowdy and Krall what makes the advent of agriculture so significant is the *expansionary* nature of the associated group dynamic. Recall from their definition of ultrasociality that "ultrasocial species are configured to actively produce and expand their food supply rather than wait for nature to provide it." This new dynamic took the form of a positive feedback loop incorporating several different elements:

1. The accumulation of surplus grain production, specifically that of high-yielding annual crops such as wheat and barley, gave rise to population growth.
2. Larger populations led to enhanced productive efficiency through greater economies of scale and divisions of labor. These divisions included groups of nonproductive specialists required to support the functioning of an increasingly complex enterprise—craftspeople,

24. Gowdy and Krall, "Ultrasocial Origin of the Anthropocene," 139–40.

25. "The imperative requirement to produce a surplus is useful for mere survival. It provides a margin that can be foregone in times of dearth. Enough is too little." Robinson, *Freedom and Necessity*, 25, quoted in Goodchild, *Credit and Faith*, 179.

26. Gowdy and Krall, "Economic Origins of Ultrasociality," 5. This qualifies their statement elsewhere that "it is surplus, not power, that drives the system." Gowdy and Krall, "Agriculture as a Major Evolutionary Transition," 192.

bureaucrats of various kinds, and a nascent army to defend stores and facilitate territorial expansion. Feeding such nonproductive members required additional surplus.

3. The sedentary mode of living necessary for surplus accumulation, combined with the priority of sustaining populations during those seasons when food locally was less readily available, provided another accumulation imperative.

4. Since the regular cultivation of annual crops leads to the degrading of soils, the consequent loss of soil fertility provided a further impetus for expansion into new areas.

As time passed the transition to agriculture became obligate for most as the larger groups with the more efficient farming practices and more effective militaries outcompeted and marginalized others.[27]

Like leafcutter ants, agrarian human societies thus developed into specifically ultrasocial superorganisms; that is, social systems in which the behavior of individuals is organized so as to pursue the collective goal of producing and expanding food supply. Gowdy and Krall emphasize that this development was fundamentally economic in nature, and that it demonstrated the operation of natural selection in favor of the emerging group: "An evolutionary transition where society takes on the characteristics of a superorganism within which individuals become cogs harnessed to further a higher-level goal which may or may not be in the interest of individual well-being."[28] Indeed the archaeological evidence is clear that the transition had detrimental effects for most individuals, accompanied as it was by shorter lifespans, a reduction in physical stature, and greater proneness to disease.[29] Jared Diamond didn't mince his words when he described the agrarian revolution as "the worst mistake in the history of the human race."[30] The well-being of the average person was sacrificed at the altar of the emerging agrarian superorganism. Quality of life was trumped by quantity of stored surplus.[31]

27. Gowdy and Krall, "Economic Origins of Ultrasociality," 10.

28. Gowdy and Krall, "Agriculture as a Major Evolutionary Transition," 184.

29. See, e.g., Larsen, "Agricultural Revolution as Environmental Catastrophe"; Sahlins, "Original Affluent Society."

30. Diamond, "Worst Mistake."

31. The ultrasocial turn thus meant the inversion of the principle of least effort which had characterized the lives of pre-agrarian groups. See Kemp, *Goliath's Curse*, 80–83, 343.

Yet this was but the beginning of woes. Many lament the appearance of capitalism as an economic system, though disagree on when it came about. Some would date it to thirteenth-century Florence;[32] others to the English countryside of the sixteenth century;[33] while others again would point to the appearance, in the eighteenth century, of a market society empowered by the industrial exploitation of fossil fuels.[34] But for Gowdy and Krall all these were simply further staging posts on a journey begun millennia previously. Capitalism, whenever it came about, is just the latest phase of "a continuum along the human ultrasocial path," being established on the foundations of preexisting market exchange made possible by surplus production.[35] Why go to the trouble of accumulating cumbersome grain when, far more conveniently, you can instead accumulate social claims on material wealth of all kinds—i.e., money—with a view to reinvestment and further accumulation? Likewise with the Industrial Revolution: the ancient sunlight stored in fossil fuels only served to resolve (temporarily) the bottleneck arising from the strictly limited energy flux available to run the capitalist machine from current photosynthesis. "In this way the ultrasocial impulse of human evolution took on a more pronounced dynamic, ushering in the Anthropocene."[36]

As ultrasocial entities, what the early agrarian society of Jericho shares with contemporary global finance capitalism is a common expansionary imperative—and therein lies their fundamental problem: "They have a constitutional proclivity to expand; and because of their tremendous interdependence, they are particularly difficult to disengage before they reach the point of collapse."[37] It's this latter feature, the intricately interdependent nature of the superorganism's parts, rather than its hierarchical structure, which makes it so resistant to reform. And the need for radical reform is urgent, since the "general message from human ultrasociality is negative—the human enterprise is driven by a mechanical evolutionary process working against individual well-being and

32. "The whole panoply of forms of capitalism—commercial, industrial, banking—was already deployed in thirteenth-century Florence." Braudel, *Perspective of the World*, 621.

33. E.g., Meiksins Wood, *Origin of Capitalism*, 95–105.

34. Polanyi, *Great Transformation*.

35. Gowdy and Krall, "Ultrasocial Origin of the Anthropocene," 142–43.

36. Gowdy and Krall, "Ultrasocial Origin of the Anthropocene," 144.

37. Gowdy and Krall, "Economic Origins of Ultrasociality," 11.

environmental sustainability."[38] Yet even its most oppressed members have an interest in its survival since any change would be highly disruptive, if not disastrous, at least in the short term. The system may demean many, yet it also "works," after some fashion, for many—for now.

Where has all this left us? Gowdy and Krall have no qualms about describing the results of the ultrasocial transition as a lock-in, and in employing the language of strong emergence:

> The transition to agriculture set into motion forces that led to a higher level of social organization around a new and distinctive bioeconomic dynamic that should be viewed as an articulate whole, a unified system. Through downward causation, the entire human economic enterprise including production systems, technologies, ideologies, laws and customs, in short the entire institutional and material fabric of economic society, has evolved as an interlocking, downward self-reinforcing entity around the bioeconomic dynamic at play. . . . We are in the grip of an impersonal self-organizing system within which humans and essential elements of the natural world are expendable.[39]

This could easily be read fatalistically, as admitting the futility of any bottom-up attempts to counter the insatiable appetite of the surplus-obsessed superorganism. Actually the authors are not *quite* so despairing.[40] In any event some might object that, in the final analysis, human beings are not ants. It's one thing to characterize an ant colony as a superorganism given that, as the authors note, individual social insects "can't survive without performing specific functions within the group."[41] But the same scarcely applies to human beings. Robinson Crusoe may be an exception that proves the rule, but characters such as this demonstrate that people can certainly survive and even thrive independently of any group context. To this extent human societies more resemble the "temporary superorganisms" which can emerge among lions, whales, and various other species when hunting.[42]

38. Gowdy and Krall, "Economic Origins of Ultrasociality," 14.

39. Gowdy and Krall, "Ultrasocial Origin of the Anthropocene," 144, 146.

40. "We are not suggesting that there is no human agency but we are suggesting that the role of human agency is much less powerful than we think." Gowdy and Krall, "Ultrasocial Origin of the Anthropocene," 138.

41. Gowdy and Krall, "Agriculture as a Major Evolutionary Transition," 192.

42. Corning, *Holistic Darwinism*, 197.

So do Gowdy and Krall then go too far by insisting on our incorporation in an economic superorganism which exercises top-down control? At this point an important distinction needs to be made between the processes of *organification* and *organization*. Strictly speaking organification only occurs in biological systems, in the sense that a part which has developed to function exclusively as an organ will die if removed from its host body. But in an organization otherwise independent individuals are arranged in such a way that the resulting whole may, nonetheless, be said to exercise causal power in its own right. This is the concept of *relational* emergence advocated by sociologist Dave Elder-Vass:

> Relational emergence theory argues that entities may possess emergent properties, which are produced by mechanisms that in turn depend on the properties of the entity's parts and how these parts are organised. This organisation allows the parts to interact in ways that are specific to entities of the type concerned and this process of interaction is the mechanism that gives the entity a causal power.[43]

So, on this view, it's the particular *organization* of parts in order to perform a given overall function which generates top-down causation. While we can still explain the behavior of the whole bottom-up in terms of the interaction of its parts, *the specific relations between these parts* possess an ontological status; that is, *they exist in their own right*. This distinguishes Elder-Vass's relational emergence from strong emergence as understood by others such as George Ellis.[44] Nevertheless Elder-Vass maintains that the kinds of emergent properties exhibited by human social groups are "strong enough" to justify the claim that such wholes exercise a form of top-down causation.[45]

In an organization, then, it's the social structure that acts, and it does so *through* its individual members. While those individuals remain so organized they could indeed be said to constitute a superorganism which acts as an agent in its own right, subordinating the agency of its parts in particular ways according to the roles required of the individuals: "The individuals that make up an organization *behave differently* than they would if they were not parts of it."[46] This is very much the case

43. Elder-Vass, *Causal Power of Social Structures*, 192.

44. Elder-Vass, *Causal Power of Social Structures*, 66–68.

45. Elder-Vass, *Causal Power of Social Structures*, 38.

46. Elder-Vass, *Causal Power of Social Structures*, 195, italics mine.

in post-agrarian transition human societies as recounted by Gowdy and Krall:

> The new group dynamic was not simply a larger aggregation of individuals that comprised the group. The economic organization of the group itself more rigidly defined the role of individuals within it and came to constitute a cohesive whole with a unique evolutionary dynamic.[47]

It's precisely this organizational feature which qualifies the agrarian transition as an example of relational emergence in Elder-Vass's sense. And it seems that what emerged back then still has a strong hold on us. Otherwise, given how grim being part of a superorganism can be for so many of its members, why don't they simply walk away and organize themselves differently, so producing better outcomes for themselves?[48] I've already noted the lock-in due to the proximate negative feedbacks which can accompany attempts to detach from the superorganism. But can we further hazard a deeper explanation for this in terms of ideas encountered in earlier chapters?

This is where the Maximum Power Principle (MPP), underpinned by Swenson's Law of Maximum Entropy Production (LMEP), loom large. As Gowdy and Krall point out, the ultrasocial character of large settled groups, when compared to the informal cooperation within small itinerant bands, means that these larger wholes are able to harness total food energy for useful work at a faster rate. Strikingly, this is despite the fact that per capita output rates in early agrarian societies may have been lower than those of hunter-gatherers.[49] In a competitive situation it's overall size that matters. Larger, organized agrarian groups came to dominate simply because of the greater *gross* power at their collective

47. Gowdy and Krall, "Economic Origins of Ultrasociality," 3.

48. Walking away may just not be feasible for those finding themselves somehow "caged." Much of the superorganism thesis is echoed in a more recent book by Luke Kemp, who provides an analysis of what he prefers to call "Goliath." Kemp identifies three environmental requirements for Goliath's emergence: storable and lootable surplus (as per Gowdy and Krall), weaponry which can be monopolized by a particular group, and—relevant to "simply walking away"—limited defection options for the masses. To these he adds certain psychological requirements, including a status competition dynamic, the tendency of power to corrupt, the authoritarian hankerings of stressed populations, and the "dark triad" of psychological pathologies exhibited by a subset of those rising to leadership positions. See Kemp, *Goliath's Curse*.

49. Gowdy and Krall, "Agriculture as a Major Evolutionary Transition," 190; cf. Bowles, "Cultivation of Cereals."

disposal, despite any comparative per capita inefficiency. Simply put, they prevailed because they were bigger and so more powerful than the extant foraging bands.

As with the phenomena of poorer health and decreased longevity for the majority following the agrarian turn, we find here an example of group-level, or multilevel, selection as opposed to individual-level or kin selection.[50] This counterintuitive outcome can be explained by the MPP, the expression in biological systems of the LMEP's selection of larger-scale systems.[51] The advent of capitalism and fossil-fueled industrial society have merely served to turbocharge this dynamic, so providing an even more egregious example of what appears, prima facie, a perverse outcome.

SUPERORGANISMS AND MEGAMACHINES

Gowdy and Krall are far from being the only ones to have noted how individual flourishing is too often inhibited, if not undermined, by integration into what passes for civilization. This typically anarchist trope is common to writers as varied as Christian philosopher Jacques Ellul (1912–94) and atheistic environmentalist Edward Abbey (1927–89). Abbey memorably captures what it means to be entrained within a human superorganism:

> Call it the Anthill State, the Beehive Society, a technocratic despotism—perhaps benevolent, perhaps not, but in either case the enemy of personal liberty, family independence, and community sovereignty, shutting off for a long time to come the freedom to choose among alternate ways of living. The domination of nature made possible by misapplied science leads to the domination of people; to a dreary and totalitarian uniformity.[52]

50. See Gowdy and Krall, "Economic Origins of Ultrasociality," 4–5, for a discussion of the growing consensus in favor of multilevel selection as an evolutionary process.

51. This is not to deny the probable additional role of institutional innovation—private property rights—in enabling the ascendancy of agrarian collectives as argued by Bowles and Choi, "Neolithic Agricultural Revolution." Gowdy and Krall concede that "production for surplus and the evolution of property rights may have been a co-evolutionary process." Gowdy and Krall, "Agriculture as a Major Evolutionary Transition," 191.

52. Edward Abbey, quoted in Kingsnorth, "Vaccine Moment," 35.

However, for a more systematic diagnosis along these lines, I shall turn to the writings of historian and sociologist Lewis Mumford (1895–1990), best known for his two-volume work *The Myth of the Machine* (1967/1970). In the prologue to the first volume Mumford sounds the following warning:

> In terms of the currently accepted picture . . . our age is passing from the primeval state of man, marked by his invention of tools and weapons for the purpose of achieving mastery over the forces of nature, to a radically different condition, in which he will have not only conquered nature, but detached himself as far as possible from the organic habitat. . . . Instead of functioning actively as an autonomous personality, man will become a passive, purposeless, machine-conditioned animal whose proper functions, as technicians now interpret man's role, will either be fed into the machine or strictly limited and controlled for the benefit of depersonalized, collective organizations.[53]

For Mumford, the machine rather than the organism provides the dominant metaphor for understanding our predicament. Yet, as the above quotation hints, the end result is much the same.[54] By my role in a technocratic organization, the organization acts through me: I express its will via my own desires for sustenance, belonging, wealth, social status, and so forth as emphatically as my heart spontaneously executes my unconscious will by beating some sixty to a hundred times every minute of the day and night.

Megamachine is in fact the term preferred by Mumford to describe this "organization of an archetypal machine composed of human parts,"[55] each part "assigned to his special office, role, and task, to make possible the immense work output and grand designs of this great collective organization."[56] By the same token he stresses that human components are integrated with nonhuman parts too: "It is a machine in the orthodox technical sense, as a 'combination of resistant bodies' so organized as to perform standardized motions and repetitive work."[57] In other words

53. Mumford, *Technics and Human Development*, 3.

54. Mumford does in fact use the term "superorganism" once in these two volumes, when referring to Teilhard de Chardin's vision of an evolutionary end-state, and in so doing equates it with his preferred term of "megamachine." Mumford, *Pentagon of Power*, 319.

55. Mumford, *Technics and Human Development*, 11.

56. Mumford, *Technics and Human Development*, 189.

57. Mumford, *Pentagon of Power*, 240.

the megamachine functions by yoking both material and social power in harness together in order to achieve its ends.

According to Mumford the megamachine's origins lie at the start of the Bronze Age in the fourth millennium BCE. The onset of this new and fateful social dynamic lies not so much with the dawn of agriculture as such, as per Gowdy and Krall, but more specifically with the rise of large, complex agrarian societies. He pays particular attention to ancient Egypt and the way in which the divining of a cosmic order—"a product of myth, magic, religion, and the nascent science of astronomy"[58]—came to underpin a regimented social order epitomized in the wherewithal to build the pyramids and develop the elaborate irrigation system which famously, in due course, made Egypt Rome's breadbasket. Agricultural progress came at no little cost to the average worker (as Gowdy and Krall also emphasize) with the ruler and his retinue enjoying vastly disproportionate benefit from the megamachine's operation.

By contrast the bulk of the population became reduced to acting as cogs in the service of the megamachine. As well as manual labor, a large and well-developed military and civilian bureaucracy was required to facilitate its functioning. Membership of administrative cadres required unqualified obedience, so much so that in the later Roman iteration of the megamachine these posts were commonly staffed by slaves, free citizens being unwilling to undergo the associated humiliation.

With the collapse of the Roman Empire the megamachine receded from view, in the West at least, only to return in its modern guise, Mumford argues, in the form of Thomas Hobbes's Leviathan. Hobbes envisaged fusing "the new science and the old politics of the seventeenth century" so as once again "to transfer autonomy from each individual member and group in the community to the organized whole in which they would function only as obedient, machinelike parts."[59] The ground for this had been prepared in part—and inadvertently so—by the Benedictine monastic order, with its requirement of voluntary submission to a punctiliously structured daily regime.

Although he doesn't use such terms, it's clear from Mumford's account that the megamachine is very much a locus of top-down control, as symbolized visually in ancient Egypt by the pyramids themselves. He speculates that this arrangement may have developed from the role of the

58. Mumford, *Technics and Human Development*, 11.

59. Mumford, *Pentagon of Power*, 100.

leader in earlier hunter bands, and in any event he sees a military precedent underlying this paradigm: "*Through the army, in fact, the standard model of the megamachine was transmitted from culture to culture.*"[60] Writing in the 1960s he saw its modern incarnation strengthened by two world wars in rapid succession and an ensuing permanent Cold War, in which (top-down) propaganda too played a key role in promoting conformist outlooks and behavior within society.

As already mentioned Mumford's megamachine operates on a necessarily material, or biophysical, platform. Every machine exists in order to do work, and the megamachine represents a fine example of the MPP in operation, maximizing the rates of both human labor and nonhuman energy consumption "for ends that are relevant chiefly to the power complex's restrictive purposes: the expansion of its own structure and the extension of its own mode of control."[61] Just as the MPP implies that there is no ceiling to the rate of doing useful work, so also the megamachine exists simply to pursue limitless expansion. Its human components, along with the various artifacts and endeavors devised by them to progress this drive, are simply surface manifestations and instruments of its "fundamental animus."[62] Limitless expansion: the congruence with Gowdy and Krall's central thesis is here explicit.

Lacking a terminus, what can we nonetheless say about the trajectory of this animus? Whatever direction it takes it will be characterized by "speed, uniformity, standardization, quantification."[63] Of these, speed obviously coheres with the MPP; and the other three traits share a common tendency towards abstraction from concrete, qualitative, lived human experience. In this regard money, the general equivalent, embodies the animus perfectly; as sheer quantity it knows no bounds. Mumford observes:

> Physical power, applied to coerce other human beings, reaches natural limits at an early stage: if one applies too much, the victim dies. So, too, with the command of purely material goods or sensual pleasures. . . . But when human functions are converted into abstract, uniform units, ultimately units of energy or

60. Mumford, *Technics and Human Development*, 192, emphasis in original.
61. Mumford, *Pentagon of Power*, 303.
62. Mumford, *Technics and Human Development*, 207.
63. Mumford, *Technics and Human Development*, 239.

> money, there are no limits to the amount of power that can be seized, converted, and stored.[64]

The animus of the megamachine is therefore expressed in the maximization of flows of energy and money. In an earlier chapter I drew attention to how money is unusual as a form of social power. As sheer quantity it much resembles material power, the rate at which energy performs useful work. But notice also the link with another point made in that chapter, namely the role played by stocks, the storage of surplus. Gowdy and Krall also stress this essential element in humanity's ultrasocial turn: accumulation, not for its own sake, but for the sake of its readiness-to-hand, the ability to turn on the tap as and when one wishes, so liberating those with access to surplus from the contingent flows of the natural world. The industrial era would not have been possible without the unanticipated legacy of millions of years' worth of ancient sunlight stored in the bowels of the earth. And now, as those stocks get harder to come by and human attention returns to nature's capricious flows, the need for proactive storage, in the form of chemical batteries this time, asserts itself once again.

Because only on the basis of a reliable store of energy—or of money as a fungible energy token—can the megamachine's utopia of artificial regularity be realized. Mumford asserts that "almost all utopias emphasize regularity, uniformity, 'dirigisme' or authoritarianism, isolation, and autarchy,"[65] along with a hostility towards nature perceived as that which eludes programming and control, the as-yet-unconquered. As in ancient Egypt so now the megamachine enacts a regime of control, imposing hierarchical order on human and nonhuman worlds alike.

And there is no alternative. That at least was, and is, the myth of the machine, namely "the notion that this machine was, by its very nature, absolutely irresistible—and yet, provided one did not oppose it, ultimately beneficent."[66] Yet efforts at resistance there have been. Mumford notes that the Jewish people, sucked into the maw of the megamachine during both Egyptian captivity and Babylonian exile, took a stand through the introduction of two institutions, Sabbath and synagogue. By these means the drive for unlimited power was limited—no labor on the seventh day—and the top-down deployment of human components curtailed—at synagogue all meet as peers, as the people of God rather than subjects

64. Mumford, *Pentagon of Power*, 165.

65. Mumford, *Pentagon of Power*, 210.

66. Mumford, *Technics and Human Development*, 224.

of an alien sovereign. Here we glimpse an alternative narrative which undermines the machine and its myth, about which more will be said in later chapters.

Before leaving Mumford's account of our predicament, it's worth asking what, in his view, lies at its roots. Human history, he says, has a "broad streak of superior irrationality" running through it, demonstrated in "a chronic disposition to error, mischief, disordered fantasy, hallucination, 'original sin.'"[67] All this he sees as a tragic and inevitable correlate of the extraordinary and distinctive creativity of our species:

> In escaping organic fixations, man forfeited the innate humility and mental stability of less adventurous species. Yet some of his most erratic departures have opened up valuable areas that purely organic evolution, over billions of years, had never explored. . . . Man's proneness to mix his fantasies and projections, his desires and designs, his abstractions and his ideologies, with the commonplaces of daily experience were, we can now see, an important source of his immense creativity. There is no clean dividing line between the irrational and the superrational; and the handling of these ambivalent gifts has always been a major human problem.[68]

This is surely the least satisfactory element in what is otherwise a compelling account. Terminology aside, much of Mumford's analysis aligns with and enriches that of Gowdy and Krall. But whereas the latter is situated squarely on a fairly secure foundation in evolutionary biology—the consequences of the operation of multilevel selection processes—Mumford can only gesture vaguely at a primordial ambivalence which simply comes with the territory of being human. What both accounts share, however, is a niggling sense that humanity is all but doomed to continue down a path of destruction to its eventual downfall.

Can we really not dodge this bullet? Or could theology offer the prospect of redemption for the superorganism and the megamachine? To begin to explore this possibility I turn to the New Testament's understanding of social structures and their ambivalent influence on the human lot.

67. Mumford, *Technics and Human Development*, 10.

68. Mumford, *Technics and Human Development*, 10–11.

SUPERORGANISMS AND THE POWERS

The language of megamachines and superorganisms was scarcely available to the New Testament writers, yet I'm going to argue here that they were nonetheless fully aware of such phenomena, and that they articulated a particular kind of response to them. To do this I shall draw on the work of Walter Wink in his 1980s–90s trilogy on what he termed *the Powers*. Who or what are the Powers? Perhaps the best way to answer that question would be to consider five key texts from the Epistles to the Colossians and to the Ephesians as classically expounded by someone who broadly shares Wink's exegetical perspective, namely biblical commentator G. B. Caird.

> In him [Christ] all things were created, in heaven and on earth, visible and invisible, whether thrones or dominions or principalities or authorities—all things were created through him and for him. He himself is before all things, and in him all things hold together.[69]

Caird treats these four categories—thrones, dominions, principalities, and authorities—synonymously as expressions of the social, economic, and political structures which order collective human life. For the sake of conciseness I shall follow Wink by referring to them as "the Powers." Behind the idea of the Powers lies a blend of two influences: first the ancient conception of a heavenly council of inferior national deities presided over by a supreme God, the Israelite YHWH; and secondly a quasi-astrological sense of correspondence between what happens in earthly human experience and invisible heavenly dramas.

While he can describe the Powers as symbolic representations of the power structures of the current world order, Caird is equally clear that we aren't merely dealing with imaginative metaphor, the personification of essentially impersonal forces. Rather they are indeed, in some sense, *spiritual beings* abroad in "the heavens," this region being neither the sky nor some immaterial parallel dimension but rather "a realm of human topography, standing for man's invisible, spiritual environment, as contrasted with the visible, tangible environment we call earth."[70]

Whatever we make of that, the writer of Colossians clearly asserts that, fundamentally, the Powers are aspects of God's good creation

69. Col 1:16–17.

70. Caird, *Language and Imagery*, 239, 242. Caird, *Paul's Letters from Prison*, 34, 46.

intended, as Caird puts it, "to subserve the true ends of man; and, since those ends are all summed up in Christ, it can be said that they were created *through him and for him*."[71] The Powers are supposed to provide an enabling order which gives human beings *potentia*, *power to* live alongside each other well, according to the model of Christ. Failure to provide in this way therefore implicitly reflects the Powers' rejection of Christ.

> For we are not contending against flesh and blood, but against the principalities, against the powers, against the world rulers of this present darkness, against the spiritual hosts of wickedness in the heavenly places.[72]

However the Powers have departed from their divine mandate, becoming disordered and so acting in opposition to humanity's best interests. Interestingly Caird describes this as a malfunction[73] deriving from an idolatrous attitude towards the Powers, that is, an absolutizing of the Powers' status by human individuals. This renders the Powers ends in themselves, divorced from both their divine origin and their ordained purpose, so delivering their helpless human parts over to destruction.[74] Notice the two-way traffic here: the bottom-up attitudes of individuals lead to a change in the nature of the top-down constraints imposed by the presiding Powers.

> God put this power to work in Christ when he raised him from the dead and seated him at his right hand in the heavenly places, far above all rule and authority and power and dominion.[75]

God, then, has acted to repair this malfunction of the Powers through Christ. Commenting on this verse, Caird identifies the malfunction precisely as an abuse of the delegated power to administer good order; indeed the Powers "constantly act in opposition to God's real purpose," but even so remain entrusted with their divine commission. Does the corruption lie with the Powers or with those individual humans whose idolatrous attitudes underlie the Powers' malfunction? Caird answers that this is a false dichotomy since, he argues, the Powers "are responsible for all those institutional and corporate wrongs which are

71. Caird, *Paul's Letters from Prison*, 178, emphasis in original.

72. Eph 6:12 (RSV).

73. Caird, *Paul's Letters from Prison*, 178–79.

74. Caird, *Paul's Letters from Prison*, 39, 46, 92; *Language and Imagery*, 241.

75. Eph 1:21.

human in origin but cannot be laid at the door of individual sinners."[76] The latter phrase is significant. The Powers arise from human interactions; they do not exist independently of them. Equally they are irreducible to the particular actions, the vices and virtues, of individuals; they are emergent products of human society.

> [God erased] the record that stood against us with its legal demands. He set this aside, nailing it to the cross. He disarmed the rulers and authorities and made a public example of them, triumphing over them in it.[77]

Here we have an account of the way in which God has acted to correct the Powers' malfunction by exhibiting, making plain, their failure. Caird's comments on this are worth reproducing at length:

> Paul believed that these powers, like their human agents, had acted in good faith in bringing about the crucifixion, but in ignorance of the true purpose of God (1 Cor 2:6–8). The Roman authorities were responsible for the maintenance of public order to which the activities of Jesus seemed a threat; and the Jewish authorities were charged with the administration of their law . . . which Jesus seemed to undermine. Jesus was sentenced to death as a criminal by the combined action of the highest religion and best government the world had till then known. By crucifying him who subsequently proved to be God's own Son, the powers showed that they had totally misrepresented God's will. In the cross, therefore, which appeared to be the exercise of their authority, God in fact *disarmed* them, stripped them of their authority. In the cross he had *made a public example of them*, exposing them as usurpers who had tried to make their limited authority absolute and had succeeded only in making it demonic.[78]

Notice that Jesus deals with, and effectively disempowers, the Powers neither by competing with them *on their terms* nor by colluding with them *through acceding to their terms* but rather by acting out his calling *in defiance of the terms* on which they operate.

> Although I am the very least of all the saints, this grace was given to me to bring to the Gentiles the news of the boundless riches of Christ, and to bring to light what is the plan of the

76. Caird, *Paul's Letters from Prison*, 46–47.

77. Col 2:14–15.

78. Caird, *Paul's Letters from Prison*, 196, emphasis in original.

> mystery hidden for ages in God who created all things; so that through the church the wisdom of God in its rich variety might now be made known to the rulers and authorities in the heavenly places.[79]

The point of the church, the Christian community, is to demonstrate the reconciliation of Jew and non-Jew, two groups whose estrangement epitomized the manifold divisions blighting human society. In other words the church is called to embody a redeemed way of living alongside others, one delivered from the hostilities and rivalries stemming from the idolatrous attitudes towards particular Powers typical of fallen humanity. And this amounts to nothing less than the unveiling of an age-long mystery, the displaying of God's wisdom to the otherwise ignorant and foolish Powers.

So much for Caird's exposition of the Powers. What does Walter Wink add? "The Powers are good. The Powers are fallen. The Powers must be redeemed."[80] Thus Wink summarizes his reading of the New Testament witness on this topic, and the broad sweep of the thesis of his three volumes. He finds the language of power in the New Testament to be pervasive, and its use highly unsystematic and fluid. So, like Caird, he makes no substantive distinction between terms like "powers," "thrones," "authorities," and so forth.[81] The Powers are "socio-spiritual entities,"[82] possessing both visible and invisible aspects, "an outer, physical manifestation (buildings, portfolios, personnel, trucks, fax machines) and an inner spirituality, or corporate culture, or collective personality,"[83] though any given biblical usage may stress either or both aspects.

Some would argue that Wink doesn't do justice to the New Testament's imputing of intellect and will to the Powers.[84] In fact Wink declares himself agnostic as to whether "actual metaphysical being"

79. Eph 3:8–10.

80. Wink, *Engaging the Powers*, 10.

81. Wink, *Naming the Powers*, 7–12.

82. Wink, *Engaging the Powers*, 8.

83. Wink, *Engaging the Powers*, 3.

84. See, e.g., Moses, *Practices of Power*, 32–38. C. S. Lewis coins the term *Macrobes* for the Powers in the last of his science fiction trilogy, *That Hideous Strength*. This captures the increased dimensionality of emergent forms nicely. Compared to humans, "they are more permanent, dispose of more energy, and have greater intelligence." In terms of the discussion offered in chapter 7 below, the enhanced intelligence attributed to them here by the character Frost is however strictly limited to narrow-boundary goals. See Lewis, *That Hideous Strength*, 155.

can be predicated of them, though he seems clear that they are inherently impersonal.[85] Happily, our earlier discussion of the phenomenon of emergence can cast some light on this point. As we've seen, human groups can exhibit superorganismic properties whereby particular kinds of organization lead to the relational emergence of a higher-order entity, one which expresses top-down control over its members. For Gowdy and Krall this was incipient with the agrarian turn during the early millennia of the Holocene; for Mumford it was inaugurated with the advent of large, complex societies in the fourth millennium BCE. In any event the larger social wholes so constituted came to exercise a dominant, subordinating agency in their own right. Since the whole acts purposefully via the recruiting and transmuting of the heterogeneous smaller-scale purposes of its members, and since purpose is commonly associated with personal qualities such as intellect and will, it isn't hard to see why it was natural for the New Testament writers to describe the Powers' actions in personal terms, even if the underlying goal—boundless quantitative expansion—is essentially impersonal.

Wink's reading of the Powers dovetails neatly with ground covered earlier in this chapter. He links the origins of what he terms the Domination System—that which emerges "when an entire network of Powers becomes integrated around idolatrous values"[86]—with the rise of the great city-states of Sumer and Babylon c. 3000 BCE. In doing so he aligns himself roughly with Mumford's dating of the first sightings of the megamachine.[87] Wink's account of the mechanism at work here echoes that of Gowdy and Krall: competition motivated by group-level self-interest in the context of newly scarce resources. Whereas my appetite for my daily bread is naturally limited, once an ethos of open-ended accumulation has set in "enough" ceases to have meaning. This renders all resources artificially scarce, and intergroup competition for them becomes the norm. Other cultural possibilities become foreclosed and a particular, unchosen pattern of life gets imposed on unwitting populations. We need to realize that this process was, and is, spontaneous, independent of both individual volitions and the schemings of any cabal:

> No one person or group of people imposed the Domination System on us; it came wholly unbidden. People inadvertently

85. Wink, *Engaging the Powers*, 8, 9.

86. Wink, *Engaging the Powers*, 9.

87. Wink, *Engaging the Powers*, 39.

> stumbled into a struggle for power beyond their ability to avoid it or to stop. . . . It was the *experience* of a total system operating (as it seemed) autonomously and even, at times, malevolently, that gave rise to the perception of the role played by the Powers in human destiny.[88]

Although this process throws up visible human leaders, including the ostensibly influential, charismatic ones which enliven the news and popular histories, their freedom is always circumscribed: "They appear to choose, but the selective process generated by the ungoverned system confers upon them that role."[89] Time and again, and regardless of who is notionally in charge, the course of action followed ends up being the one which increases competitive power.[90] Put differently, the MPP—or at least one particular way of expressing the MPP—seems ineluctable. The process is primary; the human actors, and the specific outcomes of their highly constrained actions, secondary.

> People have thus become slaves of their evolving systems, rather than civilized society being the servant of its members. Not that the selection for domination systematically selects what is injurious to people. The process is not hostile to human welfare; it is simply indifferent.[91]

As a trait, an indifference to human welfare is obviously common to both the biblical Powers—both good and fallen, as per Wink's telling—and our prevailing economic system. Wink provides a contemporary example of how this works.[92] Consider, first, a small farmer. *In order to sell to the market and make a profit*, the farmer is obliged to buy cutting-edge machinery, till to the edge of her fields, and pile on commercial fertilizer. She will also want to see higher-yielding strains of seed and more effective herbicides and pesticides developed. But this is fundamentally

88. Wink, *Engaging the Powers*, 41–42, emphasis in original. Wink draws here on Schmookler, *Parable of the Tribes.*

89. Wink, *Engaging the Powers*, 42.

90. Luke Kemp would qualify this by stressing the parts played by minorities exhibiting particular psychological traits. See Kemp, *Goliath's Curse*, 149–70.

91. Wink, *Engaging the Powers*, 42. Much the same could be said of Artificial Intelligence systems, which therefore reveal themselves less as novel developments and more as the latest stage in the unfolding human performance of the MPP. See Bostrom, *Superintelligence.*

92. Wink, *Engaging the Powers*, 79–80.

the desire of the market system at work, expressing itself via the farmer's desire to remain in business.

Now consider, in addition, an agricultural researcher. *In order to remain in employment and so generate an income for himself*, he responds to the farmer's demand by producing a hybrid corn variety which will increase yields. But the researcher is employed by one of only a couple of large seed manufacturing corporations, and these have mandated the production of self-terminating seeds. This means that the farmer has to buy new seeds each year rather than recycle some of last year's harvest, so cutting into her profits and possibly driving her into debt. She may even go out of business since, thanks to increased yields across the board, the price of corn has fallen.

The last thing the researcher wants to do is to ruin the life of a fellow human being, and yet the top-down constraints of the system are such that this is the inevitable tendency of their combined actions. Agency in the fullest sense lies neither with the researcher nor the farmer but with the economic system, the ruling Power, of which they are merely parts.

Two things are striking in this fictional example. First, the quest for increasing surplus. For all the prospect of security and freedom from the vicissitudes of the seasons accompanying the agrarian transition, the farmer's living remains precarious enough. Embedded as a small part of a surplus-based system the lure of profit is always offset by the threat of loss. The system as a whole may prosper but, in the process, many human components of that system will fall by the wayside. As Gowdy and Krall remark, "An invisible hand is at work, but it is very different from the benign, bottom-up conception of Adam Smith that individual self-interest will lead to the common good."[93]

Second, notice the central role played by money. Wink observes that, in contemporary society, this is the prevailing medium by which power is expressed; and the valuing of power as such is characteristic of the Domination System. The way money works provides much insight into the workings of human superorganisms. Money has already been discussed as a medium of social power and as abstract surplus, and its quintessentially quantitative nature will be further explored in the following chapters. For now I merely note Wink's wry comment: "Mammon is wiser in its way than the dictator, for money enslaves not by force but

93. Gowdy and Krall, "Economic Origins of Ultrasociality," 15.

by love."[94] The linkage here of money, power, freedom, and desire leads to the heart of the issues discussed in this book.

Individual powerlessness in the face of malfunctioning Powers: what lies at the root of this sorry situation? I think that both Wink and Caird would answer "Idolatry," understood as giving a part the regard due to the whole; treating what is limited as absolute. For the biblical writers the absolute is God's own self, and the whole is God's creation in its entirety. The Powers, as idols, are the manifestations of bids for the strictly *local* expansion of surplus accumulation, necessarily adversarial and confrontational in character. "Local" need not mean nearby or geographically confined, rather the merely partial. It includes the transnational corporation and the military-political hegemon. Each Power only has regard for itself, not for its myriad parts or for creation as a whole. Latently, the Powers therefore constitute a mutually adversarial bloc. As such they stand in opposition to the universal as rooted in the Christ who grants each Power its rightful role. The common strand of their idolatry is a particular kind of performance of the MPP, one which makes absolute the lust for accelerating flows *here and now* so as to perform work which is no longer useful for the whole but rather diverted to serve the perceived interests of the part—*our* part—only.

Thus at the roots of institutional idolatry lies a rejection of Christ, since in Christ "all things were created, in heaven and on earth, visible and invisible, whether thrones or dominions or principalities or authorities . . . and in him all things hold together."[95] In the same way that the Powers were created to serve human beings as structures which enable collective *potentia*, *power to*, so also Christ is the gift of superordinate ordering of the Powers. In him they receive their systemic place.[96] Take away Christ and what you're left with is what Wink calls the Domination System, "an entire network of Powers . . . integrated around idolatrous values."[97]

The church's mission, then, is to proclaim and provide an example of the meta-ordering dynamic of Christ. This is what the making-known of God's wisdom, as per Ephesians 3:10, amounts to. I'll return to the meaning of wisdom vis-à-vis power in the final chapter, but for now note how witnessing to a universal wisdom of this kind constitutes the

94. Wink, *Engaging the Powers*, 54.

95. Col 1:16–17.

96. Wink, *Engaging the Powers*, 67.

97. Wink, *Engaging the Powers*, 9.

church's raison d'être. In practice this must mean challenging the absolutizing claims of the various superorganisms which demand the exclusive allegiance of their members. Not least among these must surely be those national and transnational alliances which arrogate to themselves the right to make war, overt and covert, so reducing their citizens to mere pawns for manipulation and sacrifice. Mumford noted that the standard model for the megamachine is provided by the army; and Gowdy and Krall join Wink in claiming limited evidence of warfare before the rise of the Powers manifested in large, complex states.

Not that we should imagine a golden age of peace and harmony prior to this point.[98] Rather we should conclude that, with organized warfare, the sin of the Powers lies in their betrayal and inversion of the divinely appointed vocation of securing justice, peace, and prosperity for all. While history amply demonstrates that "just as cells are expendable for a body and individual bees are expendable for the hive, human beings, under some circumstances, are expendable for their group,"[99] in God's kingdom the social structures over which the Powers preside exist to serve their individual members, and not the other way around.

SUMMING UP

That something is amiss with the human lot is a theme which we find in the ancient writings of diverse cultures: Adam, Eve, and the apple; Pandora's box; the current Kali Yuga . . . In this chapter we've explored three accounts of humanity's fall from grace, two secular and one biblical. Lewis Mumford offers us the image of human individuals reduced to the status of cogs in a megamachine bent on ever-accelerating, quantitative expansion. John Gowdy and Lisi Krall prefer the term "superorganism," a population ultrasocially organized for surplus production. The New

98. Although Selin Kesebir in her study of human superorganisms acknowledges that warfare "represents the pinnacle of human superorganismic potential," she also points to more recent archaeological evidence, congruent with studies of contemporary hunter-gatherer societies, suggesting that both intra- and intergroup violence was and remains by no means restricted to complex societies post the agrarian transition. Kesebir, "Superorganism Account of Human Sociality," 245–46; see also Morris, *Foragers, Farmers and Fossil Fuels*, 41–43. This is clearly an area of continuing debate however. Gowdy and Krall, for example, note that "a strong case has been made that warfare did not exist in hunter-gatherer societies." Gowdy and Krall, "Economic Origins of Ultrasociality," 10, 44–45.

99. Kesebir, "Superorganism Account of Human Sociality," 250.

Testament shows an inchoate awareness that life in society is both enriched and immiserated by the rule of mysterious Powers expressed in and through the political, economic, and cultural structures of the day. What these accounts share in common is a depiction of ordinary people doomed to live under the thumb of an oppressive, superordinate animus.

Following Dave Elder-Vass, we can helpfully understand these phenomena as examples of relational emergence, the arising of social wholes which exert top-down influence on their individual human parts through the various roles which these individuals are organized to play. Here, as in hierarchical complex systems generally, "the lower level proposes, the higher level disposes." The possibilities generated by the often-chance turn of historical events are sorted, again by a mixture of accident and human design, such that some modes of social organization end up selected over others on the basis of competitive outcomes. In this way settled agriculture came to predominate over the millennia of the Holocene, giving rise in due course to the great state societies in which Mumford sees the first evidence of the megamachine's operation. In this way capitalism—financial, agrarian, and industrial—arose, subordinating the lives of individuals to the goal of profit for reinvestment, the endless increase of (surplus) money. In this way the MPP found new expressions through spontaneously evolving patterns of human social organization.

Power, as observed earlier, is all tied up with potential, the accumulation of surplus, stocks which can be tapped to release flows. With social power, these ultimately material flows and motions embody human desire. The propensity to amass ever-larger stocks, whether they be of energy, grain, or money, reveals an underlying desire for ever-greater power. And greater power can only be realized, again as noted previously, through organ-ization, lamented by Gilles Deleuze and Félix Guattari as the suppression of freedom to enter into new, life-giving connections with the world.

While Gowdy and Krall provide an elegant and parsimonious explanation of this process in terms of multilevel selection and evolutionary biology, we owe it to Mumford for coining the phrase "fundamental animus" to name the dynamic underlying these millennia-long developments. What can be described cogently, up to a point, in the language of the natural sciences requires the humanities' vocabulary to bring out the lived experience of this reality. "Animus" is a felicitous choice, combining as it does the neutral sense of "motivating or governing spirit" with the more evaluative "spiteful or malevolent ill-will." Very obviously,

Mumford's insight is not so distant from the New Testament's accounts of "the spiritual hosts of wickedness in the heavenly places."[100]

Which sets the stage for Wink's discussion of the biblical Powers: good, fallen, and redeemable. In an earlier chapter we noted how the *power to* achieve the otherwise impossible can arise from large-scale collaborative effort. This *potentia* may be yoked to different ends. History and everyday experience suggest that these ends tend towards the sheerly quantitative, expressed either through physical force or through money, so resembling the simple, material outworking of the MPP. *This is the nature of the megamachine's animus.* In stark contrast Wink reads the New Testament as providing a vision of qualitative beatitude and a corresponding social order which, far from compromising the well-being of its individual members, instead provides a context for their fulfillment. Such an enabling of necessity requires corresponding constraints, as we saw in chapter 1, but these constraints are necessary not least to guard against the degeneration of presiding Powers into idols, that is, ends in themselves which sacrifice the lasting good of the whole to the short-term, merely apparent benefit of certain parts.

Whether the machine or the organism offers the best metaphor for the current human lot is of course debatable. "Machine" captures its impersonal character well. On the other hand, unlike a machine, no one deliberately set out to build it, whereas organisms "arise through self-organisation in a particular environment and so their structure and behaviour are intrinsically context-dependent."[101] Perhaps the term *cyborg* has some merit: a collective entity defined by mechanical prostheses operating (for now) on an organic substrate, alien to it and parasitic upon it. As such it follows a truncated version of the organic fecundity principle. Although its human parts can breed and reproduce, it as an entity cannot, so all that remains for a cyborg is the absolute drive for survival and growth. As a description of our collective de facto *conatus*, this doesn't seem too inaccurate. And whereas humans, individually and as groups, can (and do) entertain goals which transcend the fecundity principle, an emergent cyborg cannot. For all its awesome power, a cyborg is in key respects a lesser being than its mature human parts: a toddler wielding a chainsaw.

100. Eph 6:12.

101. De Bari et al., "Thermodynamics, Organisms and Behaviour," 2. On the difference between machines and organisms more generally see also Rosen, *Essays on Life Itself*.

Even for a cyborg, then, enabling and constraint go hand in hand; and, according to the New Testament, the constraint required to resist and redeem the cyborg Powers' animus is spelled out in the story of Jesus of Nazareth. Jesus demonstrates a power different in kind to theirs because it's in the service of a different kind of goal, qualitative rather than quantitative. Pursuing this end means two things: not competing in the contest for quantitative *power over*; and, equally, not acquiescing to being part of a whole committed to the pursuit of merely quantitative power—even though that may still mean submitting to authorities which have betrayed their divinely appointed vocation.

This story will be reviewed and explored more fully in a later chapter, but first we need to attend to a question prompted by much of the ground already covered: if the de facto human performance of the MPP has historically proven so exploitative, what would a different kind of performance require? Encouragingly, we saw in earlier chapters how, in biological and ecological systems, the expression of the LMEP and the MPP can take unexpected forms. In our current human-dominated eco-social system, what conceptual tools do we have for thinking about the possibility of a different, better kind of performance? Curiously perhaps, it turns out to be a question of how you join the dots.

5

The Dots and the Numbers: Two Articulations of Being Human

What really frightens and dismays us is not external events themselves, but the way in which we think about them. It is not things that disturb us, but our interpretation of their significance.[1]

Let me take you back to a childhood experience. A well-meaning aunt has just bought little Johnny a new puzzle book. He opens it, and this is what he finds on the first three pages.

1. The first page just contains a random jumble of dots. Try as Johnny might, he can't make out any particular shape among them. It's a picture of nothing. Or, equally, since Johnny is blessed with a vivid imagination, it could be a picture of anything. By arbitrarily joining the right dots he could produce anything you like—a leg, a nose, a wing . . . you name it.
2. On the second page is another jumble of dots, but this time the dots aren't scattered so evenly. They're clustered here and there, suggestive of shapes such as perhaps a flower . . . or maybe a wheel . . . or just a nasty rash? Joining the dots on this page would be a less arbitrary business; there's an incipient order here—potentially several, in fact—but it's still not clear what particular thing is depicted, leaving plenty of room for Johnny and his little sister to argue about it.

1. Epictetus, c. 50–135 CE.

3. Turning to the third page Johnny finds a proper join-the-dots puzzle: the same spread of dots that we found on the second page but, magically, numbers have now appeared next to some of them. His pulse racing, he picks up his pencil to join the numbered dots, and . . .

Bingo: complete with trees, flowers, squirrels, and a summer sun beaming down, unambiguously and incontrovertibly, we have a picture of a charming woodland scene (Why not?). His watercolors to hand, Johnny is well away.

What a difference those numbers made. The disordered jumble of dots on the first page was lifeless and dull. It held out no potential for the young artist. On page 2, though, things started to get interesting. It was as if a breath of wind had passed through, disturbing the dots' symmetry and generating incipient order. Many possible orders, in fact, as the imagination got to work. The previously random distribution wasn't random anymore. Suddenly there were possibilities, prospective associations between dots.

But things really moved up a gear when the numbers appeared. As a result some of the prospective associations on page 2 got selected and so stood out in relief, while others did not. It wasn't obvious in advance which ones these would be; there was a discontinuity of sorts here. The numbers provided a code, a set of instructions which did two things: they highlighted some of the dots, not all; and they told Johnny in which sequence those dots should be connected. In other words, the figure on page 3 took the incipiently ordered distribution on page 2 and provided a specific pattern for ordering it into what appeared as Johnny went to work with his pencil: the final product, the well-defined picture of some recognizable thing.

What a difference those numbers made. Notice the pronounced shift between the second and third pages. A new factor came into play at this point. So we might say that what we had here was a two-stage process. The first stage (pages 1 and 2) provided the conditions for the emergence of certain possible shapes; the second stage (page 3) selected one specific shape from among the many possible ones for eventual actualization by Johnny's pencil.

This trivial example acts as a bridge to the subject of this chapter, since the two-stage process apparent here illustrates a theoretical framework applicable to many aspects of how the world works. As we shall shortly see, it usefully provides a common way of understanding some of the diverse ideas encountered elsewhere in this book. Although the framework might seem rather jargon-heavy at first sight, it's really just a convenient shorthand for describing significant commonalities which we might otherwise miss; and, as we have seen, in the end it's no more complicated than a join-the-dots puzzle.

THE WARP AND THE WEFT

This join-the-dots conceit shows the process of *assembling* in action. Gilles Deleuze and Félix Guattari, whom we came across in chapter 1, discuss this process at length and from several different angles in their book *A Thousand Plateaus*. They see assembling's two-stage pattern cropping up everywhere: in the formation of sedimentary rock, in the combining of organs into organisms, in the establishment of particular customs in human societies. For the things assembled need not all be of the same kind, as in join-the-dots. Far from it. Deleuze elsewhere describes the process of assembling as leading to "a multiplicity which is made up of many heterogeneous terms and which establishes liaisons, relations between them, across ages, sexes and reigns—different natures. . . . [Its] only unity is that of a co-functioning: it is a symbiosis, a 'sympathy.'"[2] In each instance, some miscellaneous things somehow wind up in the vicinity of each other and so come to constitute a certain *content*. Their contingent characteristics mean that they lend themselves to being linked together in a variety of possible ways. Certain of these links then happen to get selected by incidental factors with the result that a particular, ordered *expression* of that content is produced. Deleuze and Guattari call this the *double articulation* of an assembling.[3]

Recall the example of the lake ecosystem from chapter 3. The transition between pages 1 and 2 of the puzzle book is paralleled by the opening of a hitherto stagnant pool to a flow of fresh water bearing a miscellany of organisms. Various associations between organism and

2. Deleuze, *Dialogues II*, 69.

3. Deleuze and Guattari, *Thousand Plateaus*, 45–46. See also Adkins, *Deleuze and Guattari's* A Thousand Plateaus; Bonta and Protevi, *Deleuze and Geophilosophy*. Note that although the conventional English translation of Deleuze and Guattari's *agencement* is "assemblage," I render it here as "assembling" in order to emphasize that we are dealing with a process rather than with a thing, or with the end product of that process. See DeLanda, *Assemblage Theory*, 1.

substrate, predator and prey spontaneously arise in the new ecosystem: this is the first articulation of the assembling. These associations lead to the establishment of autocatakinetic feedback loops, whereby some (not all) associations prosper and grow. A mature ecosystem typically expresses its content through a signature of well-established flow circuits (such as bladderwort-algae-water flea) and this represents the assembling's second articulation, mirroring as it does the transition from the numbered dots of page 3 to the final sketched picture. Hence the two stages can be helpfully summed up in the maxim which we encountered earlier: the lower level proposes, the higher level disposes.

Human societies, or social assemblings, have been a particular focus for the work of philosopher Manuel DeLanda.[4] Here human bodies provide the basic content of the so-called *pragmatic system*, or system of things. These, along with various nonhuman bodies, provide the essential building blocks of a social assembling. Together they make up what, in Deleuze and Guattari's terminology, is known as the assembling's *substance of content*—its raw materials, if you wish.

These bodies are incipiently ordered by virtue of certain physical and biological needs: for food and shelter, primarily, such that any human society must involve some collaborative method for acquiring food—for example by foraging, hunting, cultivating land—and also forms of clothing, however rudimentary. Universal human needs like these impose fundamental limits on the kinds of variety which human societies can exhibit if they're to be at all viable. And such needs can only be met if humans are part of a larger ecosystem, that is, an assembling which also includes other kinds of things, living and otherwise. General requirements like these order the substance of content of human societies (people and artifacts) and constitute the *form of content* of a social assembling.

Living interdependently alongside others in society also entails common restrictions and requirements on the otherwise arbitrary behavior of individuals. For example, a certain measure of civility towards acquaintances is expected; you can't just go around smacking anyone who irritates you, or walking away with their stuff. But different cultures express the loosely ordered content of a social assembling in very different ways; as we noted in chapter 1 when considering desire, we all need to eat, but what and how we eat are shaped by the precedents of those around us. It was at this point, in the join-the-dots analogy, that the numbers

4. DeLanda, *New Philosophy of Society*.

came in. The numbers "transform the . . . assemblages of bodies without changing the bodies themselves."[5] Certain possible ways of expressing the form of content get selected and established as normative. In this way each culture embodies a *semiotic system*, or system of meanings, in which society as a structure of meaningful actions gets organized according to a particular set of codes; so *we* happen to say grace before eating noodles with chopsticks together around a table, while *you* use a fork to eat a takeaway on your own in front of the TV. These codes together make up the *form of expression* of a social assembling, and can vary from relatively trivial implicit conventions (when you meet a stranger you shake hands) to explicit laws forcefully applied (if a soldier sent to battle runs away he will get court-martialed).

Since codes are specific to cultures they vary, sometimes markedly, from place to place and from time to time. Over there, they chop your hands off if you do that; over here, we just slap your wrist. The outcome in each case is an emergent social whole, the *substance of expression*, a particular way of life arising from the basic requirements of embodied, social existence "overcoded" by the *specific* ethical, legal, economic, and other norms which happen to make up a given culture. Expressive codes represent "the takeover of content, putting it to work in a 'functional structure,'"[6] the functional structure being the substance of expression. Or, in Deleuze and Guattari's metaphor, forms of expression provide the warp around which the weft of content is woven.[7]

The elements of the double articulation of a social assembling process are summarized in the following table.[8]

Content (pragmatic system)		Expression (semiotic system)	
Substance	Form	Form	Substance

Table 2: The double articulation of a social assembling.

In a social assembling, then, the form of expression is that set of social codes which gives definite procedural shape to the form of content. Or, in Deleuze and Guattari's jargon, it performs an *incorporeal transformation* on the form of content so producing the substance of expression, that is, an actual lived social order.

5. Adkins, *Deleuze and Guattari's* A Thousand Plateaus, 71.
6. Bonta and Protevi, *Deleuze and Geophilosophy*, 83–84.
7. Deleuze and Guattari, *Thousand Plateaus*, 95.
8. Based on Adkins, *Deleuze and Guattari's* A Thousand Plateaus, 50, 72.

Given the variety of actually existing forms of expression, the human interpretations of, and engagements with, the world are extraordinarily diverse. For example, an atmospheric scientist, looking at a sunset, could provide one kind of account of the phenomenon in terms of well-defined physical processes expressible in quantitative, mathematical terms. Ask another scientist and she should give you an exactly identical account.[9] By contrast a painter, looking at the same sunset, would provide a different *kind* of interpretation altogether, one which is qualitatively different to that of the scientist. And you wouldn't expect another painter, even one of the same school, to produce an identical painting—that would be denounced as a forgery, an incorporeal transformation that has gone wrong. Art is all about celebrating the qualitative diversity that characterizes the system of meanings.

On the other hand material power, as outlined in chapter 1, is all about quantity—wattage pure and simple. As the rate of performance of humanly useful work it is, strictly speaking, a second articulation phenomenon, the product of applying a particular form of expression onto the manifold content of experience, that form being defined by the conventions of the natural sciences, and of physics in particular.[10] Granting that human purposes are always there in the background, I shall nonetheless generally associate material power with the first articulation in what follows since it deals most directly with motions and flows in the pragmatic system, the system of things.

In describing the assembling process Deleuze uses the term *symbiosis*. This is significant, having as it does a bearing on how organisms differ from ecosystems—an issue which has already cropped up in earlier chapters. For example, in chapter 1, I pointed out how Deleuze and Guattari commend the social ideal of a "body without organs." In terms of the double articulation, this means shunning rigid forms of expression since these lock people into particular roles and identities, so precluding

9. This is not to deny that science too has its sociology of knowledge, with different interpretive paradigms sometimes locked in competition. An example of this, relevant to the discussion in chapter 4, would be the recent controversy among biologists regarding multilevel selection.

10. Within the natural sciences it's understood that physics alone can't adequately express the range of phenomena presented in the system of things, hence the need for chemistry and biology. As mentioned in chapter 3, the phenomena captured and expressed by these various scientific disciplines are qualitatively diverse, so reinforcing the conclusion that substances of expression in a social assembling have an inherently qualitative character (biology and chemistry resist being reduced to mathematical physics).

other, potentially life-enhancing, associations. In *A Thousand Plateaus* Deleuze and Guattari describe such a truncated existence as *stratified* in the same sense that the component elements of a stratum of sedimentary rock are firmly cemented into place. Stratification, as the terminus of an assembling process, very much represents a dead end.

And this is precisely the condition of an organism's organs. Each organ is hardwired into a given position and function. More congenial to Deleuze and Guattari is the ecosystem, in which the component organisms remain free to enter into various nonprescribed symbiotic associations with each other. In this sense the internal flexibility of an (immature) ecosystem makes it a good example of what the authors term a *consistency*, an assembling which preserves the heterogeneity of its components. The stratum-consistency binary parallels the hierarchy-heterarchy binary we encountered in chapter 3, and Manuel DeLanda has likewise proposed regarding strata and consistencies as ideal types representing assembling at its two polar extremes of minimal and maximal internal freedom. In practice a social assembling can move between these poles in real time, for example in interpersonal exchanges when the rules governing conversation spontaneously relax as strangers become friends.[11]

A PANARCHY OF REGISTERS

Although social assemblings are the main focus of our concern here it's important to note that Deleuze and Guattari regard these as representing only a subset of one of the three major strata, or registers, which make up the world. These major strata are: the inorganic, the register of matter and material processes; the organic, the register of life; and the alloplastic, in which living things use signs to produce territories, the register of culture.[12] Human social assemblings represent a subset of the cultural register, and not its entirety, since some animals too employ territorial conventions.[13] Whichever the register, an assembling is always inherently dynamic (on some time-scale), the conjunction of its components generating a coevolution in which the assembling as a whole, and its

11. DeLanda, *New Philosophy*, 16.

12. Deleuze and Guattari, *Thousand Plateaus*, 44–82. Holland refers to these as the three mega-strata, but I shall follow Bonta and Protevi in using instead the term "registers." Note that the inorganic register lumps physical and chemical classes of phenomena together, which admittedly represents a debatable simplification.

13. Holland, *Deleuze and Guattari's* A Thousand Plateaus, 21–28; Adkins, *Deleuze and Guattari's* A Thousand Plateaus, 47–61.

component parts, undergo change. Some examples of how the double articulation process operates in these registers are given here.[14]

REGISTER	*CONTENT*		*EXPRESSION*	
	Substance	*Form*	*Form*	*Substance*
Cultural	Humans and artifacts	Actions and passions	Social codes	Social institution
Organic	Organisms	Interconnecting flows	Mutual adaptation	Ecosystem
Inorganic	Liquid molecules	Thermal diffusion	Thermal convection	Convection cell

Table 3: Examples of the double articulation in each of the inorganic, organic, and cultural registers.

The three registers can be thought of in a hierarchical manner in such a way that the substance of expression of a lower register acts as the substance of content for its higher neighbor:[15]

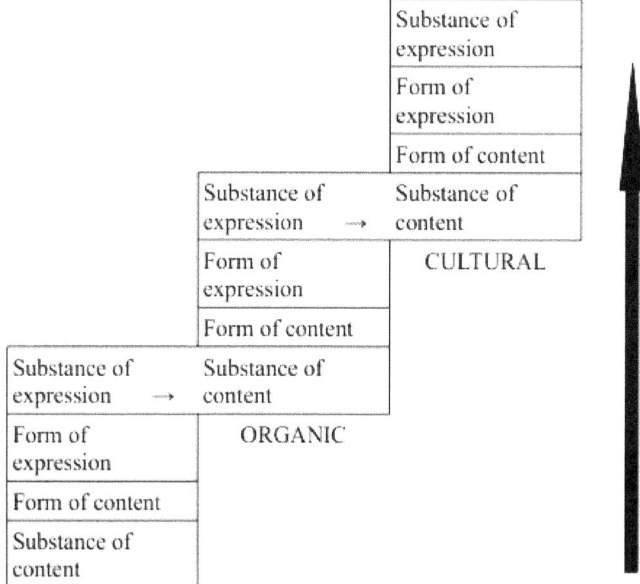

Table 4: The hierarchy of double articulations in the inorganic, organic, and cultural registers.

14. Adapted from Bonta and Protevi, *Deleuze and Geophilosophy*, 152–53. The example from the inorganic register is based on the Bénard cells described in chapter 3.

15. DeLanda, *Assemblage Theory*, 9–10.

The reader may by now have realized why we have taken this detour into the rather arcane writings of Deleuze and Guattari. Their account of the double articulation process provides a common framework which can be used to analyze what's going on in a number of otherwise diverse phenomena. For example, in chapter 3 the phenomenon of emergence was introduced: the spontaneous arising of higher-order functional forms on the basis of the interaction of lower-level components. What drives this, according to Rod Swenson's Law of Maximum Entropy Production (LMEP), is a basic natural striving to degrade global potential differences at the fastest rate by means of the emergence of local zones of sustained high-potential difference which entrain ambient environmental flows. These sustained zones can be considered entities in their own right, and their enhanced ability to degrade potentials is down to their operating on spatial and temporal scales greater than those pertaining in their environment. This obviously entails some structure of hierarchical organization. In Michael Polanyi's words each emergent level "reduces the scope of the one immediately below it by imposing on it a boundary that harnesses it to the service of the next-higher level, and this control is transmitted stage by stage, down to the basic inanimate level."[16]

Each of Swenson's self-organizing autocatakinetic structures therefore represents the second articulation of the dissipative, gradient-eroding processes entailed by the LMEP. A particular form of expression entrains the substance of content, inchoately ordered by the form of content, into an incipiently stratified assembling. To pursue the opening analogy, this assembling is the result of dots becoming numbered and joined together on a larger scale. If this assembling proves at all durable it may in turn get recruited as a component part of an even higher-level assembling. And at each new level novel properties emerge, as George Henry Lewes observed.[17] New *kinds* of things, qualitatively different, come into existence, and this process culminates in the existence of different classes of phenomena, the chemical arising from the physical, the biological from the chemical, and so on.

These new kinds of things arise because as one set of gradients is eroded another, more elaborate, set is generated in the form of a dissipative or autocatakinetic structure. Potential gradients are therefore not so much eroded as realized in new ways; potentials get transformed.

16. Polanyi, "Life's Irreducible Structure," 1311.

17. Lewes, *Problems of Life and Mind*, 413.

Deleuze and Guattari's analysis adds to this by pointing out that in the cultural register, and so in a social assembling, the second articulation involves an *incorporeal* transformation. This is to say that the emerging substance of expression has the character of *meaningful action or event* rather than uncomprehended brute fact. It embodies an interpretation of some kind, one reflecting the form of expression applied.[18]

Swenson's approach lends itself to being viewed through the lens of assemblage thinking not least because, as we saw in chapter 3, he holds a holistic view of how the universe works. The striving of living things to grow, expand, and reproduce, he claims, is in continuity with a more fundamental striving to realize biophysical potentials. In other words a property of the inorganic register is echoed, or analogically reproduced, in the organic register. This echo can also be heard in the human cultural register, and this is reflected in the fact that the German word *strebt*, "strives" (as in the universal striving to minimize potentials identified in Clausius's formulation of the second law of thermodynamics), could also be translated, in a different context, as "aspires." So, moving between the registers, the LMEP's striving is transformed from a blind, inexorable urge to minimize intensive gradients first into the *conatus* of living things and then into a responsibly owned human aspiration to achieve what is deemed a worthwhile goal, to realize a desirable potential. We shall come back to this point repeatedly in the rest of what follows.

Our three-registered world can in fact be seen as a complex, nested hierarchy of double articulations. Hierarchy isn't quite the right description, though. Better would be *panarchy*, another term which was coined by ecologist Buzz Holling. We encountered Holling in chapter 2 when we discussed the adaptive cycle, which describes how ecosystems typically pass through four developmental stages: exploitation (r-phase), conservation (K-phase), release or collapse (Ω-phase), and reorganization (α-phase). Holling and his coauthors argue that adaptive cycles pervade all time- and space-scales, so forming a nested arrangement of slower, larger cycles built on top of progressively faster, smaller ones. The reason the term "hierarchy" won't quite do is that in a hierarchy, narrowly defined, the upper levels simply dominate those below. In a panarchy, by contrast, the prevalence of adaptive cycle dynamics *at each*

18. Of course thermodynamics in general, and Swenson's autocatakinesis and LMEP in particular, like all other products of scientific endeavor, represent the outcomes of one particular kind of incorporeal transformation of the content of experience. This precludes any naively realist reading of the scientific scholarship featured here.

level complicates matters. As a result the cyclical dynamics of the various levels can become coupled, such that disturbances at one level are liable to transmission *both down and up* the panarchy. This gives rise to two significant phenomena: *remembering* and *revolt*.

Remembering is a top-down process which affects lower levels undergoing reorganization. The possibilities and constraints current during this phase can be strongly influenced by the next higher level—if the higher level is in its conservation phase, that is. The "accumulated wisdom" of the higher and slower level thereby shapes the reorganization taking place below it. So, for example, after a forest fire resources accumulated over a larger scale can slow the leakage of locally released nutrients, and the seed bank and surviving species from further afield can inform the pattern of reorganization.[19] In terms of the double articulation, what's happening is that the higher level's form of expression is overcoding the lower level's form of content as it reassembles.

Remembering is of a piece with the kind of stratifying, top-down control you might expect in a generic hierarchy. Revolt is entirely different. Holling describes it in this way:

> When a level in the panarchy enters its Ω-phase of creative destruction, the collapse can cascade to the next larger and slower level by triggering a crisis. Such an event is most likely if the slower level is at its K-phase, because at this point the resilience is low and the level is particularly vulnerable.[20]

Thus, given a suitable coincidence of phases across levels, disturbances can cascade *up* the panarchy. Even a relatively minor, local event at the right time and place can have global, long-term consequences. In terms of the double articulation, the disassembling of the substance of expression at a lower level can lead to the destabilizing of the form of content at a higher level, potentially precipitating a cascading collapse.

As an example of a revolt brewing in the human cultural register, consider the impact of cheap, plentiful fossil fuel energy on human societies over the last two hundred years. As outlined in chapter 2 there's evidence that, following a steep rise through much of the twentieth century, per capita global primary energy supply is no longer growing; and the efficiency of converting that supply into all-important useful physical work has also been on a plateau since the 1970s. This likely represents

19. Holling et al., "Sustainability and Panarchies," 76.

20. Holling, "Understanding the Complexity," 398.

the onset of the Ω-phase in a critical part of the social assembling's first articulation—its pragmatic system, the stuff from which society is built. It's reasonable to expect this to cascade up the panarchy to the second articulation—the semiotic system in which human sense-making happens. A crucial part of that sense-making involves how we order our common life so as to exchange goods and services for mutual benefit. Since the economies of much of the developed world are already arguably at the vulnerable K-phase this could readily destabilize the rudimentary conditions enabling not only the economic but also the political, social, and cultural structures which we have long taken for granted.[21]

Physicist Reiner Kümmel is among those who query whether developed capitalist economies and notions such as human rights can indeed be sustained in the absence of the expansionary dynamic enabled by the steam engine and all that has followed in its train.[22] Of course if John Gowdy and Lisi Krall are correct then this dynamic was already in place long before the steam engine came along; but if the added momentum which it and its successor technologies have provided is on the wane then that does leave an awkward question: how long can the modern world we know, our social assembling's substance of expression, remain a functional structure?

TALES OF TRANSFORMATION

So far we've noted two important features of doubly articulated assemblings. First, the marked discontinuity at the transition between articulations: how an assembling gets expressed is not pinned down by its content. Second, the tendency of assemblings to form nested panarchies: the expression of one assembling can function as the content of another, and so on in a chain of content and expression stretching off into the distance. Forms of expression and the transformations of content which they effect may be underdetermined by the assembling's content but, once in place, they can prove very hard to shift, especially when concatenated in this way. Some real-life examples of these features in the human cultural register bring this home and illustrate the value of assemblage thinking.

As a first example, the reader may dimly recall the virus-human assembling known as the 2020–22 COVID-19 pandemic. To many it

21. Matutinović et al., "Mature Stage of Capitalist Development."

22. Kümmel, *Second Law of Economics*, 16.

may still seem that the human component—a social phenomenon in the cultural register—was entailed or demanded by the viral component—a biophysical phenomenon belonging to the organic register. But where did the viral pandemic end and the human pandemic begin? Put differently, how inevitable was the particular incorporeal transformation, or expressive overcoding, of the spread of the SARS-CoV-2 virus into lockdowns, vaccine mandates, etc., as seen in many countries around the world?[23] What happened in the UK serves as a useful case study.

Left to its own devices, SARS-CoV-2 would simply have acted on the content of societies, specifically by reordering human bodies. Its direct effect would have been to produce a range of relatively minor symptoms in most but also more serious symptoms in the immunocompromised. As a result some people would have been off work for a few days; some would have been hospitalized for a while; some would have experienced infection sequelae; some would have died. Some hospitals might have been severely stretched and there would have been some economic impact. In terms of our join-the-dots analogy, the distribution of some of the dots (people) would have changed, temporarily, and some dots would have been erased altogether. That would have been it.

But the UK government response after March 23, 2020, expressed the virus-ordered content so as to produce a much more consequential outcome. The results of this overcoding were manifold. On a physical level, human bodies were largely constrained to a form of house arrest, and even when allowed out in public were required to observe a spatial separation of at least two meters. Meetings with nonfamily members were restricted to electronically mediated internet calls. Domestic violence increased. Education was disrupted, with life-changing consequences. Businesses went bust. Government debt skyrocketed . . . and so on. All of this was in addition to, not instead of, the direct biological impact of the viral pathogen.

Much of what became the consensus response to the pandemic followed from adopting a particular version of the virus-human story which owed a lot to a report by a team from Imperial College, London entitled "Impact of Non-Pharmaceutical Interventions (NPIs) to Reduce

23. Many dissenting rejoinders have been produced to what became the consensus response to the pandemic. Those continuing to believe that this consensus was inevitable may wish to consult, e.g., Woolhouse, *Year the World Went Mad*; Dodsworth, *State of Fear*; Craig, *Expired*; Desmet, *Psychology of Totalitarianism*; Green and Fazi, *Covid Consensus*.

COVID-19 Mortality and Healthcare Demand."[24] It told a story about how a recently discovered virus, if left unchecked, would infect most UK citizens and go on to kill more than half a million of them in short order. It told how the then current, and more moderate, government policy response would lead to as many as a quarter of a million deaths and the widespread overwhelming of hospital services.

As a result of this story UK government policy changed from the mitigation of overall social harms to the attempted suppression of viral spread.[25] Unprecedentedly, much of British society and its economy were shut down for several weeks, with legal restrictions remaining in place for two years. The result of the Imperial College report had been, in effect, to number the dots of the unfolding epidemic so as to produce a picture so scary that what emerged was lockdown—certainly a qualitatively novel outcome in George Henry Lewes's sense. Human history over the two years following underwent a remarkable and unexpected twist, not so much because of the virus itself, but because of what became the prevailing story told about it, the incorporeal transformation of the virus' potential action on human bodies.

This episode powerfully demonstrates the role of narrative in a social assembling's form of expression. Storytelling is central to how human beings tackle the future. It enables "lookahead" or anticipation.[26] We operate on the basis of stories we tell ourselves about what may happen when we encounter a particular situation or if we do so-and-so (if I glimpse a group of hooded youths up ahead in the park on a dark evening I might well take a detour). As well as comprising assimilated habitual responses to past experience, stories present an overarching view of what the world is like as per prevailing norms—what matters, what doesn't, what's good, what's bad.

In fact we can say that in a social assembling the form of expression has three dimensions, all of which were apparent in the response to the pandemic: the cognitive, the affective, and the effective. Narratives provide information about the world and ourselves, in this case presenting a picture of a deadly, highly infectious disease which could overwhelm health services. They also influence how we feel, in this case causing apprehension, fear, even downright panic. Most consequentially they can

24. Ferguson et al., "Report 9."

25. In terms of the discussion in chapter 3, this parallels a shift from an attempted optimal response balancing several factors to a simple minimization exercise.

26. Holland, *Complexity*, 86.

change our behavior, in this case through curtailing freedom of movement and, for a while in the UK, generating the Thursday-evening mass ritual of "clap for carers."[27]

So in a social assembling, for good or ill, the diverse stories people tell interact and some end up becoming socially normative. These get to impose definitive form on some content, an inchoately ordered jumble of bodies and artifacts, so as to express an emergent whole. And this whole may end up forming the basis of a further double articulation animated by the same, or a different, normative story.

Economist John Maynard Keynes once provided an illustration of how this concatenation of expressive overcoding can come about, one far more mundane than a pandemic yet in its own way even more remarkable: dabbling in stocks and shares. Reflecting in part on his own experience, he compared investing in the stock market to the then popular newspaper competitions

> in which the competitors have to pick out the six prettiest faces from a hundred photographs, the prize being awarded to the competitor whose choice most nearly corresponds to the average preferences of the competitors as a whole; so that each competitor has to pick, not those faces that he himself finds prettiest, but those that he thinks likeliest to catch the fancy of the other competitors, all of whom are looking at the problem from the same point of view. It is not a case of choosing those which . . . are really the prettiest, nor even those which average opinion genuinely thinks the prettiest. We have reached the third degree where we devote our intelligences to anticipating what average opinion expects the average opinion to be.[28]

This is a particularly striking example of how the double articulation can operate in a social assembling. In this case the first articulation is provided by the objective financial performance of the companies listed on the stock market. Any amount of detailed information is available to the investor about this, and it may play some part in helping her decide where she puts her money. However, says Keynes, what's decisive in these decisions is not company performance as such but rather *judgments about*

27. This involved the public being encouraged to stand at their doorways at 8 p.m. on Thursday evenings to applaud members of the caring services exposing themselves to infection by COVID-19 through contact with patients.

28. Keynes, *General Theory of Employment*, chap.12, quoted in Keen, *Debunking Economics*, 238.

others' judgments about company performance. Indeed it goes beyond that, to the third degree of "anticipating what average opinion expects the average opinion to be"; and, comments Keynes wryly, "there are some, I believe, who practice the fourth, fifth, and higher degrees."[29]

Such a heaping up of double articulations, one on top of the other, shows how decoupled the ultimate substance of expression (investment decision) can become from the underlying basic substance of content (intrinsic company performance). The latter gets mediated by stories about stories about stories, with the result that the outcome may fairly be described as pure fiction. Crucially, though, it's a *shared* fiction. Here we have the explanation for financial bubbles of all kinds, and they reflect a characteristic feature of social assemblings, that is, the dense and often determining mediation of social factors over and above the underlying material realities. As a result, rather than putting their elements to work in some functional structure, social assemblings too often end up becoming entirely *dys*functional.

Recall how in our original join-the-dots example the numbers appeared out of the blue, without any prior indication of which number would go where. This reflects the way in which, in the double articulation, the form of expression is underdetermined by the form of content. In the context of biological evolution, for example, a variety of possibilities may get thrown up in the short term through random mutational variation but only a few—or one, or none—will get selected for longer-term survival by the context. The context in this case is the organism's environment, which is entirely contingent, such that it simply isn't obvious in advance which variants will prove successful and come to define a species.

In the context of a social assembling the degree of underdetermination can be vastly more pronounced. The highly social (indeed ultrasocial) nature of human life means that others' opinions make up a large chunk of the environmental landscape, the form of expression, determining which outcome gets performed. Keynes's memorable analogy provides an extreme, but not necessarily unusual, example of how a social assembling may well comprise not just a single double articulation but a whole panarchy of them: an open-ended, compound chain of increasingly ethereal semiotic systems in which each substance of expression comes to function as the substance of content for a yet further articulation.

29. Keynes, *General Theory of Employment*, 156.

Mention of ultrasociality leads us to briefly revisit the work of John Gowdy and Lisi Krall as described in chapter 4, this time through the lens of assemblage thinking. Gowdy and Krall, we noted, draw our attention to the step-change in social organization which accompanied the transition from a hunter-gatherer mode to a fully agrarian mode of collective life following the end of the last Ice Age. This is the ultrasocial turn, at which point societies became organized for the primary purpose of surplus resource production and accumulation.

In terms of the double articulation process this novel bioeconomic dynamic represented a new form of expression overcoding the loosely ordered societies emerging from the freezer of the late Paleolithic. But it would be a mistake to imagine the agrarian transition happening suddenly, out of the blue and simultaneously everywhere. There's evidence of sedentary patterns of life and of experiments with horticulture as long ago as the last glacial maximum, some 20,000 years BCE. When plant domestication did begin to develop in earnest, spreading from its origins in the fertile crescent of the Middle East around 9,500 BCE, it took fully five millennia for farming to become established as far afield as the British Isles, with the drift towards domestication often reversed; and there's sparse evidence of associated institutionalized social inequalities or organized warfare before around 5,500 BCE.[30]

This complex story can be seen as the millennia-long outworking of only the first articulation of a fully agrarian social assembling, with various consistencies, in Deleuze and Guattari's jargon, emerging and mutating at different times and in different places only to dissolve again. Stratification, the establishment of the definite and lasting social forms of a second articulation, only began to set in around the sixth millennium BCE. It's at this point that top-down causation began to definitively assert itself as ultrasociality, the constitutional proclivity to expand. This was when well-defined social hierarchies started to appear and to gradually replace the relatively heterarchical arrangements which had previously prevailed whereby, as we noted in chapter 3, social relationships are "unranked, or . . . possess the potential for being ranked in a number of different ways, depending on systemic requirements."[31]

Prior to this transition, as anthropologists David Graeber and David Wengrow vigorously point out in their best-selling book, *The Dawn of*

30. Morris, "Against Method"; Kemp, *Goliath's Curse*, 77–111.

31. Crumley, "Heterarchy," 2.

Everything: A New History of Humanity, patterns of life for many people groups showed a distinctly seasonal pattern.[32] This "institutional plasticity" was still apparent as recently as the nineteenth and twentieth centuries among peoples as otherwise diverse as the Kwakiutl of the American Northwest, the Nambikwara of the Brazilian Mato Grosso, and the Inuit of the Arctic. For example, a contemporary anthropologist wrote that the Inuit "have two social structures, one in summer and one in winter, and . . . in parallel they have two systems of law and religion."[33] During the summer months, the Inuit dispersed into small hunting bands, each under the coercive authority of a single male elder, in which there was a clear sense of what belonged to whom. But during the winter months a radically egalitarian ethos prevailed when the wanderers reassembled in large houses, sharing wealth and even sexual partners. In sum,

> the ability to consciously alternate between contrasting modes of social and political organization . . . [was] a distinctive, emergent property of human societies in the highly seasonal environments of the last Ice Age. Dual or alternating social structures of this kind were also widely reported in early 20th century studies of recent hunter-foragers.[34]

Vehemently antievolutionist, Graeber and Wengrow insist that there was therefore no "childhood of Man" in which small, itinerant bands of foragers lived in innocent community prior to an inevitable fall into the captivity of a hierarchically exploitative agrarian feudalism. Rather, they maintain, we have a riddle: having spent so much of our history moving back and forth between different social systems—behaving as consistencies, in Deleuze and Guattari's terms—how did people get stuck in the stupendously unequal arrangements which obtain today?[35]

The underlying mechanism at work here is of course autocatakinesis, the spontaneous emergence of energetically dissipative social structures conditioned by the Law of Maximum Entropy Production and the Maximum Power Principle. But Graeber and Wengrow do us a service in pointing out that, strictly speaking, this development was and still is *not* inevitable. Consistencies are not fated to become stratified.

32. Graeber and Wengrow, *Dawn of Everything*.

33. Marcel Mauss, quoted in Wengrow and Graeber, "Farewell to the 'Childhood of Man,'" 606.

34. Wengrow and Graeber, "Farewell to the 'Childhood of Man,'" 599.

35. Wengrow and Graeber, "Farewell to the 'Childhood of Man,'" 615.

Surplus-orientated expansionism was in part a historical accident made possible by the mild and stable climates of the Holocene yet underdetermined by the looser forms of content, the flexible economic and social experiments, which preceded it. In order to become fully established as a form of expression it needed to acquire a semiotic dimension, that is, a socially normative story—in the case of ancient Egypt, "a product of myth, magic, religion, and the nascent science of astronomy."[36]

Having performed its incorporeal transformation and become established, the practice of surplus-orientated expansionism has very much taken over the world, albeit integrated with different normative stories which have arisen from time to time. As we saw in chapter 2, the underdetermination of human conduct by the MPP is also stressed by Jem Bendell, who notes that the modern industrial exploitation of fossil fuels required not only access to substantial coal deposits (belonging to the first articulation system of things) but also the prior existence of an expansionary monetary system (belonging to the second articulation system of meanings).[37] Latterly this monetary system gave rise to the unquestioned ideology of economic growth, which has served as the sacred story by which we all live. We've become socially habituated to living out this story, entrained and put to work in functional structures from which it may seem there is no escape. Indeed we're locked into them, as Gowdy and Krall emphasize, as much if not more by our levels of acute interdependence as by any deliberate exercise of top-down social power by groups or individuals. All this may have originally come about by chance, but having become established the predicament of lock-in remains.

This lock-in, and the nature of our current global socioeconomic assembling, is illustrated in the story of the silicon chip as narrated by Ed Conway in his book *Material World*.[38] The story starts at a mine and nearby refinery in Galicia, Spain, where quartz rock is quarried and heated to 1,800 °C in order to produce 99 percent pure silicon. On then to Germany, where the silicon is further refined to produce polysilicon of various grades, the highest being the premium semiconductor grade, 99.99999999 percent pure. Converting this highest-grade polysilicon to monocrystalline wafers involves a journey across the Atlantic to the Western Seaboard of the US where a Japanese company rearranges the silicon atoms into a perfectly regular structure. This process requires the

36. Mumford, *Technics and Human Development*, 11.

37. Bendell, *Breaking Together*, 330–38.

38. Conway, *Material World*, 87–121.

use of a crucible made from a particular hyper-pure kind of quartz which is virtually unique to a location in North Carolina. The final stage of the chip's journey takes it across the Pacific to a factory in Taiwan where, in a fantastically intricate process, the circuitry is etched onto it by a machine made by a Dutch company with the crucial assistance of subordinate technologies produced by two separate German companies.

A summary this brief can't do justice to the extraordinary journey so well described by Conway. Yet the point is that it is *not* extraordinary. Conway's book is replete with examples of how contemporary supply chains of all kinds span the globe, creating mind-bending networks of intimate interdependence. This is the practical outworking of the form of expression which we collectively, and for the most part unconsciously, perform. It impinges on our daily lives in ways, and to an extent, that we scarcely appreciate. Since the appearance of the first computer chip in 1971 these microscopic artifacts have become ubiquitous and utterly essential for what we've come to regard as normal life. And this is only one example—albeit a highly nontrivial example—of what our current entrainment, or lock-in, looks like. No one sat down and planned all this, but its hold on us is no less real for that.

So much for tales of transformation. Many more could be added, but these serve to give a flavor of two obvious ways in which the second articulation of the social assembling can go wrong. First, the emerging substance of expression can lose its moorings in the material world and drift off into the stratosphere, pragmatic and semiotic systems having become decoupled. This risk stems from the incorporeal nature of the transformation from one articulation to another. A process of abstraction from concrete reality necessarily occurs here, essential for the construction of meaning but, by the same token, susceptible to fantasy. Whereas, as we shall see in the final chapter, imagination is among other things integral to the exercise of wisdom, it can also lead astray. The result is a human world severed from its biophysical roots and so, ultimately, doomed to death.

Secondly, the emerging substance of expression may become sclerotic and unyielding, imposing a straitjacket on its human and nonhuman parts. This is Deleuze and Guattari's stratification, the comprehensive entrainment of flows, the thorough organ-ization of the emergent whole, lock-in. Of course biological evolution is full of examples of this, and as organisms we can scarcely regard it as an intrinsically bad thing; after all, our own bodies would promptly disintegrate without the glue of top-down causation holding our organs together in a duly organized way. But what about the *social* assembling? Is it our destiny as individual humans to become incorporated into a superorganism of some kind, and so subordinated and restricted to an inherently anonymous function within it? Or could the emergence of the fully ecosocial human mean a different outcome? If so, how do we begin to imagine how that might be?

We shall explore one particular set of answers to those questions in the next chapter. But finally here I return to the theme of power, and to a form of expression which can give rise to both these articulative infelicities in combination: money.

THE POWER OF TRUST: PREDICTABILITY OR COMMITMENT?

Back in chapter 1 we noticed some of the ways in which social power resembles its material counterpart. It also differs in important ways, and assemblage thinking can help bring this out. Material power, which characterizes the system of things as expressed by the forms of the physical sciences, is power as *quantity*. To the scientist it's a matter of wattage pure and simple—a single number. In a solely material contest, the party which can harness energy for useful work at the fastest rate will tend to prevail. Social power, which characterizes how power is expressed in that subset of the system of things comprising humans, and as expressed by the forms of the social sciences, is a matter of *potentia*, collaborative *power to* achieve some humanly meaningful end. Although we commonly speak about some people being more powerful than others, so superficially implying a simple quantitative difference, a single number—even a complex of numbers—cannot possibly suffice to describe what's going on here. To begin with, the whole notion of what constitutes "useful" work is up for grabs, to the extent that human purposes can't be reduced to the mere *conatus* of remaining alive and reproducing. What's more social power, even when expressed as *potestas*, *power over*, cannot wholly dispense with *trust* in some form or other; and trust, at first glance, would seem to be very much a qualitative phenomenon, a creature of the second articulation.

Yet one of the most consequential ways in which trust features in all our lives is as money ("I promise to pay the bearer on demand the sum of . . ."). And money, by its very nature as the general equivalent, is purely quantitative, inherently devoid of qualities. It presents a flattened vision of the world in which particular things differ from each other only in respect of representing differing amounts of the same abstract stuff. Any given thing is therefore interchangeable with any other thing on the basis of simple arithmetic. Consequently money is eminently associated with *power over* others since, as abstract quantity, it can be accumulated as a stock such that contests based on monetary wealth will be decided by who can release the strongest flows.

In this respect money recalls that mode of social power named *force* by Steven Lukes, the securing of compliance by the removal of the option not to comply. Here social power functions akin to material power, the exercise of power over a mere body—whether that's a human being or a sack of coal—rather than over a person. This affinity is confirmed by the Chartalist interpretation of money as a vehicle by which the state, the entity which asserts a territorial monopoly on the legitimate use of force, secures the subjection of individuals via taxation. As we saw in chapter 1, "I promise to pay the bearer on demand the sum of $10" actually boils down to "The bearer is remitted $10 of tax liability on presentation of this token."[39] We can trust the government to take an interest in us if we fail to pay our taxes. In other words money has the remarkable property of effectively reducing social power to material power, *potentia* to wattage, the second to the first articulation of a social assembling.

If we view the world as a panarchy of double articulations, the human cultural register emergent from antecedent organic and inorganic registers, money then appears to represent the reverse engineering of this emergence. Qualitative distinctions fall away and literally *everything* becomes interchangeable. Differences in kind get dissolved into a difference in amount according to a single scale or metric. Whether that metric be watts, amperes, gross domestic product, or any other unit of account is a secondary issue. What's happening is that a higher-order, emergent social relationship is being pared down to the level of its lower-order material constituents *but with a particular, contingent purpose in view*—the mediation of power between human beings.

In considering trust in relation to power we can usefully think in terms of two poles, or opposite modes, in which it's expressed. The first pole is represented by money. We've just noted how, as money, trust gets quantified: a debt of $1,000 embodies exactly one hundred times the

39. See, e.g., Ingham, *Nature of Money*, 47–49.

trust embodied in a debt of $10. It also gets reduced to *predictability*. I'll only exchange something useful—say an apple—for money if I trust that I can exchange that money for another apple tomorrow. Money, then, has the character of a machine, which only works to the extent that I can rely on it to (sufficiently) retain its exchange value over time (which is why hyperinflation is so disastrous). Trust as money is a technology for erasing time, in the sense that an otherwise unknown future can be made predictable, and therefore manipulable, in the present.[40] And the same therefore goes for those others to whom I relate exclusively via the medium of money. Once money comes between us you become a predictable automaton whose future behavior can be anticipated—and so exploited. The lens of money makes it look as if I can put *you* to work in a functional structure of *my* choosing, relating as object to subject rather than as persons. Accordingly I can rely on you to react in a certain way to a given financial stimulus, and so be trusted in the way that money can be trusted.

Trust's second and opposite pole of expression is referred to in the Greek of the New Testament as *pistis*. Although commonly translated as "faith," *pistis* is far from narrowly religious in scope. Rather it relates to interpersonal relationships generally, and its range of meanings includes confidence, fidelity, commitment, and trust. *Pistis* is very much a creature of the second articulation. To trust in this sense isn't about my being able to predict your behavior, far less about regarding your future behavior as amenable to exploitation. On the contrary it's about placing *myself* in *your* power by acting on the assumption that you have my interests at heart and will keep your promises. To trust is to commit myself to you in some way. Equally, *pistis* refers to that of which I am persuaded;[41] and since to persuade is "to cause another person by argument, advice or entreaty to believe" it implies an interpersonal relationship between rational peers rather than the machinic manipulation of object by subject. This second pole carries the positive, benign connotation commonly associated with the idea of trust.

40. Manipulation of a highly sophisticated nature is possible these days via derivatives, "financial weapons of mass destruction," in which predictability amounts to little more than gambling on the future value of an underlying asset. See, e.g., Fernando, "Understanding Derivatives"; Brown, "Casino Capitalism and the Derivatives Market." On a more basic level, our global financial system, being based on interest-bearing debt, assumes—treats as predictable—that the economy will keep on growing forever. Loss of trust in this founding assumption would naturally mean the collapse of the system.

41. *Pistis*, trust, is etymologically linked to *peithō*, to persuade.

Although *pistis* isn't restricted to religion, it is widely used in the New Testament to refer to one's relationship with God specifically. So it's worth contrasting trust as *pistis* with trust as *mamōnas*, or mammon. The word "mammon" occurs four times in the Gospels: three times in Luke chapter 16, the last of these being in the well-known adage "You cannot serve God and mammon," and once in Matthew chapter 6, where the adage is reproduced.[42] Actually mammon has a negative connotation in all these passages, qualified in the first two instances as "unrighteous mammon." Commonly translated into English as "wealth," "money," or "property," *mamōnas* is itself a Greek transliteration of an Aramaic word derived from the verb "to trust," such that mammon literally means either "that which is entrusted" or "that in which one trusts."[43]

Mammon in Jesus's usage therefore brings us back to trust's first pole of expression identified above, but this time we find it painted in a darker hue. While essential for social interaction of even the most basic kind, and intrinsic to a right relationship with God, trust has a deeply ambivalent character. As mammon it precisely rivals God as an object of service. And since service clearly has to do with *power over* others, what Jesus is saying is that human life, whether we like it or not, always already entails being caught up in some web of power or other. We may feel that money is simply something that we use, which serves our arbitrary ends, which enables us to exercise power so as to realize our prior desires. But Jesus claims that things are the other way around; when we use money, we also are being used.

In fact, as we saw in chapter 1, to exercise power at all is to locate oneself in a particular field of power in which enabling and constraint go hand in hand. So in claiming that "you cannot serve God and mammon" Jesus issues a challenge: In *which* field of power will you place yourself? To which set of constraints will you submit? Which incorporeal transformation, which system of meanings, is it to be? In what functional structure will you put your body to work? Who, or what, will you trust? For power in the second articulation of a social assembling comes in many different *kinds*, each with its own field, and perhaps mammon's greatest deceit is to

42. Luke 16:9, 11, 13; Matt 6:24.

43. Mammon's negative connotation in Jesus's teaching is reinforced by his comments regarding wealth elsewhere, and contrasts with a more neutral usage of the term in rabbinical writings and those affirmative accounts of riches as God's blessing found in the Hebrew Scriptures. See Dominy, *Decoding Mammon*, xvii–xx.

deny this and kid us that everything, inevitably, is both predictable and indifferently interchangeable.

SUMMING UP

The world is a process of becoming in which different things, different kinds of things, are forever coming together, assembling, and by their conjunction creating new possibilities. Some of these associations get selected by contextual factors which happen to pertain at the time and so come to constitute, by their structured interaction, new realities of a higher order. Every process by which a new reality emerges is in this sense a twofold process, a double articulation of proposing and disposing, the assembling and expressing of content. These new realities vary greatly in coherence and, over time, will unravel and/or enter new assemblings with other things.

Within this flux of becoming we can discern a threefold hierarchy of major strata, or registers: the inorganic, the organic, and the cultural, the latter including the sphere of human social life. Each register builds on that below it, but never in a way that can be predicted. In truth this hierarchy is better described as a panarchy, inasmuch as each register comprises countless nested, dynamic adaptive cycles drifting in and out of phase with each other in endless successions of exploitation, conservation, collapse, and reorganization. Atop this, human bodies and societies wax and wane according to the relative phase conjunctions across the threefold panarchy.

"What really frightens and dismays us is not external events themselves, but the way in which we think about them. It is not things that disturb us, but our interpretation of their significance." Epictetus's words capture the basic experience of the double articulation in the human cultural register. The assembling of bodies lends itself to being interpreted in many different ways, eliciting diverse responses. Assembled bodies may be put to work in functional structures of many different kinds, hence the great variety of human cultures across time and space, and regardless of the common basic requirements for the sustaining and reproducing of bodies. Within the human cultural register the product of each double articulation lends itself to becoming an ingredient in a yet further assembling, so that the human world often ends up comprising a vertiginous concatenation of interpretations only distantly coupled to their underlying bodily foundations.

Since the last Ice Age certain functional structures have come to dominate how bodies interact in the human cultural register. These are summarized in the notion of surplus-orientated expansionism, as described by John Gowdy and Lisi Krall. This represents a selection from among the many possible ways of organizing societies exemplified in archaeological and anthropological studies. The selection process involves the phenomenon of autocatakinesis and the Law of Maximum Entropy Production discussed by Rod Swenson, but these factors didn't determine the current outcome since, both within and across the registers, the second articulation remains underdetermined by the first. In the organic and cultural registers the LMEP is expressed in part by the Maximum Power Principle; and in the human cultural register the expression of the MPP happens to have become defined primarily by money and physical force in combination. Both of these represent the atavistic ascendancy of the merely quantitative over the qualitative, harnessed to an ambition to determine future events rather than trust in their gracious unfolding.

Could things have gone differently? Even now, can a different articulation of our ecosocial system be imagined and enacted? In Epictetus's terms, can we think about external events differently so as to fashion a different response? If so, what narratives are available to inform how the human assembling may be otherwise expressed? The next chapter will examine one candidate for this daunting yet vital task.

6

The Victory of the Cross: Jesus and Power

The Buddha, the Roman god Bacchus, and Jesus of Nazareth walk into a bar. The Buddha calmly asks, and pays, for an orange juice. Bacchus thumps the bar, demands a bottle of Chianti, and opens a tab. Jesus looks at the water tap in the corner, smiles, and says to the barman, "My friend, you and I are going to get very rich."

What bearing can the life of Jesus of Nazareth, a "marginal Jew" from the first century, possibly have on how we understand evolutionary biology's Maximum Power Principle (MPP)?[1] This book has been written in the conviction that the account of that life handed down by the Christian church is indispensable for grasping how the MPP can be performed well in human societies. This chapter will begin the task of explaining why that is, mainly by reference to the picture of Jesus painted in the four Gospels.

But do the Gospels paint a single consistent picture? How do these pictures, shot through with Christian faith, relate to the historical figure of Jesus? And which historical Jesus are we dealing with anyway? After all there is no shortage of candidates for the role, each championed by a prominent contemporary scholar. These candidates can vary a lot in how far they resemble the Christ of traditional Christian faith. Take, for example, Reza Aslan's failed revolutionary; or John Dominic Crossan's

1. As described in the title of Meier, *Marginal Jew*.

Jewish Cynic philosopher; or Dale Allison's millenarian prophet; or N. T. Wright's orthodox Christian messiah.[2]

I don't propose trying to sort the chaff from the wheat here—that would be a book in itself. Instead I'll allow various perspectives to cast light on what will be a straightforward reading of the Gospels as we have them, all with a view to bringing out the various ways in which power gets expressed in Jesus's life and ministry. Some of the categories introduced in chapter 1 offer a helpful preliminary framework here. I'll then go on to draw on ideas introduced in the intervening chapters in order to bring out how it's specifically the *story* of Jesus which saves, how that story changes the way we understand power, and so also the social implications of the MPP and the superorganismic tendency deriving from it.

JESUS AND POWER IN THE GOSPELS

Ask the person in the street what they know about Jesus and they're likely to mention his miracles. These, along with his preaching, seem to have been why he caused such a stir and drew huge crowds as he traveled around Palestine and its neighboring territories. The Greek word translated as "miracles" is actually *dunameis*, literally "powers," "deeds of power," or "mighty works" as commonly rendered in English translations. The conceit with which this chapter opened contains a reference to what is perhaps Jesus's best-known miracle, the turning of water into wine at the wedding in Cana.[3] This is an example of a nature miracle, in which Jesus acts in a paranormal way on the nonhuman world, albeit thereby also having an impact on human lives.[4] Other examples include the stilling of a storm, walking on water, the feeding of multitudes, and the production of an extraordinary haul of fish.[5]

Jesus's other miracles all involve his acting directly on human bodies. These include several healings, exorcisms, and even some instances of the dead being raised.[6] With both these and the nature miracles Jesus

2. Recent summaries of the historical Jesus debate include Bond, *Historical Jesus*; Belby and Eddy, *Historical Jesus.*

3. John 2.

4. I prefer the term *paranormal*, "beyond the scope of normal objective investigation or explanation," to *supernatural* given the latter's connotation of departure from some lawlike natural propensity.

5. E.g., Mark 4:35–41; Mark 6:30–52; Luke 5:1–11.

6. Luke 7:11–17; Matt 9:18–26; John 11.

demonstrates material power, power impinging on bodies, human and otherwise, so bearing primarily on the first articulation of the social assembling.[7] Of course the miracles also impinge on the second articulation: these are meaningful acts, apprehended as such by others—both "patients" and onlookers—whose actions often change as a consequence. Should we then also regard these as examples of Jesus deploying social power, in one or more of the three dimensions discussed by Steven Lukes?

Lukes's first dimension of power involves getting people to do things they otherwise would not do (as distinct from things they *could* not do). Jesus's miracles generally don't feature power in this way as they're consistently presented as ends in themselves. For example, Jesus heals blind Bartimaeus in order to give him what he, Bartimaeus, wants. The fact that Bartimaeus then responds by following Jesus is incidental—there's no indication that was part of what Jesus wanted or expected to happen.[8] An exception to this rule is found in Luke the evangelist's account of the calling of the first disciples, which he (unlike Mark and Matthew) links to an extraordinary catch of fish.[9] This call to abandon livelihoods and follow Jesus, whether or not accompanied by a nature miracle, would seem a notable example of the first dimension of power in operation, specifically through the exercise of charismatic, as distinct from institutional, authority.

Likewise Jesus does not appear, on the face of it, to exert social power in the second sense described by Lukes, that is by delimiting the range of options available to his audience. In Lukes's usage this typically involves the narrowly political power of being able to set an agenda which serves to both include and exclude what may be discussed, and so what actions are possible. However here too there's at least one significant exception. By arriving in Jerusalem for the Passover festival very deliberately, as per messianic prophecy, on the back of a donkey, Jesus is knowingly acting in a highly provocative manner.[10] The effect of this action is reinforced, in Matthew, Mark, and Luke, by his then proceeding to cause a fracas in the outer precinct of the temple; and, in John, by his having just raised

7. In this chapter I shall be drawing freely on the vocabulary of assemblage thinking introduced in chapter 5. As mentioned in that chapter, although material power, as the rate of performance of humanly useful work, is strictly a second articulation phenomenon, I associate it here with the first articulation since it deals most directly with actions in the pragmatic system, the system of things.

8. Mark 10:46–52.

9. Luke 5:1–11.

10. E.g., Mark 11:1–11; cf. Wright, *Jesus and the Victory of God*, 490–91.

a man (Lazarus) from the dead. It's John who makes it explicit that such actions effectively constrain the options open to the Jewish authorities: either do nothing, and risk a popular insurrection; or join the crowds in proclaiming Jesus as messiah, thereby guaranteeing a merciless Roman crackdown; or act decisively to dispose of the threat posed by Jesus.[11] We should notice that this agenda has been imposed on them by Jesus. Had he attended the festival surreptitiously or stayed away altogether then they would not have acted as they did.

Lukes's third dimension of social power has to do with the forming of others' desires. In this case Jesus very obviously *does* seek to exercise social power through his teaching ministry and, more particularly, in his recruiting of the Twelve, his inner circle of apprentices (in context a more appropriate translation of the Greek *mathētēs* than "disciple").[12] This is clearly an attempt not only to train them in the skills Jesus is already demonstrating but also to educate the apprentices to desire as he, Jesus, desires, to "seek first the Kingdom of God and its righteousness."[13] This is important: unlike the commercial advertiser and the government Nudge Unit Jesus isn't aiming to foster desires that suit his own, rather different, ends.[14] Rather, analogously to Nicola's peer group in chapter 1, he recruits his apprentices to join him in his own mission of bringing the kingdom of God to bear on people's lives.

Jesus, then, certainly exercises social *power over* others in the ways just noted. But, staying with the categories introduced in chapter 1, in doing so does he also contribute to a collective *power to* achieve certain goals? True, the recruitment of apprentices does mean that more people get healed and exorcised; but this development seems secondary to the main thrust of the Gospel narratives. First and foremost the Gospels are about what *Jesus* says and does. Yet the Gospels do suggest a sense of a collective *power to* when they state that Jesus was "filled with the power of the Spirit," and that "the power of the Lord was with him to heal."[15] Jesus's source of power doesn't lie within himself but rather derives from his being part of a larger, divine set of relationships. Jesus's *power to* therefore evokes the fourth dimension of power mentioned in chapter 1, namely

11. John 11:45–53.

12. Mark 3:13–19; 6:7–13; cf. Luke 10:1–20.

13. Matt 6:33.

14. On the UK government's "Nudge Unit," or Behavioral Insights Team, see Dodsworth, *State of Fear*.

15. E.g., Luke 4:14; 5:17.

power as that which constitutes subjects, or "makes up" people. Jesus is who he is, and does what he does, by virtue of being situated within a set of more-than-human relationships. He is the vehicle of a particular kind of power, the main artery through whom flows the transforming life of God.

But this isn't the only field of power in which Jesus is situated. John's Gospel makes it clear that, though this is Jesus's native and constituting domain, he has been sent into "the world" and so is caught up in the power dynamics of a very different world order, one to which he does not belong. The ruler of this world order has no power over him since Jesus is constituted as a subject by another, divine field of power. So, contrary to appearances, Jesus retains power to lay down his life and to take it up again. When Pilate boasts that he has power either to release Jesus or to crucify him, Jesus points out that Pilate is not the origin of such powers, any more than Jesus is the origin of his. Pilate as Roman governor, like everyone else, is constituted by prior fields of power. Their source, ultimately, is God, but God's power is mediated and distorted by human structures: the "ruler of this world," as John puts it.[16] Constraints which at root exist to enable the channeling of God's life thus become chains which bind some to the arbitrary will of others. Even the bond of friendship makes betrayal possible.[17]

We encountered these distorted structures previously in chapter 4, rendered there in the plural as the Powers, "the world rulers of this present darkness . . . the spiritual hosts of wickedness in the heavenly places."[18] There too we encountered Walter Wink's summing up of our predicament and task: the Powers are good, fallen, and must be redeemed.[19] How does this redemption happen? Through the bottom-up effects of the actions of particular people. The template is provided by

16. John 12:31; 14:30; 16:11.

17. John 8:23; 14:30; 10:18; 19:10–11.

18. Eph 6:12.

19. We should understand redemption, in this context at least, in the sense of rehabilitation, restoration, or repair. The alternative interpretation, of ransom payment, can surely only serve to confuse. Gustaf Aulén's classic, *Christus Victor*, draws welcome attention to the prevalence of the theme of Christ's victory over the Powers and to its association with ransom. Although the ransom metaphor appears several times in the New Testament, and underlies Paul's notion of redemption, *apolutrōsis*, the victory of the cross as read here, per Wink's emphasis, consists rather in the revelation of the Powers' moral bankruptcy—which makes possible their rehabilitation, and so in turn the restoration of those individuals subordinated to them.

Jesus, who establishes this practice of redemption by accomplishing his mission on the cross.[20] Stemming from that, others too may come to share in this work. As John's Gospel puts it with disarming simplicity, "To all who received him, who believed in his name, he gave power to become children of God."[21] Jesus as the enfleshed Word of God confers *power to* become constituted as subjects of a particular kind, to receive a fundamental identity deriving from a redeemed system of power. God's children remain *in* "the world" but are no longer *of* "the world" since they are now people "made up" by a different field of power through living lives based on trust, *pistis*, in the story of Jesus rather than in the rival propaganda of the Powers.

If power is as much about constraint as it is about enabling then it's illuminating to consider what, according to the Gospels, Jesus can and cannot do. Most obviously he can perform deeds of power. Yet, though he can in this way save others, he cannot save himself.[22] Related to this is the crucial requirement for *pistis* on the part of others in order to enable Jesus's deeds of power. It's the *pistis* of the woman with a hemorrhage which saves her while, just a few verses later, the lack of *pistis* of Jesus's erstwhile neighbors means that "he could do no deed of power there."[23] This shows that Jesus is constituted as a miraculous healer not only by his relationship with his divine Father but also by the trust of those whom he serves. Indeed in the case of the woman with a hemorrhage it's the sufferer, rather than Jesus, that exercises agency by taking the initiative of touching his cloak; for his part Jesus is only aware, passively, that "power had gone forth from him." Again, he can foresee the fatal consequences of his last pilgrimage to Jerusalem, but knowledge of "the day or the hour" when the final redemption of the world will be accomplished is hidden from him.[24] And, poignantly, although by his words and actions he can draw an enthusiastic crowd and even recruit a team of effective apprentices, he cannot secure their understanding or their loyalty at the last.

20. John 19:30.

21. John 1:12.

22. Matt 27:42. Likewise his ability to turn water into wine at the wedding feast doesn't mean that he's in a position to open a liquor store.

23. Mark 5:24–34; 6:1–6; "except that he laid his hands on a few sick people and cured them," Mark 6:5. At the wedding in Cana it's his mother's *pistis* (and gentle prodding) which evokes Jesus's performance of the sign.

24. Mark 8:31; Mark 13:24–32.

We can conclude that Jesus's power, material and social, as depicted in the Gospels is extraordinary but limited—limited by virtue of the *kind* of power at his disposal, the nature of the field of relationships which makes him who he is. This is well illustrated in condensed form by Jesus's temptations in the wilderness at the very start of his public ministry. Having just been affirmed as God's beloved Son at his baptism Jesus is immediately propelled[25] by God's Spirit into the wilderness "to be tempted by the devil,"[26] where he goes without food for forty days.

Famished, the first temptation is to command stones to become loaves of bread. This would be a straightforward instance of material power, which Jesus eschews. Notably this contrasts with the later multiplication of loaves and fishes miracles in two respects. In the latter case Jesus is making more abundant what has been offered to him rather than arbitrarily changing the nature of something present at hand in order to suit his own desires. Also in the latter case, in line with the observation made at his crucifixion, Jesus acts for the benefit of others rather than himself.

Following Matthew's sequence of events, the second temptation involves throwing himself down from the pinnacle of the temple in order to oblige God to send angels to the rescue. Like the first temptation this is presented by the devil as a way of demonstrating, indeed exploiting, his recently affirmed identity: "If you are the Son of God then . . ." On the face of it this would simply be another instance of material power, that is, defying the law of gravity. But there's a sense in which the first dimension of social power is relevant here too, specifically the temptation to emotionally manipulate the actions of another—in this case Jesus's divine Father—in order to get that person to do something he otherwise would not have done. After all, God wouldn't want to see his Son get hurt, would he? This interpretation is confirmed by Jesus's riposte, "Do not put the Lord your God to the test," and reinforces the point that the field of power which makes Jesus who he is—Son of God—permits neither the satisfaction of arbitrary desire nor the pursuit of indulgent self-interest.

Finally the devil offers Jesus "all the kingdoms of the world and their glory." This time, instead of the earlier "if you are the Son of God" clause, the offer is made on the condition that Jesus worship the devil. This would amount to a complete change of identity for Jesus, as it would involve a change in his defining relationships and so a shift into a wholly

25. Mark 1:12.

26. Matt 4:1.

different field of power. Notably, in Luke, the devil bolsters his offer by pointing out that authority over earthly kingdoms "has been given over to me, and I give it to anyone I please."[27] Here we have an offer of social power par excellence, strikingly illustrating the conviction that de facto human power structures are, at some deep level, inclined away from their Creator. Jesus's response, "Worship the Lord your God, and serve only him," leaves the reader with the awkward question: can exercising political power ever be reconciled with giving God his due? Or, drawing again on Walter Wink, if the Powers are so deeply compromised in this way, how may they be redeemed?

Jesus's ministry of power, then, is integrally bookended by episodes of seeming powerlessness: starting in the wilderness and ending in Jerusalem with his unresisting arrest in the garden of Gethsemane. Yet it's precisely in this seeming powerlessness that Jesus exhibits and makes effective that field of power which makes him who he is, the beloved Son of God. How can this be? There's only one way to answer that question, and that is to tell the story of Jesus.

JESUS JOINS THE DOTS

One of the limited number of tales about Jesus which is common to all four Gospels concerns a particular deed of power: his feeding of a crowd of thousands by multiplying a few loaves and fishes.[28] John, being John, isn't content to leave it at that, and much of the remainder of John chapter 6 is taken up with a typical Johannine dialogue in which Jesus and his interlocutors talk past each other about the meaning of this deed. For our purposes the crux of the dialogue lies in the following exchange between Jesus and those members of the recently fed crowd who have chased after him along the coast of the Sea of Galilee to the town of Capernaum:

> When they found him on the other side of the lake, they said to him, "Rabbi, when did you come here?" Jesus answered them, "Very truly, I tell you, you are looking for me, not because you saw signs, but because you ate your fill of the loaves. Do not work for the food that perishes, but for the food that endures for eternal life, which the Son of Man will give you. For it is on him that God the Father has set his seal." Then they said to

27. Luke 4:6.

28. Matt 14:13–21; Mark 6:32–44; Luke 9:10–17; John 6:1–15. Matthew, Mark, and John immediately append a second deed of power—Jesus walking on the water.

> him, "What must we do to perform the works of God?" Jesus answered them, "This is the work of God, that you believe in him whom he has sent." So they said to him, "What sign are you going to give us then, so that we may see it and believe you? What work are you performing?"[29]

There are four key terms in this passage: work, or deed (*ergon*); belief, or trust (*pistis*); sign (*sēmeion*); and eternal life (*zōē aiōnios*). What's going on here, and throughout much of John's Gospel, is a debate about the character of the second articulation of the social assembling. Specifically, Jesus and his interlocutors differ over which form of expression should be applied to effect the incorporeal transformation from pragmatic system to semiotic system, from brute fact to meaningful action.

The incorporeal transformation which the crowd applies to the mass feeding event issues in physical nourishment as substance of expression, the "useful work" of maintaining the function of physical bodies. As Jesus puts it, "You are looking for me . . . because you ate your fill of the loaves." He counters this naive interpretation by applying a different transformation which generates a different outcome, or substance of expression. This is the authentic reading of the sign, *sēmeion*, of the feeding event. The form of expression required to produce this is the story of Jesus as the God-sent one; and to show trust, *pistis*, in Jesus is to subscribe to the truth of this story. Trusting like this is the only work, *ergon*, required of the crowd to enable the transformation of a mere brute fact into a particular, socially meaningful happening. And this happening is the substance of expression, the "useful work," performed by Jesus as author of the signs: the achieving of eternal life, *zōē aiōnios*, for those who believe.

<table>
<tr><th></th><th colspan="2">CONTENT
(pragmatic system)</th><th colspan="2">EXPRESSION
(semiotic system)</th></tr>
<tr><th></th><th>Substance</th><th>Form</th><th>Form</th><th>Substance</th></tr>
<tr><td>Crowd</td><td rowspan="2">Water, flour, salt</td><td rowspan="2">Bread recipe</td><td>Physical appetite[30]</td><td>Physical nourishment</td></tr>
<tr><td>Jesus</td><td>Trust in Jesus</td><td>Eternal life</td></tr>
</table>

Table 5: The sign of the loaves and fishes in John 6 as two different double articulations.

29. John 6:25–30.

30. Like trust in Jesus, physical appetite shows the three dimensions typical of forms of expression: cognitive (this is something to eat), affective (I feel hungry), and effective (I will pursue the person who produced it).

But what does trusting in Jesus actually involve? How can this trust function as a form of expression achieving this kind of transformation? We need to notice that, in the absence of direct personal revelation, we only know Jesus through the Gospel accounts which have been handed down. This is relevant because, as we saw in chapter 5, forms of expression in a social assembling commonly embody narrative accounts of life, stories which shape how we see the world, how we feel about it, and how we comport ourselves within it. So, in order for "trusting in Jesus" to operate as a form of expression, it has to involve the adoption of a story which, in turn, implies certain ways of acting.

It's at this point that René Girard's account of how Jesus saves becomes very relevant. We encountered Girard in chapter 1 via his theory of mimetic desire: my desires are "borrowed" from others and so risk becoming rivalrous and generative of social tension and violent conflict. Conflicts typically get resolved by the identification of scapegoats, individuals or minorities who get blamed for the trouble, and their expulsion or killing. Actually they are innocent, but according to the socially endorsed story they got what they deserved, the evil has been purged from our midst, and everything is now OK again. The social relief provided by this strategy must always prove temporary, however, since the pattern ends up getting repeated whenever new tensions arise, as they must, due to the underlying, unacknowledged dynamic of mimetic rivalry.

Except that this dynamic has now been exposed and paraded before the world in the Bible, and most definitively in the Gospels. Already in the Old Testament figures such as Abel, Joseph, Job, and various prophets are represented not as culprits who got their due comeuppance but, truthfully, as innocent victims. In this respect they are vindicated. The falsehood of the myth of redemptive violence is therefore already apparent here, Girard claims, but the execution and resurrection of Jesus universalize this, "drawing our attention to the pervasiveness of Passion-like murders that have taken place, and continue to do so, all over the world."[31]

> The Gospels *represent* this event as it is, in all its reality, and they make this reality, this truth, which human societies had never identified, available to all humanity. . . . The crucifixion of Jesus is a victim mechanism like all the others; it is set in motion and develops like all the others. Yet its outcome is different from all the others. Until the Resurrection no one could foresee the

31. Fleming, *René Girard*, 128.

> reversal of the violent contagion that almost completely overcame the disciples themselves. The princes of this world could rub their hands in satisfaction, and yet it turned out that their calculations were undone. Instead of conjuring away once more the secret of the single victim mechanism, the four accounts of the Passion broadcast it to the four corners of the world, publicizing it wherever they were read and proclaimed.[32]

What saves, then, is not the death of Jesus in itself as a bare biophysical event but the *story* of that death as recounted in the Gospels, its biblical representation. The Gospels provide a form of expression which overcodes the empirical event of one man's execution not as due punishment meted out by the Powers, the "princes of this world," as per their divine remit but rather as travesty of justice decisively displaying the failure of those Powers. The content provided by yet another crucifixion is taken over and put to work in a wholly different functional structure; the weft of this content gets woven around a wholly different warp, so producing a wholly different pattern. And it's by assimilating *this* incorporeal transformation, by accepting the truth of *this* story, by becoming part of *the Gospels'* semiotic system, that I am saved. This is what it means to put my trust in Jesus.

So it is that Jesus joins the dots represented by the killing of yet another outcast so as to produce a picture which means that we can never see the world in the same way again. More accurately, the story of Jesus as per the Gospels numbers the dots in a particular way and invites us to creatively complete the picture ourselves. The truth has been revealed: not only the truth of this historically unique event but the tragic truth about the default modus operandi of social assemblings in general; and, salvifically, the way to forestall the otherwise endless cycle of scapegoat elimination, which is to attend to our desires and the ends which they ultimately serve. As Jesus put it on that occasion in Capernaum: are we interested simply in eating our fill of loaves, or in the food that endures to eternal life?

FECUNDITY . . . OR ABUNDANT LIFE?

In chapter 2 we had occasion to touch on Charles Darwin's account of the evolution of organisms by natural selection. This, we noted, is the logical

32. Girard, *I See Satan Fall Like Lightning*, 141–42, 148–49, emphasis in original.

consequence of three axioms, these being the finitude of resources, the heritability of differences, and, most fundamentally, the fecundity principle: "All organic beings are striving to increase at a high ratio and to seize on every unoccupied or less well occupied place in the economy of nature," as Darwin put it.[33] Fecundity of some kind would seem to be central to Jesus's story too, inasmuch as he declared his mission to be about bringing life in all its abundance.[34] But how do these two goals—biological fecundity and abundant human life—relate to each other?

Let's recap. The striving implied by the fecundity principle is integral to the MPP which is itself an expression of the Law of Maximum Entropy Production (LMEP). According to the LMEP, systems select paths which dissipate energy (maximize entropy), or degrade potentials, at the fastest possible rates under the given conditions. It therefore favors the emergence of living things since, by their performance of useful work—staying alive and reproducing—they amplify the *overall* rates at which potentials get degraded, although they themselves are organized as zones of persistently high potentials. Importantly, the MPP is only one among several goals deriving from the LMEP which combine to govern the overall growth and development of biological systems. With the emergence of a new level of organization the expression of principles apparent at lower levels changes, becoming richer, more elaborate. Rather than see the universe as bent on maximizing some particular goal, therefore, we do better to think in terms of an *emergent optimality under constraints*. This raises the question of what happens to the expression of these principles when human beings appear on the scene. In terms of the vocabulary introduced in chapter 5, the question at this point is how principles operative in the inorganic and/or organic registers—such as the fecundity principle—play out in the specifically human cultural register.

Returning to Jesus's biography, superficially at least this would seem to run quite counter to the fecundity principle. Simply on a biological level, Jesus was a failure. He died at a relatively young age leaving no evidence of having produced physical offspring. He often spoke and acted recklessly, inviting a hostile, even lethal, response. He correctly anticipated that this would lead to his untimely demise yet still insisted on attending the Passover festival despite attendant risks, entering Jerusalem ostentatiously, and seriously disrupting the functioning of the temple. He

33. Darwin, *On the Origin of Species*, 98.

34. John 10:10.

then passively allowed himself to be arrested, making no attempt to escape or argue for his release. To the uninitiated he must have seemed to be harboring a death wish.

Culturally too his teaching shows what is at best an ambiguous attitude towards growth, prosperity, and, indeed, biological life itself. In the parable of the sower he seems resigned to the likelihood that much of the seed sown will bear no fruit, that is, that his ministry will have only limited impact. In the parables of the darnel and of the dragnet he seems resigned to a harvest or catch which is substantially compromised by weeds or is otherwise inedible, that is, a ministry which will produce at best only mixed results. Perhaps most strikingly, in the Sermon on the Mount Jesus urges his hearers *not* to strive after food, drink, and clothing, basic as these are for physical survival, let alone flourishing, so apparently setting himself squarely against Spinoza's basic *conatus*—the striving of living things to survive, grow, and reproduce—and the fecundity principle. Instead he teaches them to "seek first the Kingdom of God and its righteousness,"[35] whatever that may mean. Before setting off on his last journey to Jerusalem Jesus links this teaching to his own story: "If any want to become my followers, let them deny themselves and take up their cross and follow me. For those who want to save their life will lose it, and those who lose their life for my sake will find it."[36]

This seemingly ambiguous attitude towards life is resolved once we recognize that *what Jesus is doing is transposing biological fecundity—and so the MPP—into a different register, performing a particular incorporeal transformation on biological life as a pragmatic system.* Nowhere in the Gospels is Jesus's exposition of this transposed life more explicit than in John, where it's often distinguished as *eternal* life. How is this different from simple biological functioning? It's a particular *way* of living based on an experiential knowledge of the true source of life. As already mentioned this way of living is the substantial outcome of trusting in that source and in Jesus as the one sent to make that source known. And trusting, as we also saw above, is a matter of adopting a particular narrative—the story of Jesus—as the one by which one lives, the form of expression which transposes biological functioning into fully *human* living. It's by adopting this form of expression that humans are "put to work" in the specifically

35. Matt 6:33.

36. Matt 16:4–25.

human cultural register so as to express a fulfilled life. Without this trust, this particular form of expression, such a life remains out of reach.

One of the ways in which John brings out what is distinctive about the life-giving story of Jesus is through the distinction between flesh and spirit. Emphatically, "flesh" and "spirit" don't refer to two different substances. Rather they name two contrasting dispositions towards life. As Jesus explains to Nicodemus, in order to discern the kingdom of God we have to embark on a new kind of life, being "born again" of the spirit rather than the flesh which represents our default identity.[37] And towards the end of the dialogue following the feeding of the multitude Jesus declares that "it is the spirit that gives life; the flesh is useless. The words that I have spoken to you are spirit and life."[38] Again it's *words as performative utterance*, that is, a particular expressive overcoding of merely biological functioning, which make the difference.[39]

The first articulation on its own (or coded falsely) is indeed useless when it comes to properly human living; yet, equally, it remains the essential prerequisite for any second articulation. So in John, as in Paul, "flesh" doesn't always carry a negative connotation. Indeed it is dignified as the transposed medium of the divine Word;[40] and Jesus can even insist that only those who eat his flesh and drink his blood—that is, assimilate *his* story as the expressive overcoding of their human existence—can themselves aspire to the qualitatively new life which he offers.[41]

With that major caveat, we could say that the distinction between flesh and spirit boils down to this: by the notion of spirit John celebrates the genuinely new dimension of life opened up in the human cultural register following the advent of the emergent novelty of qualitative power—that is, power that can be classed ethically as better or worse rather than just as more or less. Against this, fleshly living involves either the overt rejection of this new dimension by the atavistic assertion of quantitative power in the form of brute force; or the perversion of this new dimension by the adoption of forms of expression which remain in thrall to the bare, quantitative criteria of the organic and inorganic registers—money.[42]

37. John 3:6.

38. John 6:63.

39. The well-known concept of performative utterance derives from Austin, *How to Do Things with Words*.

40. John 1:14.

41. John 6:53.

42. Interestingly it is John alone who mentions that Jesus's betrayer, Judas Iscariot,

All this has considerable implications for the way in which the MPP is expressed in the cultural register. As we have noticed, the MPP embodies the Darwinian principles of fecundity and resource finitude: all organisms strive for limitless expansion, which can only be checked by the limited nature of resources, especially when there is competition for them from other organisms. Life is imagined here as an agonistic struggle, in which periods of apparently harmonious ecological equilibrium only represent a temporary balance of power.[43] By contrast Jesus's eternal life, as a phenomenon of the second articulation, is characterized not by the quantitative measures of boundless spatial or temporal extension but rather as an infinitely rich *quality* of life. As the Gospels show, this doesn't mean the end of striving. Instead its character is changed, as exemplified in the life of abolitionist John Greenleaf Whittier; desire operates on a higher plane.[44] It's no longer a struggle for resources and territory—matters of material power—but rather for the souls, the embodied lives, of people—the domain of social power.

Transposed into the human cultural register according to the story of Jesus, the MPP changes its character. There can be no shortage of resources in this transposed state simply because there are no bounds to qualitative excellence, to the abundance of life epitomized in this particular story. Darwinian competition does not apply here. Instead the struggle is all about *whose story wins*—that of Jesus, or one of the fleshly variants (as John and Paul would put it) which at root are still operating according to quantitative, first articulation criteria.

This transposed struggle between flesh and spirit happens in both the social and the psychic spheres. The outward, social struggle is obvious enough in Jesus's ministry and those of his followers. They are in the business of living out the kingdom of God, which means inhabiting patterns of social relating at odds with the goals of maximizing quantitative power common to both brute force and money. The ensuing conflict reaches its apogee on the cross. In not compromising his mission even to

---

kept the common purse and, moreover, stole from it (John 12:6; 13:29).

43. Ecologist Robert E. Ulanowicz, who supplied the example of the bladderwort-algae-water flea ensemble used in an earlier chapter, discusses the coexistence of competition and cooperation in ecological systems in *Third Window*, esp. 57–90.

44. "Life is not fundamentally a striving for ends, for satisfactions, but rather for bases for further striving; . . . the true achievement is the refinement and elevation of the plane of desire, the cultivation of taste." Knight, *Selected Essays*, 43 (provided we do not read "taste" in a narrowly aesthetic sense), quoted in Goodchild, *Credit and Faith*, 179.

the point of violent death Jesus triumphs over the alternative systems of meaning ranged against him. His flesh, the stuff of the first articulation, is indeed killed, but his apprentices come to testify—an activity of the second articulation—to his vindication as risen Lord. This is no ghost; however we understand the resurrection, the risen Christ must of necessity be enfleshed, since there can be no second articulation without a first. By breathing his Spirit into his apprentices the risen Christ empowers them to continue his work, the embodying of his story, though this must mean continuing struggle as amply demonstrated in the book of Acts and the church's subsequent history.

The inner, psychic struggle is no less real. In the New Testament the most vivid description of this is in Paul's writings, not least the central chapters of his letter to the Romans. In chapter 7 Paul provides a rhetorical impersonation of an everyman character bemoaning the default human condition: knowing the right thing to do but being unable to actually do it; or, in Paul's words, to be "of the flesh, sold into slavery under sin."[45] But all is not lost. Happily God has achieved what unaided human effort and the most exacting ethical scruples could not: "The law of the Spirit of life in Christ Jesus has set me free from the law of sin and of death."[46]

As in John, flesh and spirit are used as binary opposites in chapters 7 and 8 of Romans to denote the difference Christ makes. And, as in John, life is associated with the spirit; indeed "to set the mind on the flesh is death, but to set the mind on the Spirit is life and peace."[47] What's at stake here is which one of two opposing patterns of life to adopt. This, Paul claims, depends on how one's mind is set, that is, how one cognitively and affectively regards the world and one's life in it. As with John it's a question of implementing the incorporeal transformation required to fashion a genuinely human life from its merely organic precursor. Fleshly transformations—the default—remain restricted by the characteristics of the inorganic and organic registers, including natural selection's fecundity principle. To fully make the jump into this new register, this new mode of being, requires the adoption of a particular story as form of expression. And this story has at its heart a violent death willingly accepted, the exact opposite of the fecundity principle's fixation on the perpetuation of my functioning, and that of my species, at all costs.

45. Rom 7:14; cf. Witherington, *Paul's Letter to the Romans*, 179–206.

46. Rom 8:2.

47. Rom 8:5–6.

According to Paul in Romans the default human condition is to be locked into this irresolvable inner struggle between fleshly and spiritual forms of expression. What breaks the impasse, what enables the full emergence of the human as new creation, is a form of expression cast in terms of a particular story. But, crucially, this isn't *just* a story. It's about something that happened in real life, "in the flesh," and therefore can feasibly be nonidentically repeated in my life and in yours. In that claim, and in its validation through actual repetition, lies its power. This is the power of the life-giving Spirit, that Other which breaks into my otherwise intractable inner conflicts and provides a way out.

Famously, nature is red in tooth and claw, the site of a struggle for resources rendered scarce if only by life's tendency to expand to the limits of possibility. Equally it's the site of cooperation, strategic alliances which serve mutually compatible ends, as we saw in chapter 3's example of the bladderwort-algae-water flea ensemble. But even here the underlying priority of expansion to the limits remains. The struggle for life is no less central to the story of Jesus, but here it's transposed into the second articulation of the social assembling both as the inner struggle to fully birth the human cultural register in oneself and as the outer struggle to establish this semiotic system, this pattern of meaningful coexistence, as a social ethos. With the advent of the human the struggle is in the end down to whose *story* wins.

This story is summed up succinctly by Paul in the renowned hymn to Christ found in chapter 2 of his Letter to the Philippians. That this may have been a preexisting hymn incorporated into the letter by Paul makes it all the more remarkable. As in Romans 8 what matters is my attitude of mind which needs to be shaped by the story of Jesus—a story which is all about power, the relinquishing of power, and the consequences of that relinquishing. Specifically, Jesus empties himself of the divine form and humbly adopts instead not just human likeness but the form of a slave, the ultimate human object of *power over*. The obedience which is the essence of that role is taken to its extreme in the ultimate humbling, indeed humiliation, of crucifixion. There, in the supreme plot-twist, Jesus acquires *power over* literally everyone and everything.

Not that this *power over* is expressed conventionally in overt ways; Jesus has not become a cosmic Caesar. This power is different *in kind* to what generally passes for social power, modeled as the latter is on its material precursor and so expressed as the *conatus* characteristic of nonhuman organic life. Jesus's *power over* is derived precisely from a transcending of such striving, and it consists in the ability to persuade, to evoke trust, *pistis*, in others.[48] The fellowship of those among whom such trust has been evoked is in turn inspired to narrate and embody the story of Jesus, Son of David, the one true Israelite and Son of Man, the one true human.

How odd that the story of a crucified outcast should prove so winning! And yet it continues to have an impact, for deep down something inside us recognizes the paradoxical truth of our human vocation beckoning us in that story: "Those who love their life lose it, and those who hate their life in this world will keep it for eternal life. Whoever serves me must follow me, and where I am, there will my servant be also."[49] In recognizing that truth, however incompletely, some of us are drawn to follow and identify with him, and so into fellowship with others likewise persuaded. We thereby acquire a particular collective *power to* by embodying the story of Jesus in the ever-new contexts in which we find ourselves. But how does this collective embodying differ from the human superorganisms which otherwise emerge among us by default? And how does its collective *power to* differ from the operation of the Powers which preside over these superorganisms?

THE BODY OF CHRIST VERSUS THE SUPERORGANISM

In the Sermon on the Mount Jesus, as we've already noted, urged his apprentices to "seek first the Kingdom of God and its righteousness." This agenda is placed in opposition to the default agenda of preoccupation with the basic requirements of physical survival—food, drink, and clothing. Take a lesson, says Jesus, from the birds of the air, which "neither sow nor reap nor gather into barns, and yet your heavenly Father feeds them"; and from the lilies of the field which, despite their indolence and lack of practical skills, are clothed more gloriously than was King Solomon himself. His rationale for such radical exhortations? "Life is more than food, and the body more than clothing."[50]

Read in the light of the ideas discussed here, Jesus is clearly distinguishing between the two articulations of the social assembling. Life, embodied human existence as a system of meanings, is *more than* the

48. As noted in chapter 5, *pistis* derives from *peithō*, "to persuade."

49. John 12:25–26; cf. Matt 16:24–25.

50. Matt 6:19–34.

product of the biophysical processes, the system of things, from which it emerges. But the critical reference to sowing, reaping, and the accumulation of surplus should ring another bell too. Jesus seems to be taking a swing here at ultrasociality as such, "the active harnessing of the inputs to food production and a reconfiguration of the group in order to do so," along with the "constitutional proclivity to expand" that goes with that.[51] When coupled with his itinerancy, Jesus's apparent admiration for a "natural" way of life detached from the mores of agrarian civilization is reminiscent of Cynic philosophers such as the colorful Diogenes. Whether or not we're persuaded by John Dominic Crossan's description of him as a Jewish Cynic sage, what we can't avoid is Jesus's opposition to the dynamics of the superorganism implied by his attitudes here and elsewhere.[52]

The Neolithic transition to agriculture, as we saw in chapter 4, set the stage for an all-out drive to accumulate storable surplus, stock which can be converted into flows of energy as and when, and at whatever rate, the emerging societal superorganism desires. This major evolutionary transition, as John Gowdy and Lisi Krall regard it, is celebrated by the rich man in Jesus's parable: his is a bumper harvest, so good that he has to build bigger barns to accommodate all the bounty. "My soul, you have ample goods laid up for many years; relax, eat, drink, be merry!" he declares to himself. These prove to be famous last words indeed. Very obviously, Jesus doesn't approve of "those who store up treasures for themselves but are not rich towards God."[53]

Being rich towards God: here again Jesus is effecting a particular, and characteristic, transposition into the second articulation. As in so many other places in his teaching he sets his face against the default overcoding which understands wealth in the essentially quantitative terms which typify the workings of the human superorganism. This becomes apparent at the very start of his public ministry, when he abandons his settled life as a woodworker with its (admittedly limited) scope for material accumulation to become a wandering prophet, healer, and teacher accumulating people instead. Jesus becomes dependent on the charity of others—the hospitality extended by villagers towards an itinerant holy

51. Gowdy and Krall, "Economic Origins of Ultrasociality," 3, 11.

52. Crossan, *Jesus: A Revolutionary Biography*.

53. Luke 12:13–21. This parable, unique to Luke, is placed immediately before his version of Jesus's teaching about prioritizing the pursuit of God's kingdom, which is better known in its setting as part of the Sermon on the Mount in Matthew.

man and his entourage, along with the resources of wealthy female members of the entourage who had themselves benefited from his ministry.[54]

And Jesus's entourage, the social movement activated by his ministry, contrasts markedly with the organization typical of the superorganism. True, he selects twelve among his apprentices as his inner circle, but apart from the apparent designation of Judas Iscariot as group treasurer there's no demarcation of roles or ranks among them. Jesus was, after all, a tradesman, so it would only be natural for him to treat his followers as a bunch of apprentices rather than as a militia or a bureaucratic cadre. Simon Peter's frequent role in the Gospels as the apprentices' spokesman surely stems from his personality, a spontaneous bottom-up phenomenon rather than a designated office. Jesus's teaching in the Synoptic Gospels shows little concern for establishing practical group norms or procedures among his growing movement; he's a storyteller rather than a manager, seemingly concerned to spark the imagination rather than stipulate regulations.[55]

The subject of much of his storytelling is the new social order he called the kingdom of God. We'd search his parables in vain for any trace of a political or economic blueprint however. The kingdom is painted in varied, allusive tones: a pearl of great price; a mustard seed; a dragnet; the yeast which leavens the loaf. *As forms of expression Jesus's teachings remain inchoate*, gesturing at ways in which the kingdom might come about rather than proposing anything resembling an a priori social structure or program. Rather, Jesus's method seems to be to allow the kingdom as semiotic system to emerge organically through the group process of traveling together with him, subject to his ad hoc correction where necessary.[56] For this kingdom is different in kind to fleshly kingdoms, which are defined by their top-down arrogation of the right to the exclusive use of legitimate violence. There is no hint of Lewis Mumford's megamachine here. This, more than anything, distinguishes Jesus's mission from that of his Zealot contemporaries: the fullness of the kingdom of God, on his telling, remains irreducibly eschatological, the abiding horizon which beckons us ever on.[57]

54. Luke 8:1–3.

55. A notable exception to this general rule is Matt 18:15–17.

56. E.g., Mark 9:33–37; 10:13–16, 35–45.

57. The eschatological perspective in Jesus's teaching and practice is stressed, albeit rather differently, by both N. T. Wright and Dale Allison. Whereas Allison thinks that Jesus was in the end mistaken in his expectation of an imminent *eschaton*, my reading

We can go further. Jesus's ministry, his story as told in the Gospels, and the social outworking of this in the common life of the Christian community all suggest a way of living together which is at odds with the ultrasocial dynamic which has increasingly become the human default since the Neolithic revolution. In various ways the body of Christ is set against the superorganism. How so?

First and foremost the body of Christ is made known on the cross. It's the broken body of the Galilean woodworker Jesus. This isn't incidental to what the body of Christ is; it is of its essence. As broken, this body—on the face of it—can do no useful work. The essence of the superorganism, in stark contrast, like any substance of expression, is that it does do useful work, the use in this case being the maximization of wattage, the rate at which work is done. Yet, viewed with *pistis*, trust or faith, the lifting up of Christ's broken body on the cross is his greatest work, the accomplishment of the ultimate sign which extends across time to include the broken body's resurrection on the third day.[58] The useful work accomplished by Christ's broken body is the revealing of the full emergence of the human in the cultural register, qualitatively new creation, spiritual rather than fleshly expression of the MPP. And not only a revealing but also an empowering, the in-spiration of others to share in this work.[59]

The body of Christ made known on the cross, broken and risen, thus gives rise to the church as the body of Christ, "the fullness of him who fills all in all."[60] This is the social outcome of the work accomplished on the cross, its substance of expression, which becomes in turn substance of content for the work of the Spirit accompanying the retelling of the story of Jesus. But this work is, and must remain, ongoing, awaiting eschatological fulfillment. In this way the church, so long as it remains the body of Christ, resists the stratifying dynamics of the superorganism. Paul's otherwise rather puzzling contention about creation's subjection to futility by God is cast in a new light when viewed in terms of assemblage thinking:

---

here is guided more by Wright's discernment of an "already—not yet" tension in Jesus's proclamation of God's kingdom. See Allison, *Jesus of Nazareth*; Wright, *Jesus and the Victory of God*.

58. John 2:18–22; 3:14–15; 8:28; 19:30.

59. John 20:21–23.

60. Eph 1:23.

> I consider that the sufferings of this present time are not worth comparing with the glory about to be revealed to us. For the creation waits with eager longing for the revealing of the children of God; for the creation was subjected to futility, not of its own will but by the will of the one who subjected it, in hope that the creation itself will be set free from its bondage to decay and will obtain the freedom of the glory of the children of God.[61]

"Futility" is a translation of *mataiotēs*, which could equally be rendered as "purposelessness," "ineffectiveness," or "uselessness." Recall that the project of the human superorganism is the fleshly performance of the MPP, which makes use of both nonhuman and human by yoking them together in order to do work at the fastest rate. Yet creation frustrates attempts to straitjacket it in this way, reduced to and locked into a particular functional structure. It overflows and undermines any and all organized forms, not least those associated with human projects which treat its human and nonhuman components as cogs in a machine. In this sense it must always retain that residual "uselessness" which is its divinely ordained condition. The true consummation of creation lies rather with "the revealing of the children of God," the *social* emergence of the fully human as prefigured and enabled by the life, killing, and resurrection of Jesus. It's only by the emergence of a social, indeed an ecosocial, whole which transcends the ultrasocial dynamics of the superorganism that the inevitable decay of created things, as reduced to mere machines serving fleshly human purposes, may be superseded and the boundless creativity of God fully brought forth.[62]

It isn't a coincidence that Jesus accomplished his work abandoned and alone, wholly disconnected from the collective *power to* which has been so fundamental to the rise of the human species. This isn't to champion an asocial heroism, but to highlight how the social outcome of his accomplishment, the church, resists operating like a superorganism. In this sense it remains the *broken* body of Christ. In Romans Paul goes on to describe how each member of the Christian community functions as part of a body, but he immediately subverts the superorganismic tendency of this arrangement by stating that "individually we are members

61. Rom 8:18–21.

62. As noted in chapter 4 machines, unlike living things, are not self-organizing, self-healing, and self-reproducing, and so are of themselves doomed to decay. See De Bari et al., "Thermodynamics, Organisms and Behaviour."

one of another."[63] In other words this is no impersonal collective whole, subordinating its individual parts. Instead *the functions exercised by each part remain in the service of each of the others, not of the emergent entity arising from their combined efforts*. In the words of one commentator, this is a "description of the political existence of the body of Christ that is as intriguing as it is radical."[64] What this means in practice remains for the church to explore, but in any event it amounts to a real social whole different in kind to the superorganism: a truly remarkable claim.

Once again it's the form of expression provided by the gospel which makes this possible. Assimilating the story of Jesus leads to a renewed mind, an incorporeal transformation of how one cognitively and affectively grasps the world and one's life in it: "Do not be conformed to this world, but be transformed by the renewing of your minds, so that you may discern what is the will of God—what is good and acceptable and perfect."[65] The social results of this transformation are further spelled out by Paul in his First Letter to the Corinthians. In Christ the functional hierarchy inherent in any complex system does *not* entail a corresponding hierarchy of rank or esteem; to the contrary, minor members of the body are deemed indispensable. Actually the church more resembles a heterarchy in some respects, inasmuch as different members may take the lead at different times according to gifting and role.[66] And certainly there is no sense in which some may be regarded as expendable for the sake of others or of the whole: the suffering of one is the suffering of all.[67] The contrast with the workings of the superorganism is stark. As Selin Kesebir notes, warfare "represents the pinnacle of human superorganismic potential" and, for Lewis Mumford, the army provides the paradigm for the megamachine. In war hierarchy of rank is essential, and those unwilling to obey orders by sacrificing themselves for the cause are condemned as cowards or traitors. Not so in the body of Christ, whose

63. *Hen sōma esmen en Christō to de kath heis allēlōn melē*, Rom 12:5; cf. Eph 4:25. See Wannenwetsch, "Members of One Another."

64. Wannenwetsch, "Members of One Another," 210.

65. Rom 12:2. Cf. Rom 8:5–8; Phil 2:3–11.

66. As discussed in chapter 3, heterarchy names "the relation of elements to one another when they are unranked, or when they possess the potential for being ranked in a number of different ways, depending on systemic requirements." Crumley, "Heterarchy," 2.

67. 1 Cor 12:14–26.

mission was precisely to end hostility, bring peace, and "create in himself one new humanity."[68]

Correspondingly, greatness too undergoes an incorporeal transformation at the hands of the gospel. As we saw in chapters 3 and 5 autocatakinesis, as a biophysical phenomenon, involves the increased scale of flows in both space and time: the convection cell is bigger and longer lasting than the energized molecule; likewise the ecosystem atop the panarchy operates at spatial and temporal scales greater than those of its constituent systems and organisms. The transformation of potentials by the gospel also entails enhancement but, this being an *incorporeal* transformation, it need not involve physical expansion.[69] Rather, as Jesus patiently pointed out to his squabbling apprentices, "You know that the rulers of the Gentiles lord it over them, and their great ones are tyrants over them . . . but whoever wishes to be great among you must be your servant."[70] Transformed by the gospel, greatness ceases to be a matter of physical size and duration in the same way that social power is no longer a matter of material power and money deployed to secure compliance with my wishes. Again, it's the change in the qualitative character of relationships which makes the church as the body of Christ the firstfruits of an emergent new humanity: the gospel codes a particular set of qualities which are wholly unshackled from quantitative first articulation criteria.

Neither should we think that the social reordering brought about by Jesus is relevant only to large-scale agrarian and industrial superorganisms, as it extends also to the most basic unit of the family: "Whoever does the will of God is my brother and sister and mother."[71] Anyone familiar with the stories of Jacob and Esau, and of Joseph and his brothers, should be wary of idealizing social arrangements simply on the basis of scale. Small isn't always beautiful. Rather than a nostalgic return to some imagined pre-Neolithic paradise, what's at stake is nothing less than the full emergence of the human; and the vision underpinning this project is rehearsed and renewed by members of the social body of Christ every

68. Eph 2:15.

69. As we saw in chapter 3 this already applies to emergent material phenomena: chemical compounds and biological organisms are not inherently larger in scale than physical processes.

70. Matt 20:25–26.

71. Mark 3:31–35.

time they gather to break bread, the Lord's body, and to share the cup, the new covenant, or form of expression, in his blood.[72]

Jesus's aim, then, was not to eliminate or replace the existing Powers. Rather, through the struggle consummated in the victory of the cross, the Powers have been defeated in that the hollowness of their pretensions has been laid bare for all to see.[73] They're not absolute after all. The stratified stranglehold of the superorganism on its members, of the megamachine on its components, has been broken and the seed of a new form of life *alongside* one another sown. While hierarchical social structures of some kind remain, so will the Powers; not supplanted but, by the power of the cross, redeemed, restored to their ordained function as subordinate mediators of God's kingdom rule.[74] The means by which such redemption, as continuing project, occurs is the social body of Christ—as it testifies by deed and word to the gospel of Jesus, that is, God's wisdom in action.[75]

Jesus has shown how the worst the Powers can do to you—kill you—is not enough to silence the life-giving Word of God. Trust in this claim liberates from the fear of death, and therefore robs the Powers of their ultimate sanction.[76] Such is the victory of the cross: "They have triumphed over him by the blood of the Lamb and by the word of their testimony, for they did not cling to life even in the face of death."[77] Obviously this runs directly counter to the fecundity principle, which is all about the urge to survive and expand to the limits. The merely fleshly expressive overcoding of this principle is, as we've seen in earlier chapters, avarice, the endless accumulation of surplus in the form of money—trust quantified and hoarded so as to give the semblance of endless life. The fallen Powers' power, expressed as brute force and money in service of endless expansion, is inherently fleshly. Against this Jesus overcodes fecundity as *qualitatively* eternal life, which renders the surplus accumulation of anything pointless. What makes this expressive shift possible is, again, *pistis*: trust that my heavenly Father knows my need for food, drink, and

72. 1 Cor 11:23–26. This isn't to argue that a drastic reduction in scale of the current human enterprise, as per Bill Rees's recommendation, is not desirable.

73. Col 2:15.

74. Phil 2:9–11; 1 Pet 3:21–22.

75. Eph 3:10.

76. "I tell you, my friends, do not fear those who kill the body, and after that can do nothing more. But I will warn you whom to fear: fear him who, after he has killed, has authority to cast into hell." Luke 12:4–5. Cf. Matt 10:28; Heb 2:14–16.

77. Rev 12:11.

clothing; or, more directly, trust in the story of Jesus as that which makes known the character of both God and true humanity.

This teaching is of a piece with Jesus's larger message in chapter 6 of Matthew's Gospel. When we pray we should pray for our *daily* bread, that is, enough to meet the day's needs—and no more. Storing treasure of any kind on earth is not the way of God's kingdom, since it shows that we wrongly understand plenty as *more* rather than *better*. Trust in the God revealed in Jesus and the trust embodied in mammon are wholly different in kind. The latter can be accumulated; the former cannot, and we have to make a choice, a choice about which field of power shall constitute who we are, how we shall be embodied. Serving the superorganism, the megamachine, the Powers traps us as parts of a body ultimately doomed to die. Serving God releases us to become "members one of another" and so discover a new, otherwise unknown, quality of life. The choice, insofar as we're free to make it, is ours.

SUMMING UP

Jesus and power: it's complicated. The Synoptic Gospels present us with something of a power/powerlessness sandwich when it comes to Jesus's life. As the filling of the sandwich we have his active ministry, in which "deeds of power" are central. He exercises material power over bodies, human and nonhuman, and so comes to exercise social power too, not least over those whom he calls to abandon their livelihoods and become his apprentices. Not that power is his in some isolated, exclusive sense; his power to change the world is a collective power, on the one hand dependent on the Spirit sent by his heavenly Father and, on the other, reliant on the trust of those over whom power is exercised. These two features are fundamental to the *kind* of power he deployed and indeed to who and what he was—his very identity.

Encasing this filling, and providing essential context, are two episodes of seeming powerlessness in which, rather than doing, he is done unto. At the start, forty days in the wilderness during which he resists the devil, the spirit of the Domination System comprising the fallen Powers, as Walter Wink puts it. And at the end, uncoerced surrender to agents of the same Powers. Counterintuitively, it's in this seeming powerlessness that lies the victory of the cross.

But this victory is only apparent when the story of his execution is told right, that is, according to the Gospels. What makes the story of Jesus good news at all is the way meaning is given to bare physical events. John's Gospel is upfront about this: Jesus's "mighty works" are signs, and the Gospels provide the framework for understanding them. It's their particular incorporeal transformation of the bare events of Jesus's biography that saves. Even the reappearance of Jesus after his crucifixion requires this framing, otherwise we're left with nothing more than a historical oddity—a botched execution perhaps or (who knows?) some high-level conspiracy to spare Jesus—but not the resurrection: for that we need the gospel.

Jesus's power, as presented in the Gospels, is not least the power to conceive and present human life in a particular kind of way. John again gets to the heart of the matter: being fully human means transcending biological survival in order to enter eternal life. Biological fecundity is transposed into qualitatively abundant life. This is what it means to live according to the Spirit. To live according to the flesh, on the other hand, is to remain semi-human, still trapped among quantitative first articulation categories which express the MPP according to the dismal doctrine that might is right.

Life according to the flesh is life trapped within the prevailing default world order, dominated by fallen Powers, who know no better than to blindly reproduce the competitive dynamics of the social assembling's first articulation. This gives rise to ultrasociality, the snatching and hoarding of resources so as to gain competitive advantage and expand indefinitely at others' expense. Jesus sets himself against this dynamic. Belonging to the kingdom he preaches, rather than to the Domination System, means eschewing accumulation and instead relying on God to provide one's daily bread. And the community he founds is called to continue embodying this message. Even as it grows in size and organization, the social body of Christ is coded by the gospel to resist the emergent dynamics of the superorganism. Its individual human parts are members not of any impersonal whole but of one another, such that their roles get structured for gracious mutual service rather than hierarchical slavery.

But what is the secret of resisting these stifling social dynamics? What are the traits of a Christian overcoding of power, and so of the MPP? And what does it mean to mediate power wisely, to exercise practical wisdom, at a point in history when human ingenuity seems to have brought us to the edge of doom? Answering questions like these will be the goal of the final chapter.

7

Maximum Power Revisited: Of Wattage and Wisdom

Arren wondered at this power which his companion now used so lightly, and once he said, "When we began our voyage you used to work no charms."

"The first lesson on Roke, and the last, is *Do what is needful*. And no more!"

"The lessons in between, then, must consist in learning what is needful."

"They do."[1]

Ged—or Sparrowhawk, to give him his use-name—has changed a lot since the reader first met him as a young lad. He is older and considerably wiser. In his younger days he used his powers recklessly, releasing an evil, a Shadow into the world. He hunted it down in the end, but the whole business was costly for him, and it left its mark. Now, years later, he is Archmage of Roke, the fabled Isle of the Wise, and perforce embarked on another quest, this time in the company of Arren, a young acolyte.

Ursula Le Guin's *Earthsea* cycle of fantasy novels has brought delight to generations of readers, young and old alike. Among their central themes are the nature of power, what it means to mediate power well, and so what it means to be a man or a woman (or indeed a dragon). The above extract, from the third book in the series, conveys the core message about power and wisdom which appears time and again in different guises: *Do only what is needful*. If only Eve and Adam had heeded this advice! As we noticed in the introduction, the fall of humanity is all tied up with

1. Le Guin, *Farthest Shore*, 147, emphasis in original.

failing to bind ethically what we can do but should not. Learning where the boundary of *should* lies, what is actually needful and no more, is a plausible definition of wisdom; and, you could argue, what the human quest is all about.

Power and wisdom, and the relationship between them, have been implicit in much of the news over the months I've been writing these chapters. This is because of the issues raised by artificial intelligence (AI) which, out of nowhere seemingly, has sprung into almost daily media prominence and settled mainstream use. There are two opposing storylines about AI: one is that it will save the world, the other that it will destroy the world—possibly very soon.

This is obviously a very big deal, though examining those possibilities here would take us too far off our present course. More relevant are the reflections concerning AI offered by Daniel Schmachtenberger, a founding member of the Consilience Project, in a series of online interviews, since central to his argument is the distinction between intelligence and wisdom.[2] AI is intelligent only according to one possible—pragmatic—definition of intelligence, namely as the ability to achieve goals.[3] Thus far these goals have been in particular fields such as playing chess, synthesizing data, or chatting to human beings. With billions of dollars being invested in it the goal of artificial *general* intelligence may be upon us sooner than we might think—or wish.

Wisdom, according to Schmachtenberger's definition, is quite different. If intelligence is the ability to achieve certain specific, *narrow-boundary* goals then wisdom is the ability to choose good, *wide-boundary* goals; wisdom "considers how our success in achieving our goals might affect the wider world, and how it might affect us in ways we hadn't imagined. . . . It tends to practice restraint, which is important, because sometimes the things we want in the near-term are meaningfully detrimental to our longer-term goals or underlying values."[4] For example, in Eden Eve and Adam achieved the narrow-boundary goal of sampling a new fruit at the cost of spectacularly failing to achieve the wide-boundary goal of remaining in paradise. What was needful for them to remain in Eden had

2. See the following interviews with Daniel Schmachtenberger from Nate Hagens's *Great Simplification* podcast series: "Artificial Intelligence and the Superorganism"; "From Naive to Authentic Progress"; "Silicon Dreams and Carbon Nightmares."

3. A range of definitions is provided and briefly discussed by Legg, "Definitions of Intelligence."

4. The Consilience Project, "Development in Progress."

already been made plain, but fixation on a particular narrow-boundary goal served to cast the required restraint to the wind.

This discussion should ring several bells with anyone who has read the preceding chapters. Most obviously the definition of intelligence as the ability to achieve goals resonates with some of the definitions of social power featured in chapter 1, such as "getting what one wants" and "the capacity to get others to do things that otherwise they would not do." The exercise of intelligence, like the exercise of power, should obviously be in the service of human interests, best understood as well-being or flourishing in the fullest sense. But in what does this flourishing consist? Simple biological fecundity? Or something else which some, as per chapter 6, would call abundant life?

Though wisdom has only made cameo appearances in previous chapters, restraint, with which Schmachtenberger associates it, should be more familiar. I'm *restrained* from eating this ice cream by the *constraints* of my self-imposed diet: that is, specific restraints always occur within a more general framework of constraint.[5] And constraint goes hand in hand with power, as we've had occasion to observe more than once. Inhabiting, operating within, a particular field of social power entails observing a pattern of constraint, much as does the generation of autocatakinetic structures through the transformation of potentials. Interestingly, in the course of his interviews Schmachtenberger cites the institution of Sabbath as an example of wise restraint, so echoing Lewis Mumford's reference to Sabbath as a strategy of resistance to the otherwise all-consuming predations of the megamachine. In thinking about power, not least given the advent of AI, it seems that wisdom is long overdue attention.

WISDOM AS CHOKMAH AND SOPHIA

Chokmah, conventionally translated as "wisdom," and its related adjective appear around three hundred times in the Hebrew Scriptures of the Christian Old Testament. Most of these appear in the three core examples of biblical wisdom literature, the books of Proverbs, Job, and Ecclesiastes. We came across one such reference at the start of chapter 4: "Go to the ant, O sluggard; consider her ways, and be wise."[6] This illustrates the first

5. *The Britannica Dictionary*, "Constrain and Restrain."

6. Prov 6:6.

sense of *chokmah*, namely having skills in, or aptitudes towards, certain activities. Even animals can be wise in this respect.[7] Among humans, the house builder and the sailor, for example, are wise to the degree that they are skillful in, "good at," performing their respective tasks.[8] These tasks need not be purely practical as they also include what these days would come under the heading of administration, that is, the skills expected of scribes and advisors staffing the bureaucracy of the royal court.[9]

While wisdom may refer in this way to particular skills the majority of references have to do with the more general, if not universal, trait which we might fairly translate as "common sense." There's nothing at all highfalutin about this; it's just the knowledge or all-round savvy which everyone accumulates in some measure as they go though life, becoming in the process gradually older and wiser. Wisdom as common sense can be expressed in a more specific way as native wit, shrewdness, or cunning even. The fabled wisdom of King Solomon is surely the epitome here, demonstrating as it does the ability to achieve a good outcome based on a deep understanding of what makes people tick.[10] This is likely the sense intended by Jesus too when he advised his disciples, as he sent them out "as sheep into the midst of wolves," to be "wise as serpents and innocent as doves."[11]

Wisdom, then, is very much a practical skill which can be acquired and nurtured via both general experience and attention to those already wise.[12] But mention of Solomon shows that it's equally something which may be bestowed on some by God as a special grace.[13] And in all cases "the fear of the LORD is the beginning of wisdom" since God, preeminently, is wise.[14] As a divine trait, God's wisdom is even personified in the book of Proverbs and other, later, works in ways that prefigure some New Testament accounts of Christ's work and origin. In particular, God's

7. E.g., Prov 30:24–28.

8. Prov 24:3; Ps 107:27.

9. See, e.g., Jer 18:18, "Come, let us make plots against Jeremiah—for instruction shall not perish from the priest, nor counsel from the wise, nor the word from the prophet."

10. Most famously, Solomon's shrewdness is shown in how he deals with the two prostitutes, both of whom claim to be the mother of the same child (1 Kgs 3:16–28).

11. Matt 10:16.

12. Hunter, *Wisdom Literature*, 20.

13. 1 Kgs 4:29.

14. Prov 9:10.

wisdom is associated with the work of creation: "The Lord created me at the beginning of his work, the first of his acts of long ago. . . . When he established the heavens, I was there. . . . I was beside him, like a master worker; and I was daily his delight, rejoicing before him always, rejoicing in his inhabited world and delighting in the human race."[15]

At its most profound human wisdom is a matter of knowing and serving God. Yet there is competition for our attention and service. As we noted in chapter 5, Jesus taught that God and mammon represent mutually exclusive objects of worship. While not positing an opposition as such, the Old Testament's wisdom literature is clear about the radical superiority of wisdom to material wealth (wisdom is "more precious than jewels, and nothing you desire can compare with her") and about what economists would term their nonfungibility ("Where shall wisdom be found? . . . It cannot be bought for gold, and silver cannot be weighed out as its price").[16] Wisdom trumps material wealth not because it is quantitatively greater but because it is qualitatively superior. This is down to its role in the knowledge and service of God, occupations in which wealth need not play any part.

Commentator Norman Whybray notes the marked contrast between Hebrew wisdom as pious living and the meaning of the related Babylonian term as skill in religious ritual and magical knowledge.[17] Recalling Daniel Schmachtenberger's distinction between the intelligence required to achieve particular, narrow-boundary goals and the wisdom associated with the wide-boundary goal of living a good life, we can see a clear parallel here. Hebrew wisdom, as divine common sense, is a very different animal to competence in any manipulative technique, any protocol exclusively concerned with achieving my own narrow goals—whatever they might be. Equally, it's a much more positive quality than the restriction-based notion described by Schmachtenberger. This is because he starts from particular goals which then stand in need of mutual qualification rather than with a more holistic primary vision of godly living then translated into particular actions by the exercise of wisdom; a wisdom, moreover, which is both fostered by experience and gifted by the God who its ultimate source.

15. Prov 8. Equally, wisdom may also be associated with destruction, e.g., Job 12:13–25.

16. Prov 3:13–15; Job 28:15–16.

17. Whybray, *Wisdom*, 6–9.

Turning to the Gospels we find references to wisdom, *sophia*, in relatively short supply. All but one are to be found in Matthew and Luke, with the large majority being in the former. We've already noted Jesus's commending serpentine wisdom to his disciples, that is, the importance of being canny in dealings with lupine people. Wisdom also features in some of the parables. To attend to Jesus's teaching and put it into practice is to build one's house on rock rather than sand, and therein lies wisdom. To be prepared for the sudden, God-induced disruption of the status quo is to faithfully discharge one's responsibilities as God's steward, and therein also lies wisdom, as it does in prudently preparing for the delayed arrival of the divine bridegroom.[18] Two other references introduce a theme which Paul takes up to notable effect: the conjoining of Jesus's wisdom with his *dunameis*, "deeds of power," as causes of astonishment among his erstwhile neighbors in Nazareth; and the obscurity of the ways of God's kingdom to those normally deemed wise and learned.[19]

In turning to Paul, his handling of the wisdom theme in 1 Corinthians is typically polemical and should be seen in the context of its more conventional use in many of those other New Testament writings which bear his name. In Colossians and Ephesians wisdom carries hallmarks familiar to the reader of the Hebrew Scriptures, chiefly through association with God and God's activity in human history. But even here there's an awareness that *human* wisdom can mislead and, indeed, act in opposition to that of God, the latter now described as secret and hidden by contrast with its more familiar human counterpart.[20] This sets the scene for Paul's intervention in Corinth:

> For the message about the cross is foolishness to those who are perishing, but to us who are being saved it is the power of God. For it is written, "I will destroy the wisdom of the wise, and the discernment of the discerning I will thwart." Where is the one who is wise? Where is the scribe? Where is the debater of this age? Has not God made foolish the wisdom of the world? For since, in the wisdom of God, the world did not know God through wisdom, God decided, through the foolishness of our proclamation, to save those who believe. For Jews demand signs and Greeks desire wisdom, but we proclaim Christ crucified, a stumbling-block to Jews and foolishness to Gentiles, but to those

18. Matt 7:24–27; 24:45–51; 25:1–13.

19. Matt 13:54; 11:25–26.

20. 1 Cor 2:7. Compare the uses of the term "wisdom" in Eph 3:10 and Col 2:23.

> who are the called, both Jews and Greeks, Christ the power of God and the wisdom of God.[21]

Paul's treatment of wisdom here is shaped by a context of sectarian divisions in the local church. Social power was at the heart of the issue in Corinth, and Paul is determined to challenge the false views of power and wisdom undermining the unity of the Christian community. Not that power and wisdom represented two separate phenomena; rather, human wisdom, expressed as rhetorical prowess, was actually the prevailing mode by which social power was being used to destructive effect.[22] Paul's argument is with "eloquent wisdom," the gift of the gab, not with *chokmah*, the divinely sourced wisdom celebrated in the Hebrew Scriptures. This, primarily, would seem to have been the "wisdom" wrongly esteemed by the Greeks, and we need to be clear on this point. The Jews too were mistaken, but this was in demanding to see *sēmeia*, signs of material power, rather than in any anachronistic attachment to *chokmah* as a central part of their tradition. Of course, as we saw in chapter 6, this was precisely the error spotted by John, albeit that he unpacks the underlying error in a more nuanced way as the *misinterpretation* of signs in merely material terms.

In contrast to these misconceptions and misrepresentations, Paul insists that "we proclaim Christ crucified." Not only does the Christian message not depend on rhetorical accomplishment in order to be effective, the story it tells appears to be one of utter powerlessness, social and material. Both Greeks and Jews have to adjust their expectations. For *this* is how God's wisdom and God's power really are. Judged according to either classical rhetorical and philosophical standards or pure wattage, such wisdom and power must indeed remain hidden from, and incomprehensible to, the "rulers of this age." And yet it is this message alone, what in chapter 5 we learned to call this form of expression, which has the power to elicit true trust, *pistis*, in what God has accomplished in Jesus. It is this which persuades, not the conceptual sophistication or the flowing cadences of the orator.

On this basis we can conclude that, whatever else it may be about, wisdom is the skill of being able to discern who and what to trust. Wisdom originates in trusting God, the "fear of the LORD," a primary attitude towards life deriving from trust in the biblical story of God's

21. 1 Cor 1:18–24.

22. Keener, *1–2 Corinthians*, 27–29.

creative and saving works. This is the ultimate wide-boundary goal, in Schmachtenberger's terms, which serves to condition all others. Human wisdom is only authentic to the degree that it mediates God's wisdom in the creation and providential ordering of the world. It's expressed as skills in particular activities made meaningful by the horizon of a common sense which deals, as it must, with the business of living alongside others. Wisdom, in other words, is intrinsically social. And wisdom as common sense, though acquired through experience and learning from the wise, is in the end God's gift to humans, something made possible through having been created in God's image and likeness.

But that likeness has become sullied. What passes for human wisdom may too often mislead. It may only act as a disguise for the folly of personal or sectional ambition. Rather than straightforwardly mediate the wisdom of God, it may only serve to distort it—the characteristic flaw of the Powers. Particular narrow-boundary goals may dominate the ultimate wide-boundary goal of Godly living. So wisdom, for those who would live fearing the LORD, becomes a matter of skill in knowing what and whom to trust. Superficial plausibility, whether based on rhetorical style, conventional correctness, a glossy image, or apparent utility is not enough. God's wisdom and power can only be validly known henceforth through the lens of Christ crucified. As we saw in the previous chapter, the story of Christ crucified concerns how wisdom and power typically function—or, rather, malfunction—in human societies, and how that malfunction can be remedied.

That remedy involves exposing the failure of the Powers by persisting in public witness to the truth regardless of sanctions brought to bear by those Powers. In practice this must mean a readiness to disengage, at least in certain respects, from the superorganism over which the Powers preside. And disengagement from the superorganism will result of necessity in a corresponding loss of social power, that is, *power to*. Where does that leave us? What kind of agency, if any, remains for those wishing to live wisely as those fearing the LORD and walking the way of the cross?

LIVING OUT OF CONTROL: THE WISDOM OF DISCIPLESHIP

We all want to make a difference by our actions, if only with regard to our own lives. In other words we all want to exercise agency, in the commonly understood sense of exerting power so as to produce a desired effect. To lack agency, it would seem, is to become the mere plaything of others' agency and of chance events. But we saw as long ago as chapter 1 that exerting power in a social setting is never a simple matter of getting what I happen to want. Inevitably, the exercise of social power involves operating under certain constraints, radically so for those of us caught up in the workings of an ultrasocial superorganism: "We are not suggesting that there is no human agency but we are suggesting that the role of human agency is much less powerful than we think."[23]

It would therefore seem that there's more to agency than a conventional definition might suggest, which is why the perspective offered by Christian ethicist Stanley Hauerwas is so helpful.

Far from being simply the capacity to produce an effect, Hauerwas defines agency very differently as "our ability to inhabit our character."[24] To be an agent is to develop a skill, specifically the skill of owning events as parts of my story regardless of whether or not they happened because I wanted them to happen. It's a matter of being able to *describe*: "My act is not something I cause, as though it were external to me, but it is mine because I am able to 'fit' it into my ongoing story."[25] This may seem a puzzling claim if we recall some of the definitions of power encountered in chapter 1, that is, those proceeding from the common assumption that agency is about me, an atomistic individual, getting what I already happen to want. But for Hauerwas who I am, and so what I end up wanting, are by no means simply given. Rather, they're the result of always prior interactions with others which have formed me, my desires and my aptitudes.

> We are not "I"s who decide to identify with certain "we"s; we are first of all "we"s who discover our "I"s through learning to recognize the others as similar and different from ourselves. Our individuality is possible only because we are first of all social beings. After all, the "self" names not a thing, but a relation. I know who I am only in relation to others, and, indeed, who I am is a relation with others.[26]

23. Gowdy and Krall, "Ultrasocial Origin of the Anthropocene," 138.
24. Hauerwas, *Peaceable Kingdom*, 40.
25. Hauerwas, *Peaceable Kingdom*, 42.
26. Hauerwas, *Peaceable Kingdom*, 97.

Hauerwas thus offers a dynamic image of the formation of the agent as a "social construction rather than a singular given or project."[27] What matters is who I am becoming. In this sense I am a continuing process of assembling. Likewise character is less a preexisting mold imposed upon the self, more a dynamic factor formed over the course of time which confers a certain coherence on this assembling. Character provides the "characteristic" way in which agency is expressed, "the form our agency takes through our beliefs and intentions."[28] Agency as a skill is an emergent property of the self.

If agency derives from character, character in turn is formed through the cultivation of habits. Because, like it or not, how we act reflects the habits, good or otherwise, which we've developed over the years. In fact, insofar as who we are reflects the habits we have internalized, the distinction between what we do and who we are melts away.[29] "Learning what is needful" is then less about acquiring information than it is about assimilating dispositions to act in certain ways and not in others, and Hauerwas has argued that these are rooted in our most basic bodily existence. For example we all must eat, but *how* we eat—when, what, with which implements—reflects particular habits which make us human. For Hauerwas, all our capacities, nonrational and rational, share this common trait. "It is, therefore, never a question whether we will or will not develop habits and virtues, but *what kinds of habits and virtues* we will develop."[30]

Agency then, to repeat, is far from simply being the ability to act in order to bring about some desired effect, "the ability of human subjects to effect novel and creative changes in the world."[31] It's always subject to the fundamental constraint of being who we have become, the product of the habits we've internalized. Yet these habits are much more than just matters of the body, pertaining to the first articulation of social assembling only. Our practices are thoroughly matters of the second articulation also, bound up with the stories by which we live as individuals and as communities.

Indeed for Hauerwas the category of narrative is paramount. This is because, first, "if the self is historically formed we require a narrative

27. Thomson, *Ecclesiology of Stanley Hauerwas*, 132.

28. Hauerwas, *Peaceable Kingdom*, 39.

29. Hauerwas, *Approaching the End*, 164.

30. Hauerwas, *Approaching the End*, 161, italics mine.

31. Bonta and Protevi, *Deleuze and Geophilosophy*, 5.

to speak about it if we are to speak about it at all."[32] He's very aware that human life can be experienced as highly fragmented, comprising a host of disparate, largely unrelated plot lines. Indeed he compares the unity of the self with that of a novel replete with subplots and incidental characters.[33] In order to secure the self as a responsible agent who can own past actions, a larger, overarching narrative is essential. And to imagine such a narrative is to imagine a denouement, and so a direction of travel: "It is the sense of an end to the story that makes it possible to speak of a story at all."[34]

The second reason narrative is so important is because of the *particularity* of the denouement, and so of the story as a whole. For his argument is not that we should seek to live by any old story but rather by those of Israel and Jesus. I find myself by learning to locate myself within the biblical oeuvre, that is, by embracing discipleship. Lived out alongside others and across generations the emergent result is a tradition-formed community, which in turn forms its disciples.[35]

Everything hangs on the story's denouement. When I read a story for the first time I don't know how things will turn out, and in that sense our actual lives resemble stories lived out in real time. But Christians are called to live life on the assumption that, in a big-picture sense, they *do* know how the story turns out. Theologians call this living proleptically, that is, within the horizon generated by an eschatological perspective, an outlook shaped by a particular vision of where we're heading. Faith in this story, and so in the "future-which-has-already-happened," turns out to be essential in establishing character as such. More than that, it makes possible the widest of wide-boundary perspectives on my life and that of the creation of which I am a part, and the stewardship of which I share.

It's the particularity of the story which informs a peculiarly *Christian* wisdom. Hauerwas makes much use of the ethical approach set out in Aristotle's writings as mediated and supplemented in the Middle Ages by St. Thomas Aquinas.[36] The Christian story provides a particular narrative context for living a good life, fundamental to the exercise of which

32. Hauerwas, *Peaceable Kingdom*, 26.

33. Hauerwas, "Character, Narrative and Growth," 245.

34. Wells, *Transforming Fate*, 150.

35. Hauerwas, *Peaceable Kingdom*, 24–25. Note the ongoing two-way dialectic here between bottom-up and top-down causation.

36. "It is as if Aristotle is all dressed up for a strenuous journey yet requires the medieval theologians to provide somewhere to go." Wells, *Transforming Fate*, 33.

is what Aristotle called *phronēsis*, practical wisdom, the skill of being able to discern and enact the specific, immediate, narrow-boundary goal which will best serve the general, long-term and wide-boundary goal which is my life's overarching purpose.[37] Aristotle called the latter *eudaimonia*: blessedness, ultimate flourishing.

Narrative context makes a big difference. As we saw in chapter 6, Jesus's story is crucially bounded by episodes of complete material powerlessness, in the wilderness and at the Passion. Partly for that reason, the significance of the self as *agent* is, for Hauerwas, matched by that of the self as *patient*. Both the individual Christian and the church corporately have to learn the wisdom of living out of control.[38] This reflects the fact that we no longer live in Christendom, a culture informed by basic assumptions about how we should live deriving from Christian tradition. But, more fundamentally, it reflects Hauerwas's long-standing concern to work out what it means to live out my calling hopefully in inimical situations which I am powerless to change—that is, ones in which I lack agency as conventionally defined.

So being assembled as a Christian means internalizing a story which not only conditions our actions as agents, but also—and perhaps more fundamentally—our patience as patients. This isn't a matter of becoming indifferent or fatalistic; neither is it about simply being passive. Rather, Christian patience is all about fortitude, courage underpinned by the theological virtue of hope. Far from being passive, Hauerwas stresses that Christians are called to be the most *passionate* of people.[39] The organic link with Jesus's Passion is surely obvious. Salvific agency is perfected in the seeming powerlessness of Gethsemane and Golgotha.

For patience is not without its rewards. The grain of wheat, dead in the earth, will in due course bear much fruit.[40] And recall from earlier chapters that, in a well-established complex system such as a superorganism, top-down causation acts so as to severely constrain the freedom of its parts. For these parts at this point in the system's development there can be at best very limited agency in the conventional sense. But, as per Buzz Holling's adaptive cycle, the stability of any conservation phase cannot last indefinitely. A signal disruptive event at the right time and place

37. Aristotle, *Nicomachean Ethics* 6.

38. Hauerwas, *Peaceable Kingdom*, 105–6.

39. Hauerwas and Pinches, "Practicing Patience," reproduced in *Hauerwas Reader*, 348–66.

40. John 12:24.

can cause the system to unravel, so releasing its previously constrained parts such that in each case "the body being acted upon *ceases to be a mere patient*."[41] Eschatological hope shines through here, the hope noted in the previous chapter, that "creation itself will be set free . . . and will obtain the freedom of the glory of the children of God."[42]

According to the author of the Letter to the Ephesians God's ages-long design involves displaying his wisdom to the "rulers and authorities in the heavenly places" by means of Christian community.[43] What is this wisdom? If Hauerwas is right, it includes the knack of living out of control, recognizing that my agency is inherently constrained in two ways: first, by my character, the person I have become; and secondly by living, as I do, within larger systems which constrain in ways that often foreground patience. Such wisdom will likely appear folly to the Powers since they operate by a quite different understanding of agency, one based on a fantasy of power as absence of constraint and as property. But, by the preaching of the cross, the church continues to present the wisdom which is the modus operandi of the source of life itself, the wisdom known by generations past as the fear of the LORD, divinely ordered common sense.

SUMMING IT ALL UP: MAXIMUM POWER AND OPTIMAL WISDOM

That boy-racer we encountered in the introduction is still around, still zooming into the fog with his foot to the floor. It's still not sensible. It's not wise. But that sense of power, material power, at your fingertips is so exhilarating. You're living in the moment, savoring every instant, with but a single desire coursing through you: faster! Faster!

It's surely not hard to see how our boy-racer is channeling Rod Swenson's Law of Maximum Entropy Production: "A system will select the path or assembly of paths out of available paths that minimizes the potential or maximizes the entropy at the fastest possible rate given the constraints." And, with his driving test passed and his parents' protests far behind him, constraints seem notable by their absence. He feels free.

41. DeLanda, *Intensive Science*, 169, emphasis in original.

42. Rom 8:21.

43. Eph 3:9–10.

Free, that is, right up until the moment everything goes blank and he wakes up in a hospital bed encased in plaster.

Can we see the Maximum Power Principle at work here too? Strictly speaking, no, since Alfred Lotka's version of the MPP involves the operation of natural selection processes, and the genes of someone driving like this are unlikely to get passed on for obvious reasons. Had this been a race undertaken under less suicidal conditions though, the MPP could be said to apply inasmuch as the winner would have been the one able to harness energy for useful work at the fastest rate. "Useful" here means producing enough speed to achieve the goal of crossing the finishing line first. "Useful" means something very different to the boy's father when driving the family on vacation because his goals are different; goals such as getting to the destination safely and living long enough to collect a pension. With goals like that, work which involves driving with your foot to the floor just isn't useful anymore; in fact it's downright counterproductive. What counts as useful for some goals can be quite the opposite for others. *Purpose* is everything.

While the joyride lasted the boy was one of the human race's r-strategists, seizing every opportunity to get ahead as fast as possible. In the nonhuman biological world r-strategists have their place and their day. But eventually ecosystems, like human beings, learn to slow down. There's a trade-off between harnessing energy for useful work at the highest instantaneous rates—the bright but brief flaring of the shooting star—and doing so at a lower rate but for longer and at a larger scale—the steady, reliable beaming of the morning star in the winter dawn. With the onset of life the expression of the LMEP changes: new goals come into play, and maximization gives way to optimization. Eden, when first planted, was like this. The fecundity principle held sway and organisms strove accordingly. There were winners and losers, and winning strategies changed as ecosystems developed.

What does winning look like once humans show up?

Well, for one thing, the scale of the operation expands. Scale, in time and space, are material factors. In a social assembling they pertain to the first articulation, its pragmatic system. As these scales expand so the semiotic system of the second articulation changes too. In other words we find that we need increasingly elaborate stories to make sense of the increasingly elaborate material systems we build for ourselves. Our lives get entangled with those of untold numbers of others, however anonymously for the most part, via the things we buy and sell. We also find ourselves caught up in the affairs of large, impersonal social entities like nation-states and transnational corporations. We need stories, and big ones at that, which will tell us, in advance of any direct experience, how we should regard these others; and what winning and losing even mean in this newly emergent register of being.

These stories also involve an enlarged awareness of time, one which stretches backwards and forwards way beyond our own lifetimes. They have to do with the deep past and the eschatological future. Many different such stories have been told over the course of the long millennia of human history. Among the most popular of late has been the story of technological progress. This is all about winning. According to this story, things can only get better; provided, that is, that we persevere with riding the wave which has gotten us here by devising ever-new ways of harnessing more and more energy, even if that means making unprecedented changes not only to our nonhuman environment but also to ourselves.[44]

In chapter 3 we briefly encountered the creed of transhumanism, and according to some of its variants the eschatological destiny of the posthuman cyborg is to colonize the stars, transforming the natural into the artificial as it does so. Its progress metrics are essentially quantitative—watts and GDP. Sure, getting where we are today has generated some adverse side-effects, social and environmental, but these are all amenable to technological fixes. And yes, continuing progress may not be possible for each and every one of the eight billion plus of us. But what matters is the human species, that it continue to evolve and expand materially, albeit perhaps in the form of an elite whose survival and flourishing trumps all else—including the survival and flourishing of others.[45]

According to the technological progress story, work is useful only to the extent that it promotes the goal of material expansion and augmentation. AI is a key part of this story in part because it promises to find quicker ways of achieving our destiny among the stars. In the short term that has significant power implications also, in the form of electricity requirements to run the data centers in which the AI systems are trained.[46] In all respects this is a story about quantitative increase, about more, about maximum material power. Wisdom, as an idea, doesn't figure prominently here; if it does at all then it can mean nothing more

44. See, e.g., Schwab, *Fourth Industrial Revolution*; Fuller and Lipinska, *Proactionary Imperative.*

45. Thomas, *Politics and Ethics of Transhumanism*, 170–78.

46. Goldman Sachs, "AI Is Poised."

than crafty schemes to promote the goal of expansion, the goal of more. According to this story endless expansion is the ultimate, overarching purpose of human life, the end to which the exercise of all power, material and social, should be directed.

Other stories are available. Other stories which also deal with the deep past and the eschatological future, but do so by insisting that human life has an irreducibly qualitative dimension, that numbers alone can't do justice to the marvel which is existence. Notwithstanding humanity's emergence from a prehuman substrate and its abiding rootedness in the dust of the earth, the advent of the human brings with it a new dimension. Just as the striving of ecosystems can't be adequately described in terms of the simple operation of the LMEP and the MPP, combining as they do the pursuit of a range of ecological goals at different points in their development, so also the interaction of people in society aspires towards an emergent optimality which goes beyond any quantitative maximization criterion. Both the transformation/realization of potential and the performance of useful work get expressed in ways unprecedented in nonhuman assemblings. Greatness, for example, is transformed by the Christian gospel from only being a matter of physical size and material power to being about service. Consequently the emergence of the human as a new order of dissipative structures need not entail increases in spatial and temporal scale; superorganisms are not inevitable. Greater no longer has to mean bigger or longer lasting, rather better, as reflected in a superior quality of mutual regard. This is possible because the realization of potential and the performing of work in a social assembling always have an incorporeal aspect; and we can aptly name the optimality emergent in the system of meanings *wisdom*.

The tragedy of human existence is that so much of our conduct, individually and collectively, is so abjectly suboptimal. We notice this not least in the operation of money. As we've seen, money is all bound up with trust. By trusting, and allowing ourselves to be trusted, we mediate power. Just as when we play a game we're both enabled and constrained by the rules which constitute it as a game, so also our mediation of power via trust is simultaneously enabled and constrained in ways that reflect the name of the social game we're playing.

When it comes to basic motivations, the money game and the God game, says Jesus, are incompatible. Their rules are different and they require contradictory attitudes. We can't play both games at once, which is to say that we can't serve both God and mammon. Does this mean that money is evil and that we should have nothing to do with it? Not necessarily. It's the love of money that's the problem, that is, allowing money to call the shots. To love money is to pretend that we can make the world we share with others predictable, and so controllable. We can choose that route if we wish, or instead we can abandon the illusion of control and so be freed to discover the world as a place of grace, a place where nothing and no one can be taken for granted, only received as gift. God or money: wisdom means being able to discern which horse to back.

Money's problems don't end with the illusory control it promises. As a store of value it has always promised the fantasy of complete future security. But credit money, the financial system we embraced early in the modern period, adds a further fly to the ointment. Trust is the issue here again, this time as trust that in the future there will always be *more* than there is now. Money becomes capital, a pseudo-living thing which can grow, reproduce, and expand indefinitely, the fecundity principle sublimated into the Dow Jones average. The growth of living things is in the end limited by finite material resources. Money, as sheer abstract quantity, knows no such bounds. Foreshadowed in Eden by that single accessible yet forbidden tree, this is what it means to succumb to the primordial temptation: if I *can* get more then I will; the question of whether I *should* simply does not arise.

Evolution by natural selection stems not only from the fecundity principle but also from the finitude of resources. There are reasons to believe that these two axioms are not independent, as we saw in chapter 2: for humans at least, even biological fertility depends on the story by which I live. If I live in fear that there will not be enough, then forever pushing against the limits of what's possible makes sense. But if I entertain a different story—a story of enough, even of plenty—then things look very different. The drive for indefinite expansion withers, and the desire, the conative potential, animating it can get directed elsewhere, in the pursuit of values based on qualitative merit rather than just quantitative amount.[47] Life becomes richer in the truest sense; more abundant.

47. The need to go beyond quantitative growth and aim rather for qualitative development is widely recognized; see, e.g., Jørgensen et al., *Flourishing Within Limits to Growth*, 58–61. However, simply "following nature's way" scarcely suffices as a corrective, since the stories comprising (second articulation) human culture will always exceed what can currently be read off the (first articulation) workings of nature. Attempts to reduce the former to the latter have in the past given us, e.g., Social Darwinism and eugenics. Cf. Milbank, "Out of the Greenhouse."

The love of money, then, whether as tool of control, impregnable store of value, or as guarantee of indefinite expansion, is profoundly unwise. The same goes for any simple metric which you might conjure to assess true progress. Wisdom, rather, lies in recognizing that whatever your stage in life, whatever your circumstances, multiple goals need to be juggled. These goals will be incommensurable. They may even, at times, be mutually incompatible. Wisdom also, therefore, is the knack of being able to work out and achieve an optimal outcome, one which assigns due relative weight to each goal. There's no formula, no algorithm, for this. And the wisdom of the outcome may well remain debatable. In any event, the wide-boundary goal of the best outcome given prevailing constraints must involve the practice of *phronēsis*, the skill acquired through long practice of practical reasoning.[48] It leads to more than just head knowledge; it forms you as a judgment-making person. Wisdom is no mere tool, or app, which can be picked up, used, and then discarded. To acquire it is to allow it to seep inside you, to inform your character and so even your unreflective responses.[49] Wisdom is emergent optimality as manifested at a particular point in a particular and unique human life.

That said, we're not all equally wise. My optimal living, as a person, may not match up to yours; you may be more skilled at discerning and responding in a given situation than I am. That would make you more powerful than me. How come? In order to perform useful work I need to be able to discern what is truly useful in a specific situation. And an act is useful to the extent that it realizes my immediate aim which, in turn, reflects something of what I take to be the overarching purpose of my life. If power is a gauge of how much of the work I do is truly useful in this sense then *to be skilled in discernment is to mediate power*, albeit a kind of power peculiar to the second articulation of a social assembling. Power in this instance is expressed as the skill of *phronēsis*, practical wisdom.

This may seem a curious use of the term "power." Applied to—for example—a condemned man dying on a cross it might imply that,

48. Aristotle, *Nicomachean Ethics* 6.

49. "In his book *Blink*, Malcolm Gladwell explores an analogous facility for perception that, say, allows an art appraiser to judge immediately, from a 'gut feeling' as it were, that a particular artwork is a forgery. As Gladwell goes on to explain, these instant 'takes' on a situation are really the product of years of acquaintance with whatever is being judged about, that coalesces in the moment of perception and judgment. Aristotle seems to describe a capacity, also born of much experience, that permits one judge aright in moral matters, and other matters related to human well-being." Wood, "Prudence," 44.

counterintuitively, he's more powerful than those who put him there, those "who know not what they do."[50] Yet if power has to do with useful work, and useful work in a social assembling serves ends which can't be reduced simply to the package of survival, growth, and reproduction, then this surprising conclusion can't be ruled out. In which case power and wisdom are here shown to be united in a single act—the culmination of a life's vocation.[51]

SUMMING IT ALL UP: IF JESUS IS THE ANSWER . . .

If Jesus is the answer, what is the question? That was the task set in the introduction. We've by now got to the point of being able to hazard a response. At its simplest the question is something like, *How do we together, as creatures of the second articulation, survive and thrive?* We used to think that we already knew the answer. It involved technological innovation, a free market, and individuals' untrammeled desires for riches leading to win-win outcomes all round. Jesus, if his name cropped up at all, was the answer to questions which seemed relevant to fewer and fewer in the affluent West, questions which had little if anything to do with the daily realities of economics, politics, and applied technology. Pie in the sky when you die; and with life expectancies increasing all the time, questions like this seemed less and less urgent. Less urgent, certainly, than that new job, that new car, that holiday of a lifetime.

It was great while it lasted, but the party's over.[52] For a whole host of reasons, some of which were mentioned in the introduction, the joyride which has been the fossil fuel era is drawing to a messy close. True believers in the transhumanist creed won't agree of course, and continue to insist that there's a yet brighter future ahead—for some, at least. But many—most?—of us, deep down, know different. As we move into an age in which there will be fewer watts per person available, we need a new story to help us make sense of our lives, as individuals and as a species, to effect a fresh incorporeal transformation of things into meanings; one which will allow us to live well alongside others near and far.

This book has been written in the conviction that the necessary form of expression has been there all along, though its relevance has

50. Luke 23:34.

51. See John 19:30.

52. Heinberg, *Party's Over*.

been largely neglected, or at least restricted, of late. It's a story which is all about power, and about how in the second articulation of a social assembling maximum power translates as optimal wisdom. This, and not the endless multiplication of quantity, is the "will of the universe." The universe's striving to transform its potentials is taken up in the human cultural register and realized in a qualitatively particular manner, a manner exemplified in the lives of John Greenleaf Whittier and his like. Ideas stemming from disciplines such as complexity studies have served to remind us that, with the human, we have to reckon with new *kinds* of reality scarcely visible to natural scientific investigations of the material world. The human is a new thing, an emergent wonder on the face of the Earth.

Yet if emergence gave us the human, it also threatens the human's eclipse. Humans, as the product of emergent processes, find at their disposal powers way beyond the reach of other living things, and therein lies great jeopardy. This has lately become true at a species level, but individual humans have suffered under the heel of emergence in its ultrasocially expressed, top-down form for millennia. The *power to* achieve the otherwise impossible depends wholly on our capacity to cooperate via specific, organized roles in joint endeavors. But relational emergence yoked to a quantitative expansion dynamic has produced a stratified and superpotent superorganism, an insatiable Goliath devouring everything in its path. The individual, for all her fleeting consumerist trappings, is eclipsed, anonymized, mechanized. Any collective thriving arising from the expansion dynamic comes at the cost of widespread individual immiseration.

Understandably, some might conclude that salvation must therefore lie in totally repudiating organized society as we know it and embracing in its stead some form of anarchism. That, for example, would seem to be the inclination of the two Davids, Graeber and Wengrow. Others, noting the same phenomenon, conclude that we simply have to learn to live with an eternal and tragic tension between the possibility of individual sainthood and the impossibility of collective goodness. The title of theologian Reinhold Niebuhr's seminal book, *Moral Man and Immoral Society*, neatly expresses the latter sentiment.

> A sharp distinction must be drawn between the moral and social behavior of individuals and of social groups, national, racial, and economic. . . . Individual men may be moral in the sense that they are able to consider interests other than their own in

> determining problems of conduct, and are capable, on occasion, of preferring the advantages of others to their own. . . . But all these achievements are more difficult, if not impossible, for human societies and social groups. In every human group there is less reason to guide and to check impulse, less capacity for self-transcendence, less ability to comprehend the needs of others and therefore more unrestrained egoism than the individuals, who compose the group, reveal in their personal relationships.[53]

In view of this the best outcome, according to Niebuhr and others like him, is damage limitation, whereby an enlightened minority, having gained a position of sufficient power, can ameliorate the worst of what the masses are capable. Suppressing what amounts to a primordial social chaos is the solution here and this, in the contemporary global context, could presumably take the form of a benevolent AI dictator.[54]

However a more hopeful, and certainly less dystopian, possibility is suggested by John Milbank's response to Niebuhr, one which evokes the universal striving to realize potential introduced in chapter 3. In that chapter we noted how John Greenleaf Whittier's striving in the abolitionist cause provides a practical example of the "straining forward," *epektasis*, towards the Christian *telos* which Paul speaks about in his Letter to the Philippians. Milbank points out that this idea was central to a "revolutionary discovery" made by the Greek church fathers, specifically Gregory of Nyssa, namely that

> *growth might itself belong to the realm of perfection* in that it arises not from a progress out of disorder, but from a permanent tension between the uncreated infinity of God and our created finitude. Gregory's notion of *epektasis*, "straining forward" to God, reveals that *perfection for finite beings is development*; but it breaks with the pagan Greek assumption that development is just a smooth path away from imperfection towards an optimal condition of balanced virtue.[55]

The universe, according to Swenson's reading of Clausius, strives to realize its potentials through a process of *entropia*, "inward transformation." Living things, according to Spinoza and others, express this by their striving to survive, grow, and reproduce, expanding indeed, as per the fecundity principle, to the limits of possibility. Milbank, drawing on patristic

53. Niebuhr, *Moral Man and Immoral Society*, xi–xii.

54. Thomas, *Politics and Ethics of Transhumanism*, 187–88.

55. Milbank, "Poverty of Niebuhrianism," 239, italics mine.

theology, identifies the straining forward embodied in growth and development as nothing less than the perfection of created things, culminating in the human. If human life is a race, as in Paul's metaphor, then it's one in which there need not be winners and losers as per natural selection and the MPP, since these are native to a different register.[56] Instead there are only degrees of excellence and the abiding aspiration for better.[57]

Likewise the human superorganismic tendency is best seen not as a permanent feature presenting a problem to be managed but as part of a process which is never yet over, the basis for a yet further transformation into a qualitatively more excellent way of living. Not that this is an automatic process of gradual evolution, a "smooth path away from imperfection"; far from it. The next step on the path of perfection depends wholly—as it always has and always will—on the contingent enacting by human communities of a particular story, one which reveals the truth of the human, indeed the cosmic, vocation. Translated into the language of Walter Wink, the Powers are to be *redeemed*, not manipulated or played off against each other in an attempt to mitigate the worst manifestations of their essential nature. For their nature, their God-given purpose, is at root good: to mediate God's just and gentle rule so that all may flourish.

The seriously suboptimal effects of the superorganism can't of course be denied, but what's required to remedy this is neither a regression to an imagined pre-agrarian idyll nor a bureaucratic limiting of the damage caused by an inevitably rampaging superorganism. *Pace* Niebuhr, complex societies need not be immoral, and so the contemporary challenge is to strive or strain forward to help de facto societies, stupid and selfish though they plainly are, to realize their potential in a particular way by growing out of the current "toddler with a chainsaw" stage. In this, as we saw in chapter 6, the church is called to play an indispensable role, subverting the megamachine's animus by acting instead as vehicle of God's Spirit, so modeling the refusal to subordinate *better* to *more*. Being the church means precisely rebutting Niebuhr's fatalism concerning social groups by showing that it's the community as such which is called to holiness. Indeed it's the community, humanity in the plural, which is the primary site of emergence of the fully human.

Yet there's a sense in which Niebuhr is absolutely right: redemption happens bottom-up, one flawed, imperfect apprentice at a time. It

56. Phil 3:10–14.

57. As noted in chapter 5, *strebt*, "to strive," in Clausius's formulation of the second law of thermodynamics can also be translated as "to aspire."

can't be simply imposed from on high, for that would be to reproduce the stratifying shackles of one-way, top-down causation. The whole may be greater than the sum of its parts but, equally, without its parts it is nothing. Take away *conatus*, the shared urge to survive at all costs, and the starling murmuration dissolves. That also is how the superorganism gets slain. But apprentices don't arrive preformed. Bare *conatus* must be transformed through the education of desire, and for this we need community, a specific kind of social body which practices the enacting of a particular story. It's thanks to this story that the constituent parts of the body get to be members not of some impersonal whole but of one another.[58]

Although in this regard Jesus as the new Adam provides the benchmark, he does so not in splendid isolation but as representative of a people, true to their historic covenant commitment; and, early in his ministry, by assembling twelve around him who are to learn, embody, and relay his ethic for fully human living.[59] At the heart of this ethic is the claim that storing up treasures, hoardable and lootable surplus, on earth is what sours human community, which implies that the church demonstrates God's wisdom principally by renouncing and denouncing the ultrasocial drive to accumulate and expand ad infinitum.

In other words, *the task of the church is to get emergence right*, not for its own sake so much as for the sake of the world. To do this requires the wisdom of God, as set out in the story of Christ crucified. This wisdom, to briefly recap what has already been said, has three hallmarks.

First, wisdom has regard for the big picture and the distant future. Considering the big picture doesn't come readily to the fallen Powers. All they know is what impacts them directly now, which is why they so easily mess up. The narrow road may lead to life, but the narrow-boundary goals to which the Powers default lead to more ambivalent outcomes.[60] You might succeed in getting what you want, but you're likely to wind up getting some other stuff you very much don't want into the bargain. Over the last two centuries the expansionary ultrasocial dynamic has gotten us cheap energy and a cornucopia of consumer durables. But it has also gotten us climate change, metabolic disease, biodiversity loss . . . the list goes on. We can't know the full consequences of our actions, but wisdom involves employing imagination to intelligently anticipate likely big picture outcomes. The faculty of imagination, of being able to entertain creative

58. Rom 12:5.

59. Wright, *Jesus and the Victory of God*, 274–319.

60. Matt 7:14.

possibilities, is not the least of the ways in which the human bears the stamp of God's image and likeness, and the intelligence accompanying the resulting anticipations is a faculty which vastly exceeds AI's mere ability to attain narrow-boundary goals. In this sense AI channels the fallen Powers all too fully.

Secondly, wisdom knows when to stop. Constraint is as essential for wisdom as it is for power. The mages on the Isle of the Wise knew that well, in the form of the adage "Do only what is needful." As young Arren surmised, discovering what is needful is indeed the quest of a lifetime, but it isn't a quest which we start from scratch. Others have gone before us, and we've inherited numerous traditions which offer to orient us as we embark on this quest. A tradition can be seen as a set of constraints which leads to attaining the overarching purpose of the human enterprise, the *telos*, our true end. It's only by reference to some *telos* that we can meaningfully speak of anything being needful, or necessary, after all. The question is not *whether* our actions will be constrained, but rather *which* constraints we shall adopt. Put otherwise, which *telos* will constraint serve? That of endless increase of quantitative power, material and/or financial; or some vision of a particular quality of life irreducible to quantitative terms?

The Christian tradition frames a particular *telos*, and it does so in a variety of ways. As we've seen, Genesis chapter 2 speaks of caring for and cultivating, bringing the best out of, that which is created. And, to cite just one other formulation, according to the Westminster Shorter Catechism "man's [*sic*] chief end is to glorify God, and to enjoy Him forever." Whether we regard human life from the perspective of creation or of the Creator, our *epektasis*, our straining forward, involves the transforming of the potentials, material and social, which we encounter. Practical wisdom, *phronēsis*, is about coming to know which potentials to transform and how in order to realize the ultimate goal of blessedness. However we act, we could always do better. But in any action there is a sense of *enough*, beyond which any more will just make things worse.

Finally, though wisdom knows when to stop, it knows no end. As gift of God, and as garnered along life's journey, there is always more wisdom to be had. Here again Jesus is our role model. Uncomfortable as it may be for some to hear it, Jesus's response to the non-Jewish woman who asks him to help her child *is* as harsh as it superficially appears:

"It is not fair to take the children's food and throw it to the dogs."[61] We shouldn't let centuries of accreted Christian piety obscure the fully human first-century Jewish tradesman. Being likewise fully divine doesn't mean having your culturally and biographically conditioned human quirks magically erased. But it should mean the capacity to demonstrate wisdom through a readiness to go on learning, even when that learning challenges inherited aspects of how you understand your identity and your vocation vis-à-vis others, and this is what we see here.

Already Jesus had marveled at the faith of a gentile centurion, yet this encounter with a woman, deep inside gentile territory, discloses even more acutely both Jesus the first-century Jew and the Jesus who in due course will send his followers to make disciples of *all* nations. Strikingly, the woman demonstrates *power over* Jesus in this encounter; she wins him round. And she does so by acting as a conduit of grace through which Jesus grows in wisdom. Luke portrays the child Jesus as both filled with, and continuing to grow in, wisdom.[62] His encounter with the Canaanite woman shows that he went on displaying these conjoint qualities into his mature years.

This encounter provides much insight into the power of *pistis*, faith or trust. As we noticed in chapter 6, when Jesus performs his mighty deeds power is flowing both ways: from Jesus to the patient, certainly, but also in the opposite direction. Jesus as healer is empowered by the faith of those who seek his help. Remembering that *pistis* derives from *peithō*, to persuade, we see how in this encounter the woman is already persuaded of Jesus's ability to heal—that is, she has faith—and also shows herself able to persuade Jesus of her persuasion. In thinking of the crucified Christ, too, as both power and wisdom of God, the reciprocality of the power relation is of the essence. By his unjust execution on the cross Jesus mediates God's saving power to those who witness this, either directly or via the testimony of others.[63] But this only becomes actual for those who believe, since an openness to being persuaded by what is true is what actuates the saving power latent in the gospel.

The truth of how we are and the truth of how God is are revealed definitively on the cross, and so the saving power of God works in human lives by the power peculiar to persuasion. How does this power work? Unlike the first two dimensions of power discussed in chapter 1, it isn't a

61. Matt 15:26.

62. Luke 2:40, 52.

63. See John 12:32; 20:29.

matter of getting others to do things they would not otherwise do, nor of restricting the options available to them. It *does* have the effect of transforming what others desire, Lukes's third dimension of power, though this is achieved by the intrinsic appeal of its manifest truth. John Milbank again:

> Truth and persuasion are circularly related. We should only be persuaded by rhetoric when it persuades us of the truth, but on the other hand truth *is* what is persuasive, namely what attracts and does not compel. And Christians only see this *entire* attraction in the figure on the cross, a specific and compelling refusal to return evil for evil, made not in a gesture of despair or resignation, nor even of mere ethical self-offering, but rather in the confidence that a giving unto death is finally to be revealed, as a "return," as a gain of the true self-expending and yet also self-realizing self.[64]

Self-realizing: on the cross a transformation takes place. In the first articulation, the system of bodies, a man suffers agony and eventually his biological functioning ceases. Similar things have happened many times before and, sadly, will go on happening. But *this* time, in the second articulation, the system of meanings, a world-changing incorporeal transformation takes place. By his physical powerlessness on the cross, and against the backstory of how he got there, Jesus exercises the social power of persuasion, he evokes *pistis*, such that this unique life and its awful ending become the underlying motif by which I now look to live my life in turn. The potential embodied in this life, death and resurrection thus becomes realized in the lives of all those in whom trust has been evoked.

Made wiser and so empowered by the cross, the boy-racer gets a second chance. He gets to mediate power in a different way. Situated in a new field of power, he's a different person. Rather than being just a mindless sinew connecting the simple desire for more to the accelerator pedal, he now understands himself as a responsible agent, accountable to another, the means by which what is already good may be both treasured and made still better. To care for and cultivate creation was of course the job description given to the human back at the start of the story, so there

64. Milbank, "Poverty of Niebuhrianism," 250, emphasis in original.

is in fact no novelty here, just the resumption of the original plot. And according to this plot the human character is no longer the driver, apparently free to go where he wants as fast as he can. Instead it's that of the watchman, the steward, the gardener granted unparalleled creative powers, powers defined by the necessary constraint of ongoing accountability to the one who entrusted all this to him—that is, who placed *pistis* in him.

Enacting this role, of caring for and cultivating the created, is how we get to survive and thrive: from the beginning, *this* was the part we were meant to play, the creatures we were created to be. It's not beyond our reach, though it does involve living out a message which will make us look weak and stupid to many. Still, on the plus side, it also means getting to encounter the power and wisdom of God; and there's a story going around that—believe it or not—God's foolishness is wiser than human wisdom, and God's weakness stronger than human strength.

Glossary of Terms

Adaptive cycle: A term coined by ecologist Buzz Holling to refer to the four-stage developmental process typically exhibited by ecosystems: exploitation (r-phase), conservation (K-phase), release or collapse (Ω-phase), and reorganization (α-phase).

Assembling (or assemblage): A dynamic mixing of heterogeneous yet interacting components. This is a key concept in Gilles Deleuze and Félix Guattari's *A Thousand Plateaus*, in which numerous different kinds of *agencement*, assembling, occurring at various levels of being, are examined. The strength of the linkages between components can vary greatly. Weakly structured assemblings are called consistencies, while highly structured ones are termed strata.

Autocatakinesis: A term coined by ecologist Rod Swenson, also referred to as self-organization (or self-ordering) and dissipative structuring. A process of positive feedback whereby different components in a system promote each other's functioning, typically issuing in the growth and development of structure at a larger scale than that of its components. Resulting flow structures act as self-amplifying sinks, generating and maintaining their own internal order by accelerating the rates of order degradation in their environments.

Body without organs: A term coined by Deleuze and Guattari for a limit-condition in which the interaction of people and things is released from the kind of specialized functioning and interdependency typified by the organs of a body, such that people and things are able to affect and be affected, that is, mediate power, fully.

Complex system: A heterogeneous "system of systems," or *assembling*, in which components typically interact in nonlinear ways, that is, with outcomes which do not smoothly and predictably reflect causes. This can give rise to thresholds at which the behavior of the system can suddenly change in pronounced ways, leading to qualitatively different regimes of operation. See *Emergence* below.

Conatus: Commonly translated as "striving," a term deriving from the writings of Baruch de Spinoza which refers to the basic animal drive to survive and reproduce.

Content and expression: The two moments in the *double articulation* of an *assembling*.

Double articulation: The two-stage process by which the components of an assembling interact to produce enduring structures. First, dynamic flows act to provisionally arrange the *substance of content*, or raw material, of an assembling in a nonrandom manner, so setting up novel associations and possibilities—the *form of content*. This arrangement may then become overcoded according to one of a range of potential *forms of expression* and so get established as a particular, well-defined *substance of expression*. The content is thereby "put to work," or expressed, as a functional whole.

Ecosocial system: An ecosystem dominated by human activity.

Emergence: The arising of novel higher-order structures and behaviors on the basis of the bottom-up interaction of a range of lower-order components (of different kinds). Once established such structures may exert top-down control over their components via *autocatakinetic*, positive-feedback mechanisms which constrain components to exercise specific functions with respect to the higher-order whole—this is known as strong emergence.

Fecundity Principle: One of the three axioms of Darwinian natural selection: the tendency of living things to multiply and expand to the very limits of the carrying capacity of their environment.

Final energy: Extrasomatic energy in the form it is delivered to the consumer, typically as electricity, gasoline, diesel, natural gas, or coal. Quantitatively, final energy equals primary energy minus various losses associated with the conversion of energy into different forms and the transfer of energy between points.

Form of content: See *Double articulation.*

Form of expression: See *Double articulation.*

Heterarchy: The interaction of the parts of a system when those parts are unranked, or may be ranked in a number of different ways according to the system's current requirements. As such it contrasts with a hierarchy, in which an element is ranked or nested in a fixed manner on one of several levels, whereby upper levels depend on the assigned functioning of lower ones, and the latter's functioning is constrained by the former.

Incorporeal transformation: The action of a *form of expression* on the content of a social assembling whereby a pragmatic system, or system of bodies, gives rise to a semiotic system, or system of meanings.

Law of Maximum Entropy Production (LMEP): Promoted by ecologist Rod Swenson as the fourth law of thermodynamics, it asserts that "a system will select the path or assembly of paths out of available paths that minimizes the potential or maximizes the entropy at the fastest possible rate given the constraints."

Maximum Power Principle (MPP): A principle of evolutionary biology, deriving from the work of Alfred J. Lotka and Howard T. Odum, which states that those systems which can harness energy flows to perform useful work at the fastest rate given current constraints will tend to prevail, i.e., get selected by processes of natural selection.

Megamachine: A term coined by Lewis Mumford for the organization of functionally specific human and nonhuman parts so as to perform standardized motions and repetitive work. Large-scale human societies have frequently been structured as megamachines since the rise of the first empires in the fourth century BCE.

Panarchy: The quasi-hierarchical organization of a complex ecosystem whereby *adaptive cycle* dynamics at different levels of the system may become coupled together, leading to the potential transmission of effects both up and down the panarchy.

Potentia: As defined by Spinoza, the simple power to exist and act so as to cause effects. In social contexts, the *power to* achieve goals arising from collaborative effort, whether enforced or freely embraced.

Potestas: As defined by Spinoza, the securing of one person's compliance with the will of another; the exercise of *power over* some people by others.

Powers, The: A general term for the "principalities, powers, authorities, thrones, dominions," etc., alluded to in the New Testament which personify the purposeful actions of the social, economic, and political structures ordering collective human life. According to Walter Wink, the Powers are created by God, fallen, and eligible for redemption.

Primary energy: Energy in the form it is initially produced or extracted, prior to any processing or transmission to consumers, typically as coal, petroleum, natural gas, nuclear energy, or various kinds of renewable energy. By convention this is an extrasomatic metric, i.e., it excludes the energy contained in food and animal fodder.

Substance of content: See *Double articulation.*

Substance of expression: See *Double articulation.*

Superorganism: A behavioral or social system in which the independent actions of the parts, at least some of which are themselves organisms, are organized so as to pursue a collective goal. This entails two basic requirements: a specific division of labor between parts and feedback mechanisms which ensure coordination of the parts towards the goal.

Thermodynamic equilibrium: Static thermodynamic equilibrium is characterized by the complete absence of intensive gradients, and so also of any flows of energy. Dynamic equilibrium is characterized by constant intensive gradients, issuing in steady flows of energy. *Complex systems* can only arise in conditions far from static equilibrium.

Ultrasociality: Defined by John Gowdy and Lisi Krall as the configuration of a social group so as to actively harness the inputs to food production, with the result that ultrasocial species are predisposed to accumulating resources and expanding their resource base.

Useful work: Energy-expending actions (i.e., actions which degrade the potential of some intensive property such as temperature) by which a system functions (in the case of biological and engineered systems) or pursues its purposes (in the case of humans). In the case of an organ, functioning involves executing specific tasks in service of the organism of which it is a part. In the case of an organism, functioning involves survival, growth and development, and reproduction.

Bibliography

Adkins, Brent. *Deleuze and Guattari's* A Thousand Plateaus*: A Critical Introduction and Guide*. Edinburgh, UK: Edinburgh University Press, 2015.

Allison, Dale C. *Jesus of Nazareth: Millenarian Prophet*. Minneapolis: Fortress, 1998.

Alter, Robert. *Genesis: A Translation and Commentary*. New York: W. W. Norton, 1996.

Anspach, Mark R. "Imitating Oedipus." Introduction to René Girard, *Oedipus Unbound: Selected Writings on Rivalry and Desire*, vii–liv. Stanford, CA: Stanford University Press, 2004.

Arendt, Hannah. *On Violence*. New York: Harcourt Brace Jovanovich, 1970.

Aristotle. *Metaphysics*. Translated by W. D. Ross. https://classics.mit.edu/Aristotle/metaphysics.html.

———. *Nicomachean Ethics*. Translated by W. D. Ross. https://classics.mit.edu/Aristotle/nicomachaen.html.

Arthur, Amy. "Leaf-Cutter Ants: The Insects That Are Farmed by Fungi." BBC Science Focus, March 7, 2022. https://www.sciencefocus.com/nature/leaf-cutter-ants-fungi.

Arto, Iñaki, et al. "The Energy Requirements of a Developed World." *Energy for Sustainable Development* 33 (2016) 1–13. http://dx.doi.org/10.1016/j.esd.2016.04.001.

Augustine. *On Rebuke and Grace*. Translated by Robert Wallis. https://www.logoslibrary.org/augustine/rebuke/index.html.

Aulén, Gustaf. *Christus Victor: An Historical Study of the Three Main Types of the Idea of Atonement*. Translated by A. G. Herbert. Eugene, OR: Wipf & Stock, 2003.

Austin, J. L. *How to Do Things with Words*. Edited by J.O. Urmson and Marina Sbisá. 2nd ed. Oxford: Oxford University Press, 1975.

Bachrach, Peter, and Morton S. Baratz. *Power and Poverty: Theory and Practice*. Oxford: Oxford University Press, 1970.

Bastani, Aaron. *Fully Automated Luxury Communism: A Manifesto*. New York: Verso, 2020.

Baum, David A., and Buzz Baum. "An Inside-Out Origin for the Eukaryotic Cell." *BMC Biology* 12 (2014). https://doi.org/10.1186/s12915-014-0076-2.

Bawden, David, and Lyn Robinson. "'A Few Exciting Words': Information and Entropy Revisited." *Journal of the Association for Information Science and Technology* 66 (2015) 1965–87. https://doi.org/10.1002/asi.23459.

Belby, James K., and Paul R. Eddy, eds. *The Historical Jesus: Five Views*. London: SPCK, 2010.

Bendell, Jem. *Breaking Together: A Freedom-Loving Response to Collapse*. Bristol, UK: Good Works, 2023.

Bond, Helen K. *The Historical Jesus: A Guide for the Perplexed*. London: T. & T. Clark, 2012.

Bonta, Mark, and John Protevi. *Deleuze and Geophilosophy: A Guide and Glossary*. Edinburgh, UK: Edinburgh University Press, 2006.

Bostrom, Nick. *Superintelligence: Paths, Dangers, Strategies*. New York: Oxford University Press, 2016.

Boulding, Kenneth. "Comment to the US Congress Hearing on the Energy Reorganization Act of 1973." 93rd Congress. First Session: 11510:248 (1973).

Bowles, Samuel. "Cultivation of Cereals by the First Farmers Was Not More Productive than Foraging." *Proceedings of the National Academy of Sciences* 108 (2011) 4760–65.

Bowles, Samuel, and Jung-Kyoo Choi. "The Neolithic Agricultural Revolution and the Origins of Private Property." *Journal of Political Economy* 127 (2019) 2186–228.

Bradshaw, Corey J. A., et al. "Lower Infant Mortality, Higher Household Size, and More Access to Contraception Reduce Fertility in Low- and Middle-Income Nations." *PLoS ONE* 18 (2023) e0280260. https://doi.org/10.1371/journal.pone.0280260.

Braudel, Fernand. *Civilization and Capitalism 15th–18th Century, Volume 3: The Perspective of the World*. Translated by Siân Reynolds. London: Phoenix, 2002.

The Britannica Dictionary. "Constrain and Restrain." https://www.britannica.com/dictionary/eb/qa/constrain-and-restrain.

Brown, Ellen. "Casino Capitalism and the Derivatives Market: Time for Another 'Lehman Moment'?" The Web of Debt Blog, January 17, 2024. https://ellenbrown.com/2024/01/17/casino-capitalism-and-the-derivatives-market-time-for-another-lehman-moment/.

Brown, James H., et al. "Energetic Limits to Economic Growth." *BioScience* 61 (2011) 19–26.

Brunet, Thibaut, and Nicole King. "The Origin of Animal Multicellularity and Cell Differentiation." *Developmental Cell* 43 (2023) 124–40. doi:10.1016/j.devcel.2017.09.016.

Buchan, James. *Frozen Desire: An Inquiry into the Meaning of Money*. London: Picador, 1997.

Burkhard, Benjamin, et al. "Adapting the Adaptive Cycle: Hypotheses on the Development of Ecosystem Properties and Services." *Ecological Modelling* 222 (2011) 2878–90.

Caird, G. B. *The Language and Imagery of the Bible*. London: Duckworth, 1980.

———. *Paul's Letters from Prison*. Oxford: Oxford University Press, 1976.

Centre for Alternative Technology. *Zero Carbon Britain: Rising to the Climate Emergency*. Machynlleth, UK: Centre for Alternative Technology, 2019.

Chaisson, Eric J. *Cosmic Evolution: The Rise of Complexity in Nature*. Cambridge, MA: Harvard University Press, 2001.

Chang, Sarah. "Rayleigh-Bénard Convection." University of Maryland, 2019. https://www.terpconnect.umd.edu/~dsvolpe/TREND/2019/Media/Chang/convection.html.

Chittka, Alexandra, et al. "Epigenetics: The Making of Ant Castes." *Current Biology* 22 (2012) 835–38.

Clayton, Philip. "Conceptual Foundations of Emergence Theory." In *The Re-Emergence of Emergence*, edited by Philip Clayton and Paul Davies, 1–28. New York: Oxford University Press, 2008.

CLEAPSS (Consortium of Local Education Authorities for the Provision of Science Services). "Oscillating Reactions—Belousov Zhabotinsky BZ Method." YouTube, April 29, 2021. Video. https://www.youtube.com/watch?v=wGJe6rhREvs.

The Consilience Project. "Development in Progress." July 16, 2024. https://consilienceproject.org/development-in-progress/.

Conway, Ed. *Material World: A Substantial Story of Our Past and Future*. London: Penguin, 2023.

Corning, Peter A. *Holistic Darwinism: Synergy, Cybernetics and the Bioeconomics of Evolution*. Chicago: University of Chicago Press, 2005.

Court, Victor. "Energy Capture, Technological Change and Economic Growth: An Evolutionary Perspective." *Biophysical Economics and Resource Quarterly* 3 (2018) 1–27.

Craig, Clare. *Expired: COVID, the Untold Story*. Stevenage, UK: Nielsen, 2023.

Crockett, Clayton. *Energy and Change: A New Materialist Cosmotheology*. New York: Columbia University Press, 2022.

Crossan, John Dominic. *Jesus: A Revolutionary Biography*. San Francisco: Harper, 1995.

Crumley, Carole L. "Heterarchy." In *Emerging Trends in the Social and Behavioral Sciences: An Interdisciplinary, Searchable, and Linkable Resource*, edited by Robert A. Scott and Marlis C. Buchmann, 1–14. Hoboken, NJ: John Wiley & Sons, 2015. https://doi.org/10.1002/9781118900772.etrds0158.

Darwin, Charles. *On the Origin of Species by Means of Natural Selection or the Preservation of Favoured Races in the Struggle for Life*. 6th ed. London: John Murray, 1876.

Davis, Tamara. "Relax, the Expansion of the Universe is Still Accelerating." The Conversation, October 27, 2016. https://theconversation.com/relax-the-expansion-of-the-universe-is-still-accelerating-67691.

Deacon, Terrence W. *Incomplete Nature: How Mind Emerged from Matter*. New York: W. W. Norton, 2013.

De Bari, Benjamin, et al. "Thermodynamics, Organisms and Behaviour." *Philosophical Transactions of the Royal Society A 381* (2023) 2022027.

DeLanda, Manuel. *Assemblage Theory*. Edinburgh, UK: Edinburgh University Press, 2016.

———. *Intensive Science and Virtual Philosophy*. New York: Bloomsbury Academic, 2005.

———. *A New Philosophy of Society: Assemblage Theory and Social Complexity*. New York: Continuum, 2006.

Deleuze, Gilles. *Dialogues II*. Translated by Hugh Tomlinson and Barbara Habberjam. New York: Continuum, 2006.

Deleuze, Gilles, and Félix Guattari. *Anti-Oedipus*. Translated by Robert Hurley et al. New York: Continuum, 2004.

———. *A Thousand Plateaus*. Translated by Brian Massumi. New York: Continuum, 2004.

Desmet, Mattias. *The Psychology of Totalitarianism*. Translated by Els Vanbrabant. White River Junction, VT: Chelsea Green, 2022.

De Stercke, S. "Dynamics of Energy Systems: A Useful Perspective." Laxenburg, AT: International Institute for Applied Systems Analysis, 2014. https://tntcat.iiasa.ac.at/PFUDB/dsd?Action=htmlpage&page=series.

Diamond, Jared. "The Worst Mistake in the History of the Human Race." *Discover Magazine*, May 1, 1999. https://www.discovermagazine.com/planet-earth/the-worst-mistake-in-the-history-of-the-human-race.

Dodsworth, Laura. *A State of Fear: How the UK Government Weaponised Fear During the COVID-19 Pandemic*. London: Pinter & Martin, 2021.

Dominy, Peter. *Decoding Mammon: Money as a Dangerous and Subversive Instrument*. Eugene, OR: Wipf & Stock, 2012.

Douthwaite, Richard. *The Growth Illusion*. Totnes, UK: Green, 1999.

Elder-Vass, Dave. *The Causal Power of Social Structures: Emergence, Structure and Agency*. New York: Cambridge University Press, 2010.

Ellis, George F. R. "Top-Down Causation and Emergence: Some Comments on Mechanisms." *Interface Focus* 2 (2012) 126–40.

Energy Institute. "Statistical Review of World Energy." https://www.energyinst.org/statistical-review/home.

England, Jeremy. *Every Life Is On Fire: How Thermodynamics Explains the Origins of Living Things*. New York: Basic, 2020.

Fath, Brian D., et al. "Ecosystem Growth and Development." *BioSystems* 77 (2004) 213–28.

Fath, Brian D. "Systems Ecology, Energy Networks and a Path to Sustainability." *International Journal of Design & Nature and Ecodynamics* 12 (2017) 1–15.

Ferguson, Neil M., et al. "Report 9: Impact of Non-Pharmaceutical Interventions (NPIs) to Reduce COVID-19 Mortality and Healthcare Demand." Imperial College COVID-19 Response Team, March 16, 2020. https://www.imperial.ac.uk/media/imperial-college/medicine/sph/ide/gida-fellowships/Imperial-College-COVID19-NPI-modelling-16-03-2020.pdf.

Fernando, Jason. "Understanding Derivatives: A Comprehensive Guide to Their Uses and Benefits." Investopedia, December 31, 2025. https://www.investopedia.com/terms/d/derivative.asp.

Fieguth, Paul. *An Introduction to Complex Systems: Society, Ecology and Nonlinear Dynamics*. Cham, CH: Springer International, 2017.

Fleming, Chris. *René Girard: Violence and Mimesis*. Cambridge, UK: Polity, 2004.

The Free Dictionary. "Mills of the Gods Grind Slowly." https://idioms.thefreedictionary.com/mills+of+the+gods+grind+slowly.

Fricker, Tyler, and James B. Elsner. "Kinetic Energy of Tornadoes in the United States." *PLoS ONE* 10 (2015) e0131090. https://doi.org/10.1371/journal.pone.0131090.

Friedemann, Alice J. *When Trucks Stop Running: Energy and the Future of Transportation*. New York: Springer, 2016.

Friedmann, Julio S., et al. *Low-Carbon Heat Solutions for Heavy Industry: Sources, Options, and Costs Today*. New York: Center on Global Energy Policy, 2019. https://www.energypolicy.columbia.edu/publications/low-carbon-heat-solutions-heavy-industry-sources-options-and-costs-today/.

Fuller, Steve, and Veronika Lipinska. *The Proactionary Imperative: A Foundation for Transhumanism*. New York: Palgrave Macmillan, 2014.

Girard, René. *I See Satan Fall Like Lightning*. Translated by James G. Williams. Leominster, UK: Gracewing, 2001.

———. *Oedipus Unbound: Selected Writings on Rivalry and Desire*. Stanford, CA: Stanford University Press, 2004.

———. *"To Double Business Bound": Essays on Literature, Mimesis and Anthropology*. London: Athlone, 1988.

Global Footprint Network. "Ecological Footprint." https://www.footprintnetwork.org/our-work/ecological-footprint/.

Goldman Sachs. "AI is Poised to Drive 160% Increase in Data Center Power Demand." May 14, 2024. https://www.goldmansachs.com/insights/articles/AI-poised-to-drive-160-increase-in-power-demand.

Goodchild, Philip. *Credit and Faith*. London: Rowman and Littlefield, 2020.

Gowdy, John. *Ultrasocial: The Evolution of Human Nature and the Quest for a Sustainable Future*. Cambridge, UK: Cambridge University Press, 2021.

Gowdy, John, and Lisi Krall. "Agriculture as a Major Evolutionary Transition to Human Ultrasociality." *Journal of Bioeconomics* 16 (2014) 179–202.

———. "The Economic Origins of Ultrasociality." *Behavioral and Brain Sciences* 39 (2016) 1–60.

———. "The Ultrasocial Origin of the Anthropocene." *Ecological Economics* 95 (2013) 137–47.

Gowlett, J. A. J. "The Discovery of Fire by Humans: A Long and Convoluted Process." *Philosophical Transactions of the Royal Society B* 371 (2016) 20150164.

Graeber, David. *Debt: The First 5000 Years*. Brooklyn, NY: Melville House, 2011.

Graeber, David, and David Wengrow. *The Dawn of Everything: A New History of Humanity*. New York: Picador, 2021.

Green, Toby, and Thomas Fazi. *The Covid Consensus: The Global Assault on Democracy and the Poor—A Critique from the Left*. London: C. Hurst, 2023.

Grubler, Arnulf, et al. *Energy Primer*. International Institute for Applied Systems Analysis, October 10, 2014. https://iiasa.ac.at/projects/energy-primer.

Guénon, René. *The Reign of Quantity and the Signs of the Times*. Translated by Lord Northbourne. 4th ed. Hillsdale, NY: Sophia Perennis, 2001.

Haberl, Helmut, et al. "A Sociometabolic Transition Towards Sustainability? Challenges for Another Great Transformation." *Sustainable Development* 19 (2011) 1–14. https://doi.org/10.1002/sd.410.

———. "A Systematic Review of the Evidence on Decoupling of GDP, Resource Use and GHG Emissions, Part II: Synthesizing the Insights." *Environmental Research Letters* 15 (2020) 065003. https://doi.org/10.1088/1748-9326/ab842a.

Hacking, Ian. "Making Up People." In *Reconstructing Individualism*, edited by Thomas Heller et al., 222–36. Stanford, CA: Stanford University Press, 1986.

Hagens, Nate. "The Great Simplification." https://www.thegreatsimplification.com/.

Hagens, N. J., and D. J. White. *Reality Blind: Integrating the Systems Science Underpinning Our Collective Futures*. Self-published, 2021. https://read.realityblind.world/view/975731937/i/.

Hall, Charles A. S., and Timothy McWhirter. "Maximum Power in Evolution, Ecology and Economics." *Philosophical Transactions of the Royal Society A* 381 (2023) 20220290. https://doi.org/10.1098/rsta.2022.0290.

Hamilton, Lawrence. "Power, Domination and Human Needs." *Thesis Eleven* 119 (2013) 46–62.

Hauerwas, Stanley. *Approaching the End: Eschatological Reflections on Church, Politics and Life*. London: SCM, 2014.

———. "Character, Narrative and Growth." In *The Hauerwas Reader*, edited by John Berkman and Michael Cartwright, 220–54. Durham, NC: Duke University Press, 2001.

———. *The Peaceable Kingdom: A Primer in Christian Ethics*. London: SCM, 2003.

Hauerwas, Stanley, and Charles Pinches. "Practicing Patience: How Christians Should Be Sick." *Christian Bioethics* 2 (1996) 202–21.

Haugaard, Mark. "Rethinking the Four Dimensions of Power: Domination and Empowerment." *Journal of Political Power* 5 (2012) 33–54.

Haugaard, Mark, and Philip Pettit. "A Conversation on Power and Republicanism: An Exchange Between Mark Haugaard and Philip Pettit." *Journal of Political Power* 10 (2017) 25–39.

Heilbroner, Robert. *Teachings From the Worldly Philosophy*. New York: W. W. Norton, 1997.

Heinberg, Richard. *The Party's Over: Oil, War and the Fate of Industrial Societies*. 2nd ed. Forest Row, UK: Clairview, 2005.

Heinberg, Richard, and Asher Miller. *Welcome to the Great Unraveling: Navigating the Polycrisis of Environmental and Social Breakdown*. Post Carbon Institute, 2023. https://www.postcarbon.org/publications/welcome-to-the-great-unraveling/.

Hickel, Jason, and Giorgos Kallis. "Is Green Growth Possible?" *New Political Economy* 24 (2019) 469–86. https://doi.org/10.1080/13563467.2019.1598964.

Hirschman, Albert O. *The Passions and the Interests: Political Arguments for Capitalism Before Its Triumph*. Princeton, NJ: Princeton University Press, 1997.

Holdaway, Robert J., et al. "Trends in Entropy Production During Ecosystem Development in the Amazon Basin." *Philosophical Transactions of the Royal Society B* 365 (2010) 1437–47.

Holland, Eugene W. *Deleuze and Guattari's* A Thousand Plateaus. New York: Bloomsbury Academic, 2013.

Holland, John H. *Complexity: A Very Short Introduction*. New York: Oxford University Press, 2014.

Holling, C. S. "The Resilience of Terrestrial Ecosystems: Local Surprise and Global Change." In *Sustainable Development of the Biosphere*, edited by W. C. Clark and R. E. Munn, 292–317. Cambridge, UK: Cambridge University Press, 1986.

———. "Understanding the Complexity of Economic, Ecological, and Social Systems." *Ecosystems* 4 (2001) 390–405.

Holling, C. S., et al. "Sustainability and Panarchies." In *Panarchy: Understanding Transformations in Human and Natural Systems*, edited by Lance H. Gunderson and C. S. Holling, 63–102. Washington, DC: Island, 2002.

Holmgren, David. "Future Scenarios." Future Scenarios. https://www.futurescenarios.org/.

Homer-Dixon, Thomas. *The Upside of Down: Catastrophe, Creativity and the Renewal of Civilisation*. London: Souvenir, 2007.

Humanity Plus. "Philosophy." www.humanityplus.org/philosophy.

Hund, Kirsten, et al. *Minerals for Climate Action: The Mineral Intensity of the Clean Energy Transition*. Washington, DC: World Bank Group, 2020. https://documents.worldbank.org/en/publication/documents-reports/documentdetail/099052423172525564.

Hunter, Alastair. *Wisdom Literature*. London: SCM, 2006.

Ingham, Geoffrey. *The Nature of Money*. Cambridge, UK: Polity, 2004.

International Energy Agency. "Data and Statistics." https://www.iea.org/data-and-statistics.

Jackson, Tim. *The Post-Growth Challenge: Secular Stagnation, Inequality and the Limits to Growth*. Guildford, UK: Center for the Understanding of Sustainable Prosperity, 2018.

Jensen, Derrick, et al. *Bright Green Lies: How the Environmental Movement Lost Its Way and What We Can Do About It*. Rhinebeck, NY: Monkfish, 2021.

Jezos, Beff. "Notes on E/acc Principles and Tenets." *Beff's Newsletter*, Substack, July 10, 2022. https://beff.substack.com/p/notes-on-eacc-principles-and-tenets.

Jørgensen, Sven Erik, et al. *Flourishing Within Limits to Growth: Following Nature's Way*. New York: Routledge, 2015.

Juarrero, Alicia. *Context Changes Everything: How Constraints Create Coherence*. Cambridge, MA: The MIT Press, 2023.

Kauffman, Stuart A. *The Origins of Order: Self-Organization and Selection in Evolution*. New York: Oxford University Press, 1993.

———. *A World Beyond Physics: The Emergence and Evolution of Life*. New York: Oxford University Press, 2019.

Keen, Steve. *Debunking Economics: The Naked Emperor of the Social Sciences*. New York: Zed, 2001.

Keener, Craig S. *1–2 Corinthians*. Cambridge, UK: Cambridge University Press, 2010.

Kelly, J. N. D. *Early Christian Doctrines*. 5th ed. London: A. & C. Black, 1985.

Kemp, Luke. *Goliath's Curse: The History and Future of Societal Collapse*. New York: Knopf, 2025.

Kesebir, Selin. "The Superorganism Account of Human Sociality: How and When Human Groups are Like Beehives." *Personality and Social Psychology Review* 16 (2012) 233–61.

Keynes, John Maynard. *The General Theory of Employment, Interest and Money*. London: Macmillan, 1936.

King, Carey W. *The Economic Superorganism: Beyond the Competing Narratives on Energy, Growth and Policy*. Cham, CH: Springer, 2021.

Kingsnorth, Paul. "The Vaccine Moment: COVID, Control and the Machine." Paul Kingsnorth, 2022. https://www.paulkingsnorth.net/vaccine.

Kitzmann, Niklas, et al., eds. *Planetary Health Check 2025*. Potsdam, DE: Potsdam Institute for Climate Impact Research (PIK), 2025.

Kleiber, Max. "Body Size and Metabolic Rate." *Physiological Reviews* 27 (1947) 511–41.

Klein, Martin J. "The Scientific Style of Josiah Willard Gibbs." In *A Century of Mathematics in America, Volume 2*, edited by Peter Duren, 99–120. Providence, RI: American Mathematical Society, 1989.

Knight, Frank. *Selected Essays by Frank Knight, Volume 1*. Chicago: University of Chicago Press, 1999.

Kooij, Pepijn W., et al. "*Leucoagaricus gongylophorus* Uses Leaf-Cutting Ants to Vector Proteolytic Enzymes Towards New Plant Substrate." *The ISME Journal* 8 (2014) 1032–40.

Kümmel, Reiner. *The Second Law of Economics: Energy, Entropy, and the Origins of Wealth*. New York: Springer, 2011.

Larsen, C. S. "The Agricultural Revolution as Environmental Catastrophe: Implications for Health and Lifestyles in the Holocene." *Quaternary International* 150 (2006) 12–20.

Legg, Shane. "Definitions of Intelligence." Calculemus. https://calculemus.org/lect/08szt-intel/materialy/Definitions%20of%20Intelligence.html.

Le Guin, Ursula. *The Farthest Shore*. Harmondsworth, UK: Puffin, 1973.

LeVasseur, Todd, and Anna Peterson, eds. *Religion and Ecological Crisis: The "Lynn White Thesis" at Fifty*. London: Routledge, 2018.

Lewes, George Henry. *Problems of Life and Mind*. London: Kegan Paul, Trench, Turbner, and Co., 1875.

Lewis, C. S. *That Hideous Strength*. London: Pan, 1955.

Lotka, Alfred J. "Contribution to the Energetics of Evolution." *Proceedings of the National Academy of Sciences* 8 (1922) 147–51.

Lukes, Steven. *Power: A Radical View*. 3rd ed. London: Bloomsbury Academic, 2021.

———. "Power and Authority." In *A History of Sociological Analysis*, edited by T. B. Bottomore and R. Nisbet, 83–139. New York: Basic, 1978.

Macquarrie, John. *Principles of Christian Theology*. London: SCM, 2009.

Mann, Michael. *The Sources of Social Power, Volume 3: Global Empires and Revolution, 1890–1945*. Cambridge, UK: Cambridge University Press, 2012.

Mansson, B. A., and J. M. McGlade. "Ecology, Thermodynamics and H. T. Odum's Conjectures." *Oecologia* 93 (1993) 582–96.

Martenson, Chris. *The Crash Course: The Unsustainable Future of Our Economy, Energy and Environment*. Hoboken, NJ: John Wiley & Sons, 2011.

Marx, Karl. *Capital, Volume 1*. Translated by Ben Fowkes. London: Penguin, 1976.

Matutinović, Igor, et al. "The Mature Stage of Capitalist Development: Models, Signs and Policy Implications." *Structural Change and Economic Dynamics* 39 (2016) 17–30.

Maynard Smith, John, and Eörs Szathmáry. *The Major Transitions in Evolution*. New York: Oxford University Press, 1998.

McCulloch, Warren S. "A Heterarchy of Values Determined by the Topology of Nervous Nets." *Bulletin of Mathematical Biophysics* 7 (1945) 89–93.

Meier, John P. *A Marginal Jew, Volume 1: Rethinking the Historical Jesus*. New Haven, CT: Yale University Press, 1991.

Meiksins Wood, Ellen. *The Origin of Capitalism: A Longer View*. New York: Verso, 2017.

Meltzer, David J. "Overkill, Glacial History, and the Extinction of North America's Ice Age Megafauna." *Proceedings of the National Academy of Sciences* 117 (2020) 28555–63.

Milbank, John. "Out of the Greenhouse." In *The Word Made Strange: Theology, Language, Culture*, 257–67. Malden, MA: Blackwell, 1997.

———. "The Poverty of Niebuhrianism." In *The Word Made Strange: Theology, Language, Culture*, 233–54. Malden, MA: Blackwell, 1997.

———. *Theology and Social Theory: Beyond Secular Reason*. Malden, MA: Blackwell, 1993.

Morgan, Tim. *Life After Growth: How the Global Economy Really Works—and Why 200 Years of Growth Are Over*. Petersfield, UK: Harriman House, 2016.

———. *Perfect Storm: Energy, Finance and the End of Growth*. Tullet Prebon Strategic Insights 9 (2013). https://surplusenergyeconomics.wordpress.com/wp-content/uploads/2018/05/tpsi_009_perfect_storm_0093.pdf.

Morris, Ian. "Against Method: A Review of *The Dawn of Everything: A New History of Humanity*." *American Journal of Archaeology* 126 (2022) E065–75.

———. *Foragers, Farmers and Fossil Fuels: How Human Values Evolve*. Princeton, NJ: Princeton University Press, 2015.

Moses, Robert. *Practices of Power: Revisiting the Principalities and Powers in the Pauline Letters*. Minneapolis: Fortress, 2014.

Mumford, Lewis. *The Myth of the Machine, Volume 1: Technics and Human Development*. New York: Harcourt Brace Jovanovich, 1967.

———. *The Myth of the Machine, Volume 2: The Pentagon of Power*. New York: Harcourt Brace Jovanovich, 1970.

National Oceanic and Atmospheric Administration (NOAA). "Rayleigh-Benard Convection Cells." https://psl.noaa.gov/outreach/education/science/convection/RBCells.html.

Niebuhr, Reinhold. *Moral Man and Immoral Society*. New York: Charles Scribner's Sons, 1932.

Nielsen, Søren N., and Robert E. Ulanowicz. "On the Consistency Between Thermodynamical and Network Approaches to Ecosystems." *Ecological Modelling* 132 (2000) 23–31.

Norrsken Foundation. "Daniel Schmachtenberger | An Introduction to the Metacrisis | Stockholm Impact/Week 2023." YouTube. Video. https://www.youtube.com/watch?v=4kBoLVvoqVY.

O'Donnell, Patricia. "John Greenleaf Whittier." Quakers and Slavery. https://web.tricolib.brynmawr.edu/speccoll/quakersandslavery/commentary/people/whittier.php.

O'Donnell, Sean, et al. "Extraordinary Predation by the Neotropical Army Ant *Cheliomyrmex andicola:* Implications for the Evolution of the Army Ant Syndrome." *Biotropica* 37 (2005) 706–9.

Odum, Howard T. *Environment, Power, and Society for the Twenty-First Century: The Hierarchy of Energy*. New York: Columbia University Press, 2007.

Odum, Howard T., and Richard Pinkerton. "Time's Speed Regulator: The Optimum Efficiency for Maximum Output in Physical and Biological Systems." *American Scientist* 43 (1955) 331–43.

Orwell, George. *The Road to Wigan Pier*. London: Victor Gollancz, 1937.

Our World in Data. "Global Direct Primary Energy Consumption." https://ourworldindata.org/grapher/global-primary-energy.

Peace, William J. *Leslie A. White: Evolution and Revolution in Anthropology*. Lincoln, NE: University of Nebraska Press, 2004.

Plato. *The Republic*. Translated by Benjamin Jowett. https://classics.mit.edu/Plato/republic.html.

Poetry Foundation. "John Greenleaf Whittier." https://www.poetryfoundation.org/poets/john-greenleaf-whittier.

Polanyi, Karl. *The Great Transformation: The Political and Economic Origins of Our Time*. Boston: Beacon, 2001.

Polanyi, Michael. "Life's Irreducible Structure." *Science* 160 (1968) 1308–12.

Prigogine, Ilya. "Time, Structure and Fluctuations." *Science* 201 (1978) 777–85. https://doi.org/10.1126/science.201.4358.777.

Prigogine, Ilya, and Isabelle Stengers. *Order Out of Chaos: Man's New Dialogue with Nature*. New York: Verso, 2017.

Rees, William E. "Ecological Economics for Humanity's Plague Phase." *Ecological Economics* 169 (2020). https://doi.org/10.1016/j.ecolecon.2019.106519.

———. "The Fractal Biology of Plague and the Future of Civilization." *The Journal of Population and Sustainability* 5 (2020) 3–18.

Reynolds, Craig W. "Flocks, Herds and Schools: A Distributed Behavioral Model." *Computer Graphics* 21 (1987) 25–34.

Robertson, Robbie. *The Three Waves of Globalization: A History of a Developing Global Consciousness.* New York: Zed, 2003.

Robinson, Joan. *Freedom and Necessity.* London: George Allen & Unwin, 1970.

Rosen, Robert. *Essays on Life Itself.* New York: Columbia University Press, 2000.

Ross, Alison. "Desire." In *The Deleuze Dictionary*, edited by Adrian Parr, 65–67. Edinburgh, UK: Edinburgh University Press, 2010.

Ryan-Collins, Josh, et al. *Where Does Money Come From? A Guide to the UK Monetary and Banking System.* London: New Economics Foundation, 2012.

Sahlins, Marshall. "The Original Affluent Society." In *Culture in Practice: Selected Essays*, 95–137. New York: Zone, 2000.

Salthe, Stanley N. *Evolving Hierarchical Systems: Their Structure and Representation.* New York: Columbia University Press, 1985.

———. "Infodynamics, a Developmental Framework for Ecology/Economics." *Conservation Ecology* 7 (2003). http://www.consecol.org/vol7/iss3/art3.

———. "Maximum Power and Maximum Entropy Production: Finalities in Nature." *Cosmos and History: The Journal of Natural and Social Philosophy* 6 (2010) 114–21.

———. "The Natural Philosophy of Work." *Entropy* 9 (2007) 83–99.

———. "Purpose in Nature." *Ludus Vitalis* 16 (2008) 49–58.

———. "Summary of the Principles of Hierarchy Theory." *General Systems Bulletin* 31 (2002) 13–17.

Sandalow, David, et al. *ICEF Industrial Heat Decarbonization Roadmap.* Washington, DC: Information Technology & Innovation Foundation, 2020. https://www2.itif.org/2020-03-05-icef-ihd-roadmap.pdf.

Schmachtenberger, Daniel. "Artificial Intelligence and the Superorganism." The Great Simplification, May 17, 2023. https://www.thegreatsimplification.com/episode/71-daniel-schmachtenberger.

———. "From Naive to Authentic Progress." The Great Simplification, June 5, 2024. https://www.thegreatsimplification.com/episode/126-daniel-schmachtenberger-7.

———. "Silicon Dreams and Carbon Nightmares: The Wide Boundary Impacts of AI." The Great Simplification, July 17, 2024. https://www.thegreatsimplification.com/episode/132-daniel-schmachtenberger.

Schmookler, Andrew. *The Parable of the Tribes: The Problem of Power in Social Evolution.* Berkeley, CA: University of California Press, 1984.

Schneider, Eric D., and James K. Kay. "Life as a Manifestation of the Second Law of Thermodynamics." *Mathematical and Computer Modelling* 19 (1992) 25–48.

Schrödinger, Erwin. *What Is Life?* Cambridge, UK: Cambridge University Press, 1944.

Schultz, Ted R., and Sean G. Brady. "Major Evolutionary Transitions in Ant Agriculture." *Proceedings of the National Academy of Sciences* 105 (2008) 5435–40.

Schutz, Alfred. "Some Structures of the Life-World." In *Collected Papers, Volume 3: Studies in Phenomenological Philosophy*, 116–32. Translated by Aron Gurwitsch. The Hague: Martinus Nijhoff, 1975.

Schwab, Klaus. *The Fourth Industrial Revolution.* New York: Crown Business, 2017.

Sciubba, Enrico. "What Did Lotka Really Say? A Critical Reassessment of the 'Maximum Power Principle.'" *Ecological Modelling* 222 (2011) 1347–53.

Seibert, Megan K., and William E. Rees. "Through the Eye of a Needle: An Eco-Heterodox Perspective on the Renewable Energy Transition." *Energies* 14 (2021). https://doi.org/10.3390/en14154508.

Servigne, Pablo, and Raphaël Stevens. *How Everything Can Collapse: A Manual for Our Times*. Translated by Andrew Brown. Medford, MA: Polity, 2020.

Smil, Vaclav. *Energy and Civilization: A History*. Cambridge, MA: The MIT Press, 2017.

———. *Energy Transitions: Global and National Perspectives*. 2nd ed. Santa Barbara, CA: Praeger, 2017.

Smith, Daniel W. "Flow, Code and Stock: A Note on Deleuze's Political Philosophy." *Deleuze Studies* 5 (2011) 36–55.

Smith Galer, Sophia. "56 Percent of Young People Think Humanity Is Doomed." Vice, September 14, 2021. https://www.vice.com/en/article/fifty-six-percent-of-young-people-think-humanity-is-doomed/.

Spencer, Herbert. *Principles of Sociology*. Hamden, CT: Archon, 1969.

Stewart, Ken. "e: Mathematical Constant." *Encyclopedia Britannica*, December 9, 2025. https://www.britannica.com/science/e-mathematics.

Stockholm Resilience Center. "Planetary Boundaries." https://www.stockholmresilience.org/research/planetary-boundaries.html.

Swenson, Rod. "Autocatakinetics, Evolution, and the Law of Maximum Entropy Production: A Principled Foundation Towards the Study of Human Ecology." *Advances in Human Ecology* 6 (1997) 1–47.

———. "Evolutionary Theory Developing: The Problem(s) with *Darwin's Dangerous Idea*." *Ecological Psychology* 9 (1997) 47–96.

———. "The Fourth Law of Thermodynamics: The Law of Maximum Entropy Production (LMEP)." *Ecological Psychology* 22 (2010) 69–87.

———. "A Grand Unified Theory for the Unification of Physics, Life, Information and Cognition (Mind)." *Philosophical Transactions of the Royal Society A* 381 (2023) 20220277. https://doi.org/10.1098/rsta.2022.0277.

———. "Selection Is Entailed by Self-Organization and Natural Selection Is a Special Case." *Biological Theory* 5 (2010) 167–81.

Tamtik, Svetlana. "Enuma Elish: The Origins of Its Creation." *Studia Antiqua* 5 (2007) 65–76.

Tautz, Jürgen. *The Buzz About Bees: Biology of a Superorganism*. Cham, CH: Springer, 2008.

Thomas, Alexander. *The Politics and Ethics of Transhumanism: Techno-Human Evolution and Advanced Capitalism*. Bristol, UK: Bristol University Press, 2024.

Thomson, John B. *The Ecclesiology of Stanley Hauerwas: A Christian Theology of Liberation*. Aldershot, UK: Ashgate, 2003.

Tomasello, Michael. "The Ultra-Social Animal." *European Journal of Social Psychology* 44 (2014) 187–94. https://doi.org/10.1002/ejsp.2015.

Tomek, Beverly C. "Pennsylvania Hall." The Encyclopedia of Greater Philadelphia. https://philadelphiaencyclopedia.org/essays/pennsylvania-hall/.

Tooze, Adam. "What Is the Polycrisis?" World Economic Forum. https://www.weforum.org/videos/experts-explain-adam-tooze-what-is-the-polycrisis/.

Torres, Emile P. "'Effective Accelerationism' and the Pursuit of Cosmic Utopia." Truthdig, December 14, 2023. https://www.truthdig.com/articles/effective-accelerationism-and-the-pursuit-of-cosmic-utopia/.

Ulanowicz, Robert E. "The Dual Nature of Ecosystem Dynamics." *Ecological Modelling* 220 (2009) 1886–92.

———. *Ecology, the Ascendent Perspective*. New York: Columbia University Press, 1997.

———. "Increasing Entropy: Heat Death or Perpetual Harmonies?" *International Journal of Design & Nature and Ecodynamics* 4 (2009) 83–96.

———. *A Third Window: Natural Life Beyond Newton and Darwin*. West Conshohocken, PA: Templeton Foundation, 2009.

———. "Widening the Third Window." *Axiomathes* 22 (2012) 269–89. https://doi.org/10.1007/s10516-011-9181-9.

Ulanowicz, Robert E., et al. "Exergy, Information and Aggradation." *Ecological Modelling* 198 (2006) 520–24.

Varela, Francisco J., et al. *The Embodied Mind: Cognitive Science and Human Experience*. Cambridge, MA: The MIT Press, 2017.

Von Bertalanffy, Ludwig. *Problems of Life: An Evaluation of Modern Biological Thought*. London: Watts, 1952.

———. "Quantitative Laws in Metabolism and Growth." *The Quarterly Review of Biology* 32 (1957) 217–31.

Wackernagel, Mathis, and William Rees. *Our Ecological Footprint: Reducing Human Impact on the Earth*. Philadelphia, PA: New Society, 1996.

Wannenwetsch, Bernard. "Members of One Another: *Charis*, Ministry and Representation, a Politic-Ecclesial Reading of Romans 12." In *A Royal Priesthood: The Use of the Bible Politically and Ethically—A Dialogue with Oliver O'Donovan*, edited by Craig Bartholomew et al., 196–224. Carlisle, UK: Paternoster, 2002.

Weber, Max. *The Protestant Ethic and the Spirit of Capitalism*. Translated by Talcott Parsons. London: Unwin, 1930.

Wells, Samuel. *Transforming Fate Into Destiny: The Theological Ethics of Stanley Hauerwas*. Eugene, OR: Cascade, 2004.

Wengrow, David, and David Graeber. "Farewell to the 'Childhood of Man': Ritual, Seasonality, and the Origins of Inequality." *Journal of the Royal Anthropological Institute* 21 (2015) 597–619.

Wheeler, William Morton. "The Ant Colony as an Organism." *Journal of Morphology* 22 (1911) 301–25.

White, Leslie A. "Energy and the Evolution of Culture." *American Anthropologist* 45 (1943) 335–56.

———. *The Evolution of Culture: The Development of Civilization to the Fall of Rome*. New York: McGraw-Hill, 1959.

White, Lynn Jr. "The Historical Roots of Our Ecologic Crisis." *Science* 155 (1967) 1203–7.

Whittier, John Greenleaf. "The Brewing of Soma." Poetry.com, April 27, 2023. https://www.poetry.com/poem/23057/the-brewing-of-soma.

Whybray, Norman. *Wisdom: The Collected Articles of Norman Whybray*. Edited by Katharine J. Dell and Margaret Barker. London: Routledge, 2022.

Wilson, Catherine. "Darwin and Nietzsche: Selection, Evolution, and Morality." *Journal of Nietzsche Studies* 44 (2013) 353–69.

Wilson, E. O. *The Social Conquest of Earth*. New York: Liveright, 2012.

Wink, Walter. *Engaging the Powers: Discernment and Resistance in a World of Domination*. Minneapolis: Fortress, 1992.

———. *Naming the Powers: The Language of Power in the New Testament*. Minneapolis: Fortress, 1984.

Witherington, Ben III. *Paul's Letter to the Romans: A Socio-Rhetorical Commentary*. Grand Rapids: Eerdmans, 2004.

Wood, W. Jay. "Prudence." In *Virtues and Their Vices*, edited by Kevin Timpe and Craig A. Boyd, 37–58. Oxford: Oxford University Press, 2014.

Woolhouse, Mark. *The Year the World Went Mad: A Scientific Memoir*. Muir of Ord, UK: Sandstone, 2022.

Wright, N. T. *Jesus and the Victory of God*. London: SPCK, 1996.

Wu, Jianguo. "Hierarchy Theory: An Overview." In *Linking Ecology and Ethics for a Changing World: Values, Philosophy, and Action*, edited by Ricardo Rozzi et al., 281–301. Dordrecht, NL: Springer, 2013. https://doi.org/10.1007/978-94-007-7470-4_24.

Yen, Jian D. L., et al. "Thermodynamic Extremization Principles and Their Relevance to Ecology." *Austral Ecology* 39 (2014) 619–32.

York, Richard, and Shannon Elizabeth Bell. "Energy Transitions or Additions? Why a Transition from Fossil Fuels Requires More Than the Growth of Renewable Energy." *Energy Research & Social Science* 51 (2019) 40–43. https://doi.org/10.1016/j.erss.2019.01.008.

Zhang, Antong, et al. "Forecasting the Progression of Human Civilization on the Kardashev Scale Through 2060 with a Machine Learning Approach." *Scientific Reports* 13 (2023) 11305. https://doi.org/10.1038/s41598-023-38351-y.

Index

www.ingramcontent.com/pod-product-compliance
Lightning Source LLC
LaVergne TN
LVHW050618100826
845148LV00011B/1643
9798385267668